CN00419419

'A very interesting book, thorough an[...]
work with esoteric and spiritual conc[...]
curious about the subject. Christa Ma[...]
therapist and academic, who writes with conviction a[...]
she is passionate about.'

— *Avy Joseph, Principal, The College of Cognitive Behavioural*
Hypnotherapy, author of Cognitive Behavioural Therapy

'A seminal book that sheds light on the importance and practicality of integrating shamanic and spiritual practices into modern psychotherapy...an enlightened contribution to a world where individual and collective purpose must interweave if we hope to create a tapestry of survival.'

— *John Perkins, New York Times bestselling author of*
Hoodwinked *and* Confessions of an Economic Hit Man
and Founder and Director of Dream Change Coalition

'A truly compelling, well researched, yet accessible book for therapeutic professionals conveying a wealth of knowledge, insights and practical applications.'

— *John Hempstead, Chair, British Society of Clinical Hypnosis*

'An important and relevant book for the times we live in. It is a "must-read" for therapeutic professionals who look for enlightening insights and innovative methods of psycho-spiritual practice that cater for the whole human psyche.'

— *Ursula James, Visiting Teaching Fellow, Oxford University Medical*
School, author of The Source: A Manual of Everyday Magic

of related interest

How to Incorporate Wellness Coaching into Your Therapeutic Practice
A Handbook for Therapists and Counsellors
Laurel Alexander
ISBN 978 1 84819 063 4
eISBN 978 0 85701 034 6

Spiritism and Mental Health
Practices from Spiritist Centers and Spiritist Psychiatric Hospitals in Brazil
Edited by Emma Bragdon PhD
Foreword by James Lake MD
ISBN 978 1 84819 059 7
eISBN 978 0 85701 039 1

I Send a Voice
Evelyn Eaton
Illustrated by Narca Schor
ISBN 978 1 84819 100 6
eISBN 978 0 85701 082 7

Anni's Cancer Companion
An A–Z of Treatments, Therapies and Healing
Anni Matthews
Foreword by Professor Karol Sikora
ISBN 978 1 84819 067 2
eISBN 978 0 85701 044 5

CHRISTA MACKINNON

SHAMANISM AND SPIRITUALITY IN THERAPEUTIC PRACTICE

AN INTRODUCTION

SINGING
DRAGON
LONDON AND PHILADELPHIA

Epigraph on p.9 from Perkins 1994 reprinted with permission from Destiny Books.
Epigraph on p.13 from Perkins 1994 reprinted with permission from Destiny Books.
Epigraph on p.25 from Maslow 1968 reprinted with permission from John Wiley and Sons.
Epigraph on p.47 from James 1958 reprinted with permission from New American Library.
Epigraph on p.143 from Culliford 2011 reprinted with
permission from Jessica Kingsley Publishers.
Epigraph on p.289 from Williamson 1992 reprinted with permission from HarperCollins.

First published in 2012
by Singing Dragon
an imprint of Jessica Kingsley Publishers
116 Pentonville Road
London N1 9JB, UK
and
400 Market Street, Suite 400
Philadelphia, PA 19106, USA

www.singingdragon.com

Library of Congress Cataloging in Publication Data
Mackinnon, Christa.
Shamanism and spirituality in therapeutic practice : an introduction / Christa Mackinnon.
p. cm.
ISBN 978-1-84819-081-8 (alk. paper)
1. Shamanism. 2. Spiritual healing. I. Title.
BF1611.M3293 2012
201'.44--dc23
2012013210

British Library Cataloguing in Publication Data
A CIP catalogue record for this book is available from the British Library

ISBN 978 1 84819 081 8
eISBN 978 0 85701 068 1

Printed and bound in Great Britain

To my daughter Kamala, wholeheartedly loved

Contents

PART III PRACTICAL APPLICATIONS: INCORPORATING ELEMENTS OF SHAMANISM INTO THERAPEUTIC WORK

PART IV BACK TO THE 'BIGGER PICTURE'

Acknowledgements

My heartfelt thanks go to all the people who have helped me in the process of writing this book.

First and foremost I want to thank my friend, colleague and fellow author Penny McFarlane, who connected me with Jessica Kingsley Publishers, and a big hug and very special gratitude goes to my friend and colleague Diana Lodge, who read through the pages of my draft, using her skills as a freelance editor to smoothen out the edges. I furthermore owe gratitude to John Hempstead, Wenda McKee and Valerie O'Donnell for reading through sections of the book and for providing feedback.

I also thank wholeheartedly the people who have taken the time to read and endorse the book: John Perkins, valued teacher, bestselling author of *Hoodwinked* and *Confessions of an Economic Hit Man* and founder of Dream Change Coalition; Ursula James, author of *The Source* and founder and principal of Thames Medical; Avy Joseph, Principal of the College of Cognitive Behavioural Therapy and author of *Cognitive Behavioural Therapy*; and John Hempstead, the head of the British Society of Clinical Hypnosis.

Appreciation is due to the editorial staff at Jessica Kingsley Publishers, especially to Lisa, Lucy and Vicki, for their professionalism and for their prompt, friendly and always helpful responses to my questions, queries and insecurities.

Last, but by no means least, I want to thank my husband David and my daughter Kamala for their continuous encouragement, their wholehearted support, for their patience and for their belief in me. I owe them much.

There have been many teachers, colleagues, clients, students and friends who have walked with me on my path. Without their input, direct and indirect, this book would not have been written. Some of them will find themselves mentioned in the book, but my gratitude goes to all of you, mentioned or unmentioned.

INTRODUCTION

The Bigger Picture

The World Is As You Dream It.

John Perkins (1994)

Humanity has reached a critical stage in its evolution. Although our level of economic, scientific and technological development is unprecedented and has brought material benefits and freedoms for many, it has also produced a range of disturbing ecological, economic and political problems and has created 'soulless', highly developed societies in which people feel increasingly isolated, anxious and depressed, lacking a sense of meaning and purpose and of being connected to something that reaches beyond the material. We instinctively know that we have arrived at a point where our materialistic and self-serving world-view cannot aid us in tackling the many issues we need to address. Increasingly, people are becoming aware that we need to change our way of thinking, being and acting in the world, shifting our focus from developing the material and 'the outer' to developing the spiritual and 'the inner'.

It is against this background that many in the western world are searching for the spiritual, for something that takes them beyond, helps them to grow individually and restores a sense of connection, belonging and purpose. This 'psycho-spiritual' movement is developing parallel to and is enforced by scientific discoveries, mainly in quantum physics and higher mathematics, which show that the world-view of spiritual masters of all eras and creeds might come closer to the underlying reality of our world than we previously assumed. This is supporting a serious debate over whether we need an overall shift in paradigm from a material, disconnected view to an energetic, connected one if we want to come closer to understanding, not only the world, but also the human being.

Staying on the level of the world we have created, most of us can see clearly that we are facing challenges on an immense scale: our ecological systems are in disarray; the world's population is increasing at an unparalleled speed; resources are getting scarce; food is in ever shorter supply; the gap between rich and poor is widening all over the world; and our monetary system is held together more than somewhat insecurely. Lately, these problems have intensified, with the western world facing, for the first time in generations, a significant decrease in living standards, with all the social upheaval and unrest, let alone hardship, this will most certainly entail. Individually, we do not fare much better. Even before we began being affected by the economic downturn, our way of life had failed to result in satisfaction or contentment, producing ever-increasing numbers of people with mental/emotional health issues, with anxiety disorders and depression leading the field.

Nevertheless, although we know that things have gone wrong and that we need to change and find solutions, on the whole, individually and collectively, we continue to function from the materialistic, self-centred and disconnected world-view consciousness we have cultivated. Many of us feel helpless and powerless and now increasingly angry as the powerful nations and the leaders who could act on our behalf seem to either ignore the problems and/or react in an ever more self-preserving, highly dangerous manner, instead of searching for and working towards sensible and sustainable solutions.

Dangerous and heartbreaking as the current situation is, it is not surprising. It exists because we have deprived ourselves of the benefits of experiencing a wider reality, richer than the purely material one, which would enable us to step out of our reductionist view of ourselves, our place in the world and the world itself. Thus we find it difficult to search for and implement solutions to our current problems, as our so-called 'standard of living' seems to be all that is worth preserving. Individually, most of us are left feeling unsupported in our search for something that will give us a sense of belonging, purpose and meaning, while our secular, increasingly superficial societies now appear to have little to offer that helps us to address such issues. It is apparent that we are at a point where we need to find ways of being and thinking that contribute to the development of our consciousness, so that we can change how we define the world and ourselves within it. We need to move away from views that are, overall, materialistic and highly fragmented to views that can aid us in moving forward and creating a world that is sustainable, benefits all of humanity and supports us individually in our quest for more fulfilling lives.

It is, in my opinion, spirituality that can help us with this exceedingly necessary expansion of our consciousness, because spirituality (not to be confused with a set of religious dogmas) addresses the 'aspect of humanity that refers to the way individuals seek and express meaning and purpose and the way they experience their connectedness to the moment, to self, to others, to Nature, and to the significant or sacred' (Fenwick 2011, p.1). We cannot continue to ignore this vital aspect of the human psyche without paying a very high price indeed; as Abraham Maslow (1968, p.iv) states so pointedly, 'Without the transcendent and the transpersonal, we get sick, violent, and nihilistic, or else hopeless and apathetic.' The spirituality we need to strive for at this moment in time needs to be an active, inclusive spirituality, in the sense that we do not use spiritual practices solely for self-development and self-gratification, but also to reconnect with our planet, to mature as a species and to contribute to a positive overall development of mankind. This development must come, not from a fighting, violent and angry place, but from a place of inner calm, freedom and connectedness to something higher and wider than ourselves. Or as the Burmese leader of the opposition, Aung San Suu Kyi (2011), points out: 'There is certainly a danger that the acceptance of spiritual freedom as a satisfactory substitute for all other freedoms could lead to passivity and resignation. But an inner sense of freedom can reinforce a practical drive for the more fundamental freedoms in the form of human rights and the rule of law.'

The revival of indigenous teachings is just one of the strands, albeit a very important one, that will support us in this quest for connection, meaning, wholeness and belonging and the expansion of our consciousness. After having almost completely lost the wisdom of our more nature-embedded ancestors by declaring them primitive savages and destroying most of them all over the world, we now need to learn from the few that are left. Of course we cannot transfer their teachings and ways directly into modern society, but we can learn from them about natural forces and connections, about the sacredness of all life, and about the spiritual worlds we can access if we only allow ourselves to appreciate and use the capacity of our brain to alter its state. We can also learn from them how to view the human as a whole, consisting of mind, body, soul and spirit, connected to and embedded in the energetic web of life, and how to work towards integration of the many facets of existence. Most importantly though we can learn from them about 'the dream', about how, collectively, we produce 'a dream' by the way we view our world and ourselves within it and how we manifest this dream into concrete reality. The dream we have collectively produced has brought us to the brink of collapse, but has also created increasingly a new 'integral, spiritual complex' that is still growing.

I see four major reasons for advocating the inclusion of an experience-based spiritual approach, such as shamanism, that works towards integration and wholeness into our lives. First, if we want to tackle the difficult questions, issues and problems we now face as a species, we need approaches that help us to think in more holistic ways, be it within ourselves, or in connection to other people, other nations and other belief systems or to nature as a whole. We can, for instance, only begin to address such tricky questions as population growth, the over-production of senseless goods and their unequal distribution, the exploitation of the many by the few, our dwindling resources and the destruction of our natural habitat, if we fully understand that we are all part of a whole, beginning to think more holistically and putting the interest of the whole before our own.

Second, we need spirituality to help us individually to mature into more balanced and rounded personalities, moving away from the one-sided ways that are all too obvious within our lives.

Research, as I will detail, has shown that spiritual practices can aid the expansion of all facets of the human potential, whilst helping us to experience that which we cannot experience within our normal state of perception, namely the sacred, the mysterious and the higher capacities within ourselves. It aids us in developing a consciousness that values, quite naturally, the caring, the nurturing, the compassionate, the peaceful, the creative and the ecstatic. It helps us to strive for an inner and outer life that is fulfilled. It liberates us from remaining stuck in the material, conquering and exploiting mode, striving for superficial achievements that we are currently, whether we are aware of it or not, focused upon and admire.

Third, spirituality will help us to narrow the split between our vast theoretical understanding, knowledge and declarations and our emotional and moral commitments, a fragmentation that keeps us feeling inadequate and guilt stricken and, in the final analysis, incapable of taking adequate actions to resolve our problems. This split between our 'talk' and our 'walk' influences various important areas of our daily individual lives, as well as our national and international behaviours. For instance, we talk about the importance of 'emotional intelligence', but still value masculine aspects, such as power, control, action and logic, more than feminine aspects, such as intuition, emotion, caring, communication and protecting and preserving life. We state that we 'care about the earth', but in reality most of us, especially if we are city dwellers, only care as long as this doesn't negatively affect our standard of living. We talk about community, but with our hectic, demanding lifestyles we struggle to get properly involved or to serve it consistently. We talk about valuing freedom, democracy, human rights and more, but are not willing to spend the time and effort it takes to resist, adequately, when such values are threatened.

Last, but by no means least, we need spirituality because we have reached a level of 'soul starvation', which, as I will show, has a detrimental effect on our mental health and our emotional well-being. The level of isolation, stress, underlying anxieties and depression that our lifestyles seem to have produced is in stark contrast to the emotional and mental well-being we should be experiencing, at least theoretically, with reference to our relative material comforts.

Prescription levels for anti-depressants and tranquillizers are soaring, not only for adults, but now also for children. Many of us, especially our young people, drink heavily. We watch too much TV and eat more than we need. Those of us who work have to put in long hours, leaving us little time for relationships and families. Our children are, from a very early age, pushed towards achievement, with the ones who do not achieve falling by the wayside. The development of our communication devices, exciting as they are, seems to engulf us in a world that is ever more deprived of personal contact. Increasingly worshipping 'the young and body beautiful', we have neglected the old, wise and soulful. 'Keeping up with the Joneses' has brought us little more than a constant striving for more material possessions and has resulted in depression, rather than better relationships and more quality of life (James 2010).

THE CONTEXT AND STRUCTURE OF THE BOOK

Psychology worked hard to be accepted as a science, therefore subscribing increasingly to a mind/body view of the human being that ignored the spiritual dimension. Currently, however, psychologists are engaged in an intense debate over how to develop a psycho-spiritual paradigm that incorporates all aspects of the human psyche. This is no small task, given that this has to be attempted within the context of a scientific discipline and societies that have cultivated materialistic and scientific views that ignore the spiritual dimension. Whilst this debate continues, it seems to me that increasing numbers of people consult a wide range of spiritual practitioners, who are not necessarily therapeutically trained, in the hopes of accessing help that reaches beyond contemporary western mind/body approaches. Like many professionals, I have seen clients suffering from psychological conditions and disorders, who have been consulting spiritual healers and have participated in all kinds of spiritual workshops with facilitators who have little or no psychological knowledge. There is an apparent need for the fields of psychology and mental health to address the longing for the spiritual as an innate part of human existence, to address clients' search for meaning, connection, purpose and wholeness, to cater for the soul and to be able to offer clients ways and means to bring the spiritual into their lives. A growing body of research shows that spirituality contributes positively to mental/emotional and physical health, helps to develop aspects of our personality, is vital if we want to expand our consciousness and enhances our ability to cope in existential crisis, and yet the field of psychology and therapy remains divided in its response. On the one hand, there are increasingly schools and practitioners that try to develop theories and approaches that integrate the mind/body with the soul/spirit aspect, and the Royal College of Psychiatrists has a very active Spirituality and Psychiatry Special Interest Group (SPSIG). On the other hand, psychology, as a science, together with many accepted therapeutic interventions, still keeps the client firmly on the level of mind and focuses on symptom alleviation.

The modern psyche lives in a complex, fast-changing world that presents us with an array of issues. In 1992 Hillman and Ventura published a book entitled *We Have Had a Hundred Years of Psychotherapy – And the World's Getting Worse*, in which they argue that psychotherapy lacks the means to deal with the many afflictions of the western psyche. In defence of psychology, I would like to stress that, in contrast to spiritual traditions that have had millennia to evolve, psychology and psychotherapy are still in their infancy. It is nevertheless regrettable that we have allowed ourselves to ignore, even reject, the wisdom of spiritual teachings, and have failed to explore the wider capacities of the human mind. Nevertheless, there is a time for everything and, as I will show, psychology is now taking the spiritual as a vital facet of human existence much more into account.

I cannot claim to address all these issues in this book, but I aim to contribute to the now emerging psycho-spiritual paradigm by providing an understanding of traditional and contemporary shamanic approaches, concepts, teachings and tools and describing practical applications and ways of incorporating them within our therapeutic work with clients. I am convinced that the loss of a more soul-centred way of living is a major contributor to the ailments afflicting our society and that the spiritual is an innate part of human existence that has been neglected within the therapeutic field. By incorporating psycho-spiritual approaches and interventions into therapy, counselling and coaching, we can cater more beneficially for the whole person and attend more successfully to the increase of anxieties, depression, restlessness, imbalance, general disenchantment and emptiness and to the existential questions we encounter in consulting rooms.

This book has been informed by the insights and knowledge I have acquired as a spiritual seeker and apprentice to spiritual teachers and shamans in Asia and the Americas, by my own spiritual practice and by my work as a teacher and facilitator of psycho-spiritual training courses and workshops for professionals, as well as by my theoretical knowledge and practical experience as a social psychologist, therapist and trainer. The road I travelled as a spiritual seeker, which started in my twenties in Asia, where I lived in ashrams in India and received Buddhist teachings in Sri Lanka, led me to practising meditation for most of my life and yoga for part of it. Later, when exploring more nature-centred, traditional indigenous teachings in North and South America, I extended my own practice, my work with clients as well as my teachings for professionals, by combining shamanic/spiritual teachings and tools with western therapeutic approaches. This extensive experience has led me to believe that the teachings of shamanic indigenous traditions and modern psycho-spiritual shamanic approaches, provided they are used ethically and within beneficial contexts, offer us a rich and highly effective repertoire of insights and psycho-spiritual therapeutic tools. In my view, shamanism cannot replace all therapy, but it can enhance it and take it further towards the spiritual and/or embed it into the spiritual, aiding development of all human facets. It provides a compendium of teaching tools, techniques and understanding as well as knowledge about the underlying workings of life, collected over many millennia in different parts of the world. These can be used to help us with expanding our consciousness and with the quest of experiencing ourselves as an embedded part of the whole and of being whole ourselves. In this sense, it offers means for us to connect our mind and body with our soul and spirit, a connection that we need to experience directly, with our senses. Shamanism acknowledges the innate need of human beings for meaning and purpose as a fundamental to psychological well-being. It can and does work together with other spiritual approaches, such as Buddhist teachings; it is not opposed to any religious views and acknowledges people's right and responsibility to find and travel their own spiritual paths.

The book you are about to read is an introduction. It is not solely about shamanism and not solely about therapy. It is about integration. Whenever we integrate shamanic–spiritual approaches into contemporary therapeutic practices, the former will have to be altered and, in places, simplified. A traditional shamanic ceremony, for instance, is often an elaborate affair, aiming for transformation, and can take days. Naturally, ceremonial work within a therapeutic setting, especially when conducted within the constraints of a single session, is bound to be less intense, less elaborate and might only achieve a fraction of what can be achieved when it is run as a full ceremony within a nature setting in a group. Nevertheless, ceremonial work can be included within a contemporary therapeutic environment if we are not deterred by having to simplify it and only utilize some of the elements. Yet, whilst some of the tools, teachings and approaches, such as shamanic journeying or more therapeutically orientated work with the Medicine Wheel, can be integrated, others cannot. Vision Quests or sweat lodge ceremonies and other, more nature-based or complex and deep-reaching approaches will resist integration within the therapeutic field of western practices.

As this book is mainly aimed at psychologists, therapists and counsellors, I have tried to describe approaches, tools and interventions in a format that can be used within this specific setting, but many of the practical approaches described can also be used within a coaching environment and when working with groups. I have excluded 'energy work approaches', such as extractions, as they might be outside the professional framework of many therapists and counsellors and as I wanted to focus on approaches, tools and interventions that can be utilized by most trained professionals in the field. Throughout the book, I have included research, wherever this is available; especially in the third part of the book I have also used case studies for illustration and outlined step-by-step practical applications in the form of interventions, tools and exercises.

Having stated that this is not a book about shamanism, I nonetheless have provided as in depth an overview of shamanism as possible within the framework of the book and have focused less on the psychological, as the book is written for psychologists and therapeutic professionals, assuming therefore a level of given knowledge in the field.

However, Part I does provide a brief review of the current developments in psychology, with a focus on the challenges that the inclusion of a spiritual aspect provides within the current paradigm. It also outlines some of the research available, mainly that relating to the benefits of spiritual practices to mental/emotional health. It then looks at the different schools, explaining the emerging transpersonal strands and the role shamanism has played within the design and debate of those schools.

Part II is about shamanism. In Chapter 2 it provides you with an introduction to traditional shamanism, the development of western views and perceptions about it, and an outline of its chief characteristics. It briefly describes the recent development of more contemporary schools, teachings and applications and some of the diversity we encounter within the field.

The third and fourth chapters lead you to the 'heart of the matter', namely the shamanic state of perception and consciousness and the resulting paradigm that defines the world, and the human being within it, in terms of an energetic interconnected web. Without gaining a profound understanding of this 'connected energy-based world-view' and the means which informed this way of seeing, namely the profound altering of mental states, we can neither understand shamanism specifically nor spirituality generally. The third chapter is therefore quite detailed in its description of altered states of perceptions and what we experience and access within them, from the personal subconscious to the collective unconscious and the wider field. I have, in Chapter 4, described the different aspect of the view of the world resulting from those experiences and attempted to compare and underpin this with some of the current research in and models of quantum physics as well as mathematics.

The fifth and sixth chapters explain shamanic psycho-spiritual concepts of healing, therapy and wholeness, contrasting them with some psychological concepts. They show how practitioners work towards wholeness in an integrative and transformational way, and describe the tools and spirit helpers that are used. Critical to understanding shamanic integrative and transformational interventions/therapies are the interconnected maps of human reality, which dominate Chapter 6. Those maps (integrative concepts) are 'interconnected' because, to the shaman, there is no split or lack of connection between the human body/mind and the rest of our visible and invisible world, or between mind, body, soul and spirit. I describe three concrete major maps: the three-fold spirit worlds (worlds of consciousness) in the form of lower, upper and middle worlds; the mind/body/soul/spirit as the four-fold definition of the human; and the wheels of life in the form of the Medicine Wheels.

Part III, Chapters 7 to 17, provides a range of concrete tools, techniques and applications which can be used within the setting of individual therapy and counselling and also with groups. In most cases, I describe these in detail, offering case examples, underpinning them with research, if available, and provide either scripts or concrete step-by-step exercises and techniques. A few, such as soul retrieval or nature work, I only describe, without including concrete techniques, mainly because they are not easily transferable into a consulting room or because they require special training. I have included them because they are a vital part of shamanically orientated work and can provide much insight and suggest ideas to widen the field of therapeutic interventions. For example, working with and in nature, which is an important part of shamanic work, resists transference into a contemporary therapeutic setting. Nevertheless, we can adopt some of the ideas and concepts and incorporate them into 'homework', which I have done within that chapter. Something similar applies to soul retrieval. To practise it you will need training, but the ideas behind soul retrieval are substantial and can be utilized by every therapist.

Within Part III, the practical application part of the book, the first three chapters offer general tools which can be applied with every client and in every setting, introducing concepts such as sacred space, embodying energy through intent, integration techniques and how to create a sacred place of power and sanctuary with the client.

Chapter 9 also includes a trance-induction script to lead the client into an altered state of consciousness. Chapters 10 to 17 describe techniques and concrete tools, adapted for therapeutic purposes, such as journeying, how to work with the Medicine Wheel, ancestral work, working with myths and stories, and more.

In Part IV of the book I will come back to the bigger picture and address questions of meaning and purpose, individually and collectively, within a shamanic–spiritual framework, taking our current situation as described above into account, and will return to the idea of a paradigm change within the field of psychology and mental health.

I hope that you will find the book informative, that it will contribute to the enhancement of your therapeutic or coaching practice as well as to your personal life, that it animates you and gives you insights, that it encourages you to delve deeper into shamanism and, above all, I hope that you enjoy reading it.

PART I

Spirituality Matters

The exploration of the highest reaches of human nature and of its ultimate possibilities and aspirations has involved for me the continuous destruction of cherished axioms, the perpetual coping with seeming paradoxes, contradictions and vagueness, and the occasional collapse around my ears long established, firmly believed in, and seemingly unassailable laws of psychology.

Abraham Maslow (1968)

1 SPIRITUALITY AND PSYCHOLOGY

THE DILEMMA OF PSYCHOLOGY: MIND AND BODY OR SOUL AND SPIRIT

The movement towards the spiritual in the secular cultures of the western world has been steadily growing. Books on the subject matter as well as groups, workshops, seminars and training courses are flooding the markets, offering anything and everything we can think of, from meditation classes, energy balancing and quantum consciousness to shamanic trance journeying, spiritual business coaching and courses that prepare us for the year ahead. We attend yoga retreats and wilderness camps. We swim with dolphins and explore ancient spiritual sites. We are apprenticed to spiritual teachers and follow mentors and gurus of all creeds. The range of obscure and not so obscure healing practices on offer grows steadily. Energy balancing, spiritual healing, crystal healing, sound healing, chakra healing – the list seems endless. We buy CDs and DVDs on the subjects and download inspirational talks. Countless publications tell us how to 'use the laws of attraction', 'live happily in the here and now', utilize the 'powers of our minds' and 'access the quantum realm'. This search for something beyond the material in countries without spiritual traditions has been growing in influence now for many years and brings with it the questioning of our world-view.

The field of psychology is, at this moment in time, also concerned with two world-views that seem, at first glance, incompatible, namely a materialistic world-view, based on observation and science, and an energetic/spiritual world-view, based on experience through spiritual practice and traditional spiritual teachings. Psychology is generally defined as the scientific study of the human mind and behaviour, how we think, feel, act and interact individually and in groups (British Psychological Society (BPS) 2011a). It addresses the mind within the social structure of this material world of duality, utilizing scientific means of exploration and description. Spirituality is about the soul and spirit embedded within creation as a whole. It encompasses that which needs to be experienced, cannot be accessed within a normal state of consciousness and leads, for most people over time and with practice, to different, energy-based world-views that push the edges of current scientific models and means and cannot easily be fitted into the requirements of evidence-based approaches within psychology.

It is interesting in this context that the major professional bodies of psychology, such as the BPS in the UK and the American Psychological Association (APA) in the USA, do not yet list 'spirituality' as one of their topics and do not mention the transpersonal schools as a category (APA 2011; BPS 2011a), which is mainly due to the fact that transpersonal schools 'struggle' with scientific requirements.[1] Nevertheless, within the BPS we have spiritual interest groups and access to the *Journal of Transpersonal Psychology*; university courses increasingly include spirituality as a topic and research subject; the Royal College of Psychiatrists, which was in the past orientated towards a neurological and science-based view, exploring and treating the physical basis of mental illness, has a special interest group of psychiatrists working on the subject matter (SPSIG 2011), producing many interesting papers; and neuro-psychology is beginning to address the 'spiritual brain' (for overview: Fenwick 2011).

Psychology's attempt to be fully accepted as a science, its divorce from the theological, philosophical and mystical, has narrowed how we view humans, but has also contributed extensively to what we now know about the functioning of the mind, about our thought processes and the beliefs that underlie them, our emotional states and our behaviours. It has furthermore brought us a wealth of knowledge about how our childhood experiences influence and shape us and has produced much insight into the stages of individual and social development. Our mind's vast abilities, from learning and remembering, to reasoning and thinking in concepts, from the connection of our thought processes to our beliefs and behaviours, to our abilities to dissociate painful material, have been explored under the current paradigm. Without psychology's and psychiatry's extensive observations and research within the paradigm of seeing the human being as consisting of mind and body, we wouldn't possess diagnostic manuals such as the *Diagnostic and Statistical Manual of Mental Disorders* (DSM-IV-TR; APA 2000), which gives us fairly precise descriptions of conditions and disorders, outlining their symptoms, describing co-morbidities and giving us insights into differentiations, origins, prevalence, developments, patterns and other relevant features.

Nevertheless, there has been a price to pay for our scientific focus as we have stayed with the narrow idea of the human as consisting of what we understand as mind, and mostly also within the mind's normal waking state of consciousness. Questions such as, for instance, whether or not there is a soul that provides an underlying drive or if we are 'spirit in essence', with an inherent potentiality, as well as existential questions, such as those on purpose, birth, death and rebirth, and whether we are embedded into something wider and higher, could not be addressed sufficiently within such a framework. Furthermore, the mind, which is within the domain of ego and concerned with emotions, thought processes, beliefs and behaviours, cannot be segregated from the body, and the body will inevitably die. The mind, seen from a 'non-spiritual' perspective, is therefore, to a high degree, concerned with 'survival', and much of our development and our mental processes are, in one form or another, directly and indirectly, geared towards ensuring this, not only physically but also psychologically. It is highly likely, for example, that if I grow up in a spiritual system that believes in rebirth, I will, not only consciously but on a much deeper level, treat death and survival differently than if I live in a secular society, believing that this one life is all there is. Questions of how a spiritual/religious consciousness influences us and defines us, and, even more importantly, how ongoing spiritual practices shape our consciousness, our development and emotional/mental patterns, have therefore been left to philosophers and religious/spiritual scholars, and only lately touched on by psychology.

Now that we are beginning to include spirituality, we have to address such questions, leading us increasingly to the edge of what we accept currently as 'proof and evidence'. To measure the influence of spiritual components with scientific means and justify the inclusion of spirituality within psychological treatments based on current guidelines of evidence-based practice will inevitably lead to uncertainty and contradictions, but also to the exploration of new avenues. That there is a conflict can be observed in some of the recent developments: whilst the different humanistic and transpersonal psychological schools, as I will show later, as well as the ever-growing self-help movement and therapists and psychologists working outside the National Health Service (NHS), develop more and more psycho-spiritual models and approaches, the National Institute for Clinical Excellence (NICE) (2008) recommends mainly cognitive behavioural therapy (CBT) for the most common mental/ emotional health problems, namely anxiety disorders, depression, obsessive compulsive disorders and post-traumatic stress disorder (PTSD). CBT, with its focus on observable behaviours and conscious thought processes, can provide us with the necessary evidence, as long as it is solely symptom-focused, to ensure measurable outcomes. In further contrast, complementary and psychological treatments with a spiritual component, such as spiritual healing, holistic massage, meditation practices, spiritual counselling, energy psychology and psycho-spiritual approaches, have been offered, without requesting much hard evidence, in hospices for the terminally ill for quite some time as they focus on and cater for the soul/mind rather than the body/mind. Something similar applies to the field of addictions, which is the second area where the role of 'spirituality' has been accepted without being much questioned, especially in the well-established and relatively successful 12-step Alcoholic's Anonymous (AA) programme, to which I will come back later.

One restricting feature in research is the design of studies, especially those conducted along the lines of the medical model in the form of randomized controlled trials, but also certain qualitative approaches. To take spiritual practices into account will be challenging for several reasons. First, most forms of spiritual practice will induce altered states of consciousness, which will vary in depths and associations and, because we have no spiritual tradition worth speaking of, we know very little about higher states of consciousness and almost nothing about spiritual development. Thus we lack the necessary knowledge to categorize such factors and are bound to go through a phase of discussion. Second, when it comes to spirituality itself, we rely heavily on approaches developed in worlds that are not ours, such as different strands of Buddhism in the Far East or the indigenous traditions of the Americas, or on religious systems, which might not necessarily encourage 'spirituality' in the form of spiritual practice, but rather encourage 'belief'. Research not only needs to define them and distinguish between them, but also needs to take into account that we have no psycho-spiritual systems that are 'geared up' for the psyche of our western world.[2] A third reason is that it will be problematic to differentiate precisely what contributed to the effects of treatments when we include spiritual approaches and practices in various forms as adjuncts to other schools and techniques, such as we see, for example, at present with the inclusion of mindfulness within CBT.

Last, but by no means least, we face a lack of direct experience within the professional field. Spirituality, and this is one of the core problems, is a question of experience, ongoing practice and, in the final analysis, also one of description. We can have 'peak experiences' relatively easily, but lasting change, deep insights and profoundly altered views of the world come with time and, dare I say this, many of the lay people outside psychology, psychiatry and psychotherapy, and also some of our clients, will have more practical experience than the professionals they consult. Unlike thought processes and behaviours, states and symptoms, which can be observed, researched, categorized and known via descriptions of third parties, spiritual experiences are difficult to convey to somebody who has never had such an experience. Spiritual experiences can first resist description within our commonly accepted forms of language, which are geared up to describe our normal, everyday reality and, within psychology and therapy, our thoughts, behaviours, emotions and beliefs. To describe the spiritual, we often have to resort to metaphors, stories, imagery, archetypal descriptions and 'sacred' language. Second, spiritual experiences are also intensely personal, with descriptions, as I will show later, being coloured by how we individually translate those experiences. And third, a spiritual person has a different view of the world, which might be difficult to comprehend if we do not share it.

WE COULD FEEL BETTER: SPIRITUALITY AND PSYCHOLOGICAL WELL-BEING

Nevertheless, despite all the challenges, development in the field of psychology and psychiatry is accompanied by an increasing amount of quantitative and qualitative research into the correlation between spirituality/religion and mental health and emotional well-being.[3]

The scale of the global challenge posed by the rise of mental illness has been highlighted by several studies. According to the statistics publicized by the Mental Health Foundation (2011), about one in ten adults (450 million worldwide) is affected by mental health issues, accounting for over 12 per cent of the global burden of disease. One in four people is expected to experience some kind of mental health problem within the year, with mixed anxieties and depression being the most common disorders in Britain. In Europe and the Americas, the burden of mental illness is over 40 per cent of the total burden of disability, according to Andrew Powell, a member of the Royal Society of Psychiatry's SPSIG, which prompted him to pose the question 'Where else should that fundamental loss of meaning and purpose in life go except to the psychiatrist's consulting room when for many people the established faiths seem to be so divorced from the realities of daily life?' (Powell 2001a, p.2). Where indeed? Dr Lisa Rankin, a medical general practitioner (GP), describes the rather vague symptomatology that professionals observe in patients: 'We feel fatigued, depressed, listless, unfulfilled. We suffer from decreased libido, lack of spiritual connection, insomnia, anxiety, and other vague symptoms' (Rankin 2011, p.1), a description that resonates with my professional experience and that of colleagues I discuss such issues with. We seem to have reached a level of disconnection from meaning and of soul-starvation that makes us feel miserable, low, anxious, dissatisfied and unfulfilled.

Research increasingly seems to confirm that spirituality influences positively our overall mental and emotional well-being. The *Handbook of Religion and Health*, the culmination of a decade's work by Koenig, McCullough and Larson, published in 2001, includes 1200 research studies and 400 reviews. Looking into the relationship between religion/spirituality and a wide range of physical and mental health conditions, this profound review found a 60 to 80 per cent correlation between religion or spirituality and better physical health. Being embedded into a religious or spiritual context also improves people's overall well-being, happiness and life satisfaction. It furthermore increases hope and optimism, gives more purpose and meaning in life, results in higher self-esteem, greater adaptation to bereavement, lower rates of depression and faster recovery from it. Spiritual/religious people showed less anxiety, fewer psychotic tendencies, less delinquency and lower rates of alcohol and drug use and abuse (Koenig *et al.* 2001).

The success of the AA 12-step programme is by no small means due to the focus on the spiritual component of a 'higher power'. John Swindon (2001) advocates the inclusion of spirituality in *Spirituality and Mental Health Cure: Rediscovering a Forgotten Dimension* and so does Victor Schermer in his book *Spirit and Psyche: A New Paradigm for Psychology, Psychoanalysis and Psychotherapy* (2003). Both base their insights partly on work with and research into addictions, realizing that one of the key therapeutic healing factors is the development of a spiritual component within the addict's belief system and life. 'I witnessed significant healing of patients with substance misuse disorders and trauma occur through means which…could only be described as spiritual' (Schermer 2003, pp.24–25).

An emergent area of concern is our increased need to provide care for the elderly in a society that sees growing numbers of elderly people and a decrease in extended family connections. We know that caring for an elderly person in the family can be demanding, and this issue was addressed by a recent study into family caregivers for the elderly. It found that elders' and caregivers' spirituality significantly influenced their own psychological well-being, with a caregiver's spirituality significantly also influencing their elder's psychological well-being (Kim *et al.* 2011, pp.103–115).

Neurological research has also begun to explore the correlations between brain changes and spiritual practice (for overview: Fenwick 2011). For instance, Hoelzel *et al.* (2008, pp.55–61), based on functional magnetic resonance imaging (fMRI) scans of 20 mindfulness meditation practitioners and 20 controls, found, amongst other results, that the increase in size of their medial frontal cortex correlated directly with the total hours of meditation training. As the orbital frontal cortex plays a crucial role in emotion regulation by down-regulating the activity of the amygdala and is directly involved with extinction retention after fear conditioning, the researchers suggested, plausibly, that this might explain the ability of meditators to modify their emotional responses. Or, in other words, if we meditate regularly and over a period of time we will be less at the mercy of our emotions, as we will be able to calm ourselves down more easily and increase our ability to extinguish our fear responses after the fear-provoking event.

WE COULD BE MORE: SPIRITUAL PRACTICES AND PERSONAL DEVELOPMENT

Not only will spirituality help us to feel better, but spiritual practices, again, not to be confused with a set of religious dogmas and rules, but consisting of practices that aim to foster development to higher, transpersonal states, contribute to the positive development of many facets of the personality. Various researches, which I will refer to in more detail later, into Near Death Experiences, regular meditation practices or spiritually infused nature experiences confirm desirable changes in human attitudes, capacities, behaviours and values. We become more connected, less fearful, more selfless, more caring towards others, more appreciative of all life and more inclined to treat all life as being sacred (e.g. Bartlett 2008; Kübler-Ross 1997; Moody 2001; Van Lommel 2010).

Roger Walsh (2010, pp.28–35), an eminent professor of psychiatry, philosophy and anthropology at the University of California, after studying the field intensively over a period of time, lists seven positive outcomes of spiritual practices that aim at reaching the highest level of human consciousness, those levels which are described by sages with words such as enlightenment, liberation, salvation, awakening, nirvana or, as shamans would say, being connected to 'All there is'. He reiterates that spiritual practices contribute to:

- *Living ethically:* we live more ethically in the sense that we reject behaviours that inflict harm onto others and cultivate ethical intents, emotions and behaviours, such as compassion, kindness, giving and love.

- *Transforming emotions:* we practise non-attachment, which means we are being mindful of our emotions, but don't hold on to them. Spiritual practices help us to understand that emotions are the result of our thought processes and beliefs and not reflections of an objective reality.

- *Redirecting motivation:* when we redirect motivation in a spiritual sense we reduce the power our desires have over us and we change the object of our desire from things outside ourselves, such as power, fame, status or riches, to the desire of the more subtle inner knowing, to self-transcendence and to developing a unity-consciousness.

- *Training attention:* spiritual practices cultivate attention and concentration. Whatever we concentrate on, whatever we pay attention to, we can become. If we practise concentrating attention, we can begin to cultivate specific emotions, motives and intents. Eventually this practice brings a still mind, with all the benefits that this entails, such as, in spiritual terms, the mind becoming a mirror of the universe.

- *Refining awareness:* this spiritual practice is about observing and becoming the observer, creating refined levels of awareness. It brings unconscious material to the forefront, or, as some traditions would say, it holds it into the light, and whatever we 'hold into the light', whatever we make conscious, loses its unconscious hold over us. Practising refined awareness is transformative and healing. In psychological terms, it works against repression, dissociation, avoidance, exaggeration and over-association.

- *Cultivating wisdom:* wisdom, in contrast to knowledge, is a developed understanding of the processes of life with its central existential issues, such as questions of meaning and purpose, our smallness and greatness, our limits, uncertainties and sufferings, our longings and our joys, our light and our shadow and how we are embedded into the mysterious. We seek wisdom via contemplating teachings of 'wise' persons, being with wise teachers, seeking time alone in nature and, above all, looking and searching within.

- *Serving others:* most spiritual teachings emphasize the transformational power of generosity, giving and service, which strengthens positive emotions, such as compassion, love, kindness and happiness, and reduces the strengths of emotions such as anger, jealousy or hatred. Generous people tend to be psychologically healthier.

The Royal College of Psychiatrists (2010) adds better judgement, honesty, enhanced ability to 'let go', feeling more peaceful and relaxed and being able to be with people's suffering, among other outcomes of spiritual practice. Aung San Suu Kyi, the Burmese opposition leader, who has spent many years under house arrest and in Burmese prisons and is a practising Buddhist, mentioned 'freedom from fear' as the most important outcome of ongoing spiritual practices such as mindfulness meditation and practising loving kindness (Kyi 2011). Peggy Bartlett (2008) found in an extensive study that spending 'spiritual' time in nature strengthens our connection to the divine, enhances emphatic states as well as our overall well-being, produces a sense of enchantment and helps us to develop a deep understanding that we are part of this living, interconnecting system.

WE COULD COPE BETTER: SPIRITUALITY AND EXISTENTIAL CRISIS

Whilst we may be able to ignore the positive influence of spiritual practices and spiritual beliefs when it comes to everyday living, we can certainly not ignore them when it comes to existential crisis and existential questions, especially when we encounter clients who have to cope with their own life-threatening illnesses, the life-threatening illness of a loved one, or with loss.[4]

Studies find correlations between spiritual well-being and positive psychological responses when people are confronted with existential crisis situations. A recent study of 60 lung cancer patients in America, for instance, found that aspects of spirituality, namely meaning in life and prayer, have positive effects on psychological and physical responses, and an in-depth study of 160 terminally ill patients in palliative care came to the conclusion that spiritual well-being provides a sense of peace and offers some protection against end-of-life despair in those for whom death is imminent (McClain, Rosenfeld and Breitbart 2003). Two longitudinal studies (study 1 included 418 breast cancer patients and study 2 included 165 cancer survivors) confirm that it is meaning and peace that help with existential crisis. Without going into details of all the findings, which are not straightforward, the authors stress:

> Results from both studies underscore the importance of achieving meaning and peace; although not consistent for all outcomes across the two studies, having a sense of meaning and peace...and gaining meaning/peace over time (in both studies), predicted enhanced adjustment. These findings add to emerging evidence that the ability to find meaning in life is a potent predictor of adjustment to cancer...and well-being more general. (Yanez *et al.* 2009, p.1)

It doesn't take much imagination to understand that we will reach our limitations as professionals if we cannot use a wider frame of reference, a frame that reaches beyond the physical life, when it comes to existential crisis and to facing death. I will therefore not cite more research at this point but share with you an unusual case that illustrates the advantages of having a wider frame of reference at our disposal.

CASE EXAMPLE: A HIGHER POWER

When I had just finished training as a hypnotherapist, about 18 years ago, I tentatively incorporated clinical hypnosis into my practice. Soon some colleagues referred clients to me. With hypnosis not being the most professionally accepted approach at that time, it is understandable that some of my colleagues only referred clients to me after they had reached the end of the road. One of those clients was a lady who made a lasting impression on me.

She had been brought up in Jamaica and moved to the UK at the age of 12. She was a professional, middle-class, open-minded and emotionally balanced person, embedded in an extended family and community. She had been referred by her GP to a counselling colleague because she had cancelled three appointments for an operation that would most certainly save her life. She had a growth in her belly that had reached the size of a small tennis ball and she suffered. The diagnosis was straightforward: 'either we remove the growth or you will, sooner or later, die'.

The GP, her consultant and surgeon as well as her family had been trying everything, from loving persuasion to threats. My counselling colleague informed me that the client was convinced that she would die on the operating table and had developed an overwhelming fear response. The message from the other professionals was roughly, 'Well, let's try hypnosis – that's all we can do now'.

I took a case history, which revealed nothing that would give any insight into the underlying issues of her overwhelming fear response, and I was quite convinced that I would need to come up with something that was bigger and more powerful than her fear. Time was running out for this lady; the counsellor had spent three sessions with her, without much success, and another appointment for surgery was already scheduled.

When working with hypnosis, especially shortly after training, good hypnotic subjects are a gift. People who grew up in cultures where trance states are more accepted and normal are usually just that. I used very little in form of formal trance-inductions and was still contemplating what I could do, thinking along conventional lines, when I suddenly thought about religion and about God. I asked her whether she went to church when she was a child in Jamaica. And after she confirmed that I asked her to let a positive memory of a church service come to the forefront of her mind and let me know when that had happened. After receiving confirmation, I asked her to vividly remember the church, the service, the singing and clapping, the people around her and especially how she felt. I then instructed her to hold the image and feeling of the most exciting moments and to intensify them in her own way. During hypnotherapy, the therapist observes visual and other expressions, which indicate that the person is visualizing and that the altered state deepens. Both were present fairly quickly. I asked her to tell me a bit more about the experience and after she had done that I wondered aloud if it would be possible to put her faith into God and her fate into his hands. Still wondering aloud I said something along the lines of 'Well, you know that it is very important for you to have the operation we were talking about. I wonder if you could bring that trust in God back – you know – that trust from your childhood? Really trust that you can put your faith into him and your fate into his hands. Trust that all will be well.' After a few moments' silence, she nodded her head, her face lightened up and suddenly she opened her eyes, showing that far away, kind of hazy expression of being in an altered state. She said, 'I had forgotten – it's not in my power – is it? I must trust that everything will be well. That I will survive if that's what shall happen.' I reinforced that by repeating more or less her own words, adding some confidence building and reassurance.

The lady survived the operation five days later.

Needless to say, this session also provided learning for me, one which I have never forgotten. I am not a Christian, but as a professional I do know that beliefs can move mountains and I also know that it is the client's belief that will move them, not mine. The art, especially if one doesn't have much time with a client, is to elicit an appropriate and powerful enough belief to counteract a belief that will lead to suffering. In the case of this client, the belief had to be powerful enough to counteract her belief that she would die on the operating table – what else other than a 'higher power' or a 'spiritual force' can do that? I learned during this session not to shy away from taking the spiritual aspect of a person into account and realized that, as long as I work ethically, in the sense that I base the work on the client's spiritual system and not my own, it will enhance the therapeutic results.

DEVELOPING BEYOND: THE EMERGENCE OF A NEW PSYCHO-SPIRITUAL PARADIGM?

When we look at different psychological schools and psychotherapy/ counselling we are entering a complex, diverse and still-developing territory, but we can also see a movement towards an inclusion of the spiritual. Generally speaking there are four streams, psychodynamic, cognitive-behavioural, humanistic-existential and transpersonal psychology, each providing theories as well as various therapeutic applications.

A wide range of *psychodynamic therapies* have developed from psychoanalysis. They have contributed insight into the dynamics and conflicts of conscious and unconscious forces and how they influence our mental states and behaviours, as well as the self-structure we internalize during formative years in early childhood, which function as a 'blueprint' for future relationships and for how we experience ourselves and the world. The resolution of those conflicts is, quite simplified, the aim of psychodynamic therapies. Besides the three-fold structure of the person – the id, ego and superego – some widely used terms in psychology, therapy and counselling emerged from psychodynamic therapies, including conflict, neurosis, unconscious, defence mechanisms, attachment, transference, counter-transference, object relations, drives, libido and more. *Jungian psychology* (Jung 1961, 1977), which still exists in its purer form, while ideas have also been integrated into other approaches, mainly within the humanistic schools, brought concepts such as the 'self' and 'soul' as well as culture, mythology and the collective unconscious, accessible in dreams and via altered states, and was a major contribution to our understanding of our psyche. For Jung, the most important and lifelong task is wholeness, fulfilment through the process of individuation, achievement of resolution and harmony between conscious and unconscious.

Behaviourism originally placed its emphasis firmly on the study of observable behaviour, how we learn to behave in a certain way and what reinforces or hinders our learning. Placing much importance on sound research, behaviourism contributed powerfully to psychology being accepted as a science. Terms such as learning theories, conditioning, operant conditioning, stimulus-response and positive reinforcement are expressions associated with behaviourism, and therapy consisted mainly of learning adaptive behaviours via various techniques. Its developments in the form of *cognitive-behavioural* (e.g. Beck *et al.* 1979) and *rational emotive approaches* (e.g. Ellis and Dryden 2007), which focus on thought patterns and underlying belief systems, as driving our emotional responses as well as our behaviours, are widely accepted and utilized within the field of mental health.

Changing thought processes, negative, unrealistic self-talk and the underlying belief systems, and with that the painful emotions and 'maladaptive' behaviours, is the aim of therapeutic interventions.

Humanistic psychology encompasses a wide range of schools, theoretical frameworks and therapeutic approaches. Abraham Maslow (1968), who contributed theories such as the striving for self-actualization, the hierarchy of needs and higher motivation, and Carl Rogers (2003), who designed person-centred counselling/ therapy, were fundamental in initiating the movement. Fritz Perls' Gestalt therapy (1969), psychosynthesis developed by Roberto Assagioli (1965), logotherapy by Victor Frankl (1973), existential psychoanalysis by Roll May (1969) and many more are loosely connected under the umbrella of humanistic and existential schools and forms of therapy. Humanistic psychology is value orientated. It proclaims people's capacity to be self-determining and is guided by a conviction that intentionality and ethical values are strong psychological forces and major determinants of human behaviour. 'This conviction leads to an effort to enhance such distinctly human qualities as choice, creativity, the interaction of the body, mind and spirit, and the capacity to become more aware, free, responsible, life-affirming and trustworthy' (Association for Humanistic Psychology 2011, p.1). Existential schools furthermore define four existential issues, which are seen as lying at the core of the existential struggle that is considered to be at the root of most psychological difficulties: coping with death, the tension between freedom/responsibility, isolation and meaninglessness.

Transpersonal psychology, integral psychology and ecological psychology

The most recent additions, such as transpersonal psychology, integral psychology, non-dual psychology and ecological psychology, all work towards the integration of psychology with spirituality and/or ecology and present a logical development from humanistic psychology. Mariana Caplan states that transpersonal psychology draws upon ancient mystical knowledge that comes from many traditions and that it tries to integrate timeless wisdom with western psychology, translating spiritual principles into scientifically grounded, contemporary language (Caplan 2009, p.231). Transpersonal thinking and transpersonal approaches are in part influenced by various shamanic traditions and are therefore of interest here.

According to their professional body, transpersonal psychology might loosely be called the psychology of spirituality and of those areas of the human mind which search for higher meanings in life, and which move beyond the limited boundaries of the ego to access an enhanced capacity for wisdom, creativity, unconditional love and compassion (BPS 2011b).

Many of those involved in the process of formulating an integrative theory and designing therapeutic-transformational approaches stem from the humanistic stream. Abraham Maslow (1968), Stanislav Grof (1985, 1993) and Victor Frankl (1973) were early names associated with transpersonal psychology, being instrumental in publicizing the first *Journal of Transpersonal Psychology*. Major theorists and thinkers, as well as founders of schools, such as Wilber (2000, 2006), Walsh (2010), Vaughan (2000), Grof (1985, 1993, 2006), Assagioli (1965), Tart (1992) and others, have contributed to the development of the transpersonal field. Transpersonal thinking views the human psyche as consisting of a core self as well as a personal centre/ ego.[5] Within this perspective, there is both a movement of the personal (ego) to the self and a movement of the self to manifest its nature through and in the personal psyche. Thus, approaches within transpersonal psychology, theoretically at least, should include both therapeutic interventions to alleviate suffering as well as working towards individuation, drawing on a wide range of therapeutic methods towards the uncovering of psychological material within a context of the individual's potential based on spiritual insight and experience.

Transpersonal thinking has grown rather complex and diverse as different academic, philosophical and psychological thinkers, as well as practitioners, try to construct models, theories and explanations around the subject of consciousness and the integration of spirituality and psychology. Ken Wilber, originally involved in transpersonal psychology, has distanced himself and has created the term 'integral psychology' (Wilber 2000) for his approaches, and it seems that some spiritual movements criticize transpersonal approaches in psychology for staying within the world of 'maya', the world of illusion.

There are theoretical differences when it comes to models of consciousness and the development of consciousness, which are complex and exceed the capacity of this book. Nevertheless, to provide an example: Ken Wilber, who is generally recognized as one of the major philosophical contributors to the advancement of consciousness studies and integral psychology and has published many papers and books on the subject matter, postulates that human consciousness develops progressively, in the individual as well as historically, allowing for uneven processes in development. He suggests that spiritual development progresses in stages, listing four states, namely the gross, the subtle, the causal and the non-dual. We need to access the early states first before we can progress to the higher ones, which, if I understand Wilber correctly, demands ongoing spiritual practice (Wilber 2000, 2006). Grof postulates that transpersonal development requires a return to the perinatal first, before being able to progress. Grof distinguishes two levels of mind, the hylotrophic, which refers to normal states of consciousness, and the holotrophic, which refers to non-ordinary (altered) states, which we need to enter to experience the whole. In accordance with this theory, Grof developed 'holotrophic breath therapy' (Grof 1985, 1993; Grof and Grof 2010), which produces highly altered states, facilitating a regression back to birth and pre-birth to undo the birth-trauma, but also then, beyond this, to the level of the transpersonal, which he calls transpersonal regressions. It is within those levels of the transpersonal that, according to Grof, we find various:

> mythological sequences, sequences from the lives of ancestors and the history of the race, and from past lives. Here we have many of the states described in spiritual literature, of cosmic consciousness, of the perennial philosophy. This map of the human psyche shows that each individual is an extension of all of existence. (Grof 1995, p.1)

Despite theoretical and practical differences and difficulties in a field that is still developing, and will probably do so for quite some time to come, everybody involved seems to assume the existence of an underlying field, which might be pure consciousness, and which we can access when we alter our states of awareness through various means.[6] Those means range from spiritual practices, such as meditation, prayer or nature observations, to means that produce ecstatic, unusual experiences, such as trance dance, taking psychedelic drugs, strong regression techniques, shamanic journeying and intense ceremonies, as well as through sudden changes of perception produced by shock or Near Death Experiences (NDEs). Such peak experiences, those of a more 'normal' kind as well as those of a more dramatic nature, labelled, for example, spiritual emergencies or NDEs, will change our whole view of the world and of ourselves within it and, in the process, alter the way we see things, think about things and what we believe to be reality. Ongoing spiritual practice will change us, and our view of the world, over time, as we begin on many levels to develop and anchor the awareness of a wider consciousness, and this is the context from which we arise, which we are embedded in, part of and to which we will return. The transpersonal field postulates that because we have neglected exploring such 'altered states of perception' when studying the mind and human reality within psychology, we have reduced the human being to a creature of mind, without taking the innate soul and the wider connection of consciousness into account. To develop an understanding of the human as a whole we need an integration of the spiritual with the psychological.

At this moment in our thinking, the idea of defining the various functions of psychology and spirituality within a framework 'consciousness' seems helpful. As a framework, one could say that psychology addresses the content of our consciousness whilst spirituality refers to the wider context, helping us to experience the field of consciousness from which everything arises (Caplan 2009, p.225). Whilst psychology and psychotherapy/counselling in its many forms help us to unravel, heal, integrate and understand the many strands of our personal psyche, spirituality helps us to directly experience and perceive something greater, some force or forces outside ourselves into which we are nevertheless embedded, of which we are a part and from which we arise. Spirituality helps us to access that greater reality and the information held within this underlying field. With continuous spiritual practice we internalize and absorb, for want of a better word, those experiences and information within our being, a process that will alter us. The psychological and spiritual influence each other and, if we want to move forward as a species, as well as in the field of psychology, both need to be taken into account and, if possible, integrated. Transpersonal approaches share the idea that humans develop along a 'spectrum of consciousness of infinite possibilities' (Wilber 2000, p.2) and that psychology must work towards increasing wholeness, rather than focus on 'fixing' people so that they can function in accordance with socially accepted norms.

Transpersonal approaches, schools, concepts and ideas could not have come about without the ancient spiritual wisdom traditions from different parts of the world. *Shamanic studies* have been of great interest within the transpersonal approaches in psychology and have been explored also within some of the traditional medical and clinical and cognitive psychological fields (e.g. Achterberg 1985; Gagan 1998; Grof 1993; Krippner 2002; Peters 1989; Vaughan 2000; Walsh 1990, 2010; Wilber 2000, 2006). As far as we know, shamanism is the first 'psycho-spiritual' tradition that has explored altered states of perceptions and it has worked within them for many millennia. Shamans' knowledge, stemming from that work within altered states, has, as this book will show, inspired the explorations of shamanism within contemporary psychology. Peters remarked in 1989 that the study of shamanism and 'the Shamanistic State of Consciousness…is the focus of much current psychological interest' (Peters 1989, p.115). Almost a quarter of a decade later the question of 'consciousness' is becoming still more prominent within psychology, with interdisciplinary connections to contemporary physics as well as neuro-science advancing the field, a subject I will come back to in Chapter 4.

The integration of psychology and spirituality is necessary, as the spiritual doesn't automatically heal the mental/emotional, and the mental/emotional needs the spiritual to engage with the wider reality and develop the higher potentiality of human consciousness.

As we have moved away from addressing the 'whole' to explore the parts, we have made many valuable discoveries, which can help us to understand our humanness within the structure of this world and help us to heal and integrate different aspects of our 'egoic selves'. Nevertheless, we now know that we have not only neglected some parts, but have neglected to explore the whole, the whole capacity of our brains as well as the whole to which we are connected and in which we are embedded. Until we can prove that Albert Einstein's famous remark that our experiencing ourselves as separate from the universe is an illusion and William James' assertion that there is 'a continuum of cosmic consciousness into which our several minds plunge as into a mother sea' (cited in Murphy and Ballou 1960, p.324) describe reality, we might have to explore the frontiers of mind and integrate spiritual knowledge into our work without possessing ultimate proof.

Notes

1 The BPS, for example, lists cognitive-behavioural, psychodynamic, humanistic and systemic approaches.
2 I worked in Sri Lanka after the Tsunami and observed Buddhist monks providing spiritual counselling to affected families. The spiritual counselling that was undertaken would not have worked for western people – even if they followed Buddhism – who are not deeply embedded in a Buddhist culture, with extended families and strong communities, that centre around the monasteries.
3 The research is, in my opinion, still quite crude as various factors are not differentiated, but nevertheless the data seems to support the demand for further research and the integration of psychology and spirituality. Larry Culliford (2011) refers to some more of the published research when making a case for the inclusion of spirituality in psychology.
4 I will come back to this subject in Chapter 17.
5 This subject will be addressed in more detail in Chapter 3.
6 This corresponds with the shamanic world-view, which will be discussed in Chapter 4.

PART II

The World of Shamanism

One conclusion was forced upon my mind at that time and my impression of its truth has ever since remained unshaken. It is that our normal consciousness, rational consciousness, is but one special type of consciousness whilst all around it, parted from it by the flimsiest of screens, there lie potential forms of consciousness, entirely different.

William James (1958)

2 | SHAMANISM
The Continuum of Humanity's Spiritual Quest

MUCH MISUNDERSTOOD: HISTORIC PERCEPTIONS OF SHAMANISM

Shamanism is a living spiritual system, originating in and derived from various indigenous cultures, rather than a religion or a spiritual system based on a specific set of teachings and practices. Like all living systems, it is evolving, taking a range of shapes and forms in various cultures and at different times. The complexity and strangeness of shamanism have led to countless research projects and publications, from descriptions by early missionaries and explorers and articles and books by anthropologists, archaeologists, historians and religious scholars about traditional, indigenous shamanism to publications by contemporary shamans, still living in indigenous cultures, as well as western shamanically orientated practitioners.

Unfortunately, our knowledge about traditional shamanism in indigenous cultures all over the world, especially in those that were conquered or even eliminated, is not sound. The early missionaries, botanists, anthropologists and ethnographers, as well as the later religious scholars, historians, psychologists and others, were adversely influenced by the beliefs of their times, by preconceived notions and prejudices, which all influenced their methodologies, observations, descriptions and conclusions. Those early descriptions, especially those with religiously condemning connotations, have coloured popular views and have without doubt contributed to the long-standing neglect of and scepticism about the worth of indigenous knowledge and teachings.

Traditional shamans can be found in indigenous cultures all over the world, including the Americas, Russia, Africa, Asia, the Far East and China, as well as Australia and New Zealand. They vary in their practices and techniques, but also show remarkable similarities in their views of the world and their approaches to the work they do. Scholars debate the origin of the word 'shaman', although most sources indicate that the word is closely related to the word 'saman', which stems from the Evenk (Tungus) language of the Tungus tribe in Siberia, and the shamanism of this region (Siberia and Mongolia) is often referred to as classic shamanism in literature (Pratt 2007b, p.xxi). The meaning of the word 'shaman' can be roughly translated as 'one who knows' or 'one who is excited, moved, raised' (Pratt 2007b, p.xxi).[1]

In their outstanding book *Shamans through Time: 500 Years on the Path of Knowledge*, Jeremy Narby, a historian and anthropologist, and Francis Huxley, an anthropologist from Oxford University, have compiled 64 previously published works to illustrate how shamans have been perceived through the centuries (Narby and Huxley 2001). For those early European visitors, entering a world of spirits, magic, high drama, ecstatic rituals, peculiar healing practices, unfamiliar chants, the beating of drums, trancelike dances and bizarre visions must have produced strange feelings at best and fear and horror at worst. Consequently, and not surprisingly, the contributors in Narby and Huxley's compilation convey everything from suspicion, fear, condemnation, revulsion and disdain to fascination, respect, admiration and adoration. It is therefore essential to understand that there are negative and positive aspects to western attitudes towards shamanism and that both extremes – the glorification as well as the condemnation of certain aspects and practices – arise mostly from our own viewpoints, which are in turn coloured by our beliefs, our perceptions and the times and societies we live in.[2]

Narby and Huxley (2001, pp.8–10) suggest that explorers and priests from Europe and Russia in the sixteenth century were the first outsiders to encounter and discover shamanic practices, which they, on the whole and in accordance with their Christian beliefs, likened to witchcraft and consorting with the devil, characterizations that could have serious consequences during the times of witch hunts. Later, with the age of reason and enlightenment dominating western thinking, observers from the western world described shamans as jugglers and as impostors, who tricked people into believing that they communicated with spirits, but were really just fooling the people by using song and dance, tricks and sleight of hand or by manipulating the power of the imagination (Narby and Huxley 2001, pp.21–22).

The descriptions of shamans, the attitude towards them and our understanding of them began to change and develop between 1900 and 1960, when anthropologists embarked on studying indigenous cultures more intensely in various places, such as Siberia, the Canadian Arctic, British Guiana, Africa and South and North America. The reports of those anthropologists showed that different people – young and old, men and women – became shamans for a variety of reasons, including having a natural gift or being struck by illness, which resulted in a transformation. They also described how shamans could do different things: healing, charming game, hexing, predicting the future, influencing the weather and interpreting omens. Anthropological reports showed that shamans were 'different people who did different things', yet they all claimed to communicate with spirits in the interest of their community. This 'communication with spirit in the interest of their communities' gave the worldwide phenomenon the first underlying coherence (Narby and Huxley 2001, p.40).

During this period some of the anthropologists began to interview shamans, recording their own accounts of their initiations and travels into the spirit world, which led to a more differentiated and overall more positive picture.[3] It was during that period, in 1932, that Neidhardt recorded the famous life story of Black Elk, which is still being republished today (Neidhardt 1988). The debate, which had started earlier, whether shamans should be seen as mentally deranged psychotics, schizophrenics or hysterics, intensified during those years. Peter Elkin, an Australian anthropologist, casts a favourable light on the Aboriginal culture and the medicine man, calling him a man of special, and often outstanding, personality, which he attributes to his 'making' in the form of training, deeds, abilities and the special social personality ascribed to him by his fellows (Elkin 1945). Claude Levi-Strauss, the famous French anthropologist who observed shamans in Panama, stated in 1949 that shamans were more like psychoanalysts than psychotics, outlining parallels between psychoanalysis and shamanism (Levi-Strauss 1949). Elvin (1955) describes female shamans from the Soara in India as healers, whilst Devereux (1956), on the other hand, describes them as mentally deranged. On the whole, the descriptions and conclusions, although becoming more precise and positive, are still fairly controversial, with words such as savages and primitives being used when describing indigenous people generally, and alternating extremes, such as 'mentally ill and psychologically unstable' and 'gifted outstanding people', when characterizing shamans specifically.

Two major changes in perception took place in the early 1950s with Eliade's book *Shamanism: Archaic Techniques of Ecstasy*, which proved groundbreaking in its overall positive interpretation of the shamanic phenomenon. Eliade not only showed that shamans existed all over the world, but also pointed out their astonishing similarities, defining them as masters of ecstasy (Eliade 1964). After Eliade, a second, rather unexpected source began to popularize shamanism. In 1957 R.G. Wasson, a vice president of J.P. Morgan, published an article in *Life Magazine* entitled 'Seeking the Magic Mushroom', in which he describes his and his wife's participations in rituals in Mexico and their experiences during sacred mushroom ceremonies (Wasson 2011). He reached a wide audience, as several hundred thousand people read *Life Magazine*. This opened the world of shamanism to popular audiences and triggered a wave of tourism to Mexican villages, a trend that increased in the 1960s with spiritual seekers, hippies, psychologists and others from western cultures seeking to experience shamanic practices. They were driven mainly by the longing for the divine, for meaning and for ecstasy, either induced by hallucinogenic drugs or shamanic teachings, chants, drumming, meditation and dance, or a combination of both. It is interesting to note that María Sabina, the female shaman Wasson worked with, stated that after the foreigners ate the sacred children (mushrooms) to find God, they – the sacred children – ceased to elevate her and lost their magical power for her.

But, in the final analysis, it was Carlos Castaneda's first book, *The Teachings of Don Juan: A Yaqui Way of Knowledge*, published in 1969, that ignited an unprecedented interest in shamanism, achieving cult status, leading almost to a glorification of the phenomenon.[4] The book inspired a second wave of professionals and other interested people in all parts of the world to live with indigenous people, 'study' the shamans and partake in, mainly plant-induced, ceremonies and quests. Descriptions of shamans' vast knowledge, their practices and achievements now became positive and detailed, stemming from direct experience as well as minute, long-term observations, with quite eminent researchers and other interested parties trying hard to present their concepts and practices from the native's point of view.

Barbara Myerhoff accompanied the Huichol Indians of Mexico in the early 1970s, taking peyote and subsequently describing her vivid vision of the 'axis mundis', which connects the different layers of reality (Myerhoff 1974, p.156). Michael Harner wrote *The Way of the Shaman* in the early 1980s, based on his studies of Conibo Indians in the Peruvian Amazon in 1960/61 and his later work with the Shuar in Ecuador in 1968. He described the shaman as a 'man or woman who enters an altered state of consciousness – at will – to contact and utilize an ordinarily hidden reality in order to acquire knowledge, power, and to help other persons' (Harner 1982, p.25). His descriptions of shamanic techniques and approaches that everybody can practise still underpin much of contemporary shamanic practice. Blacker, a lecturer from Cambridge University, who conducted an in-depth study of Japanese shamanic practices, describes the shaman as a gifted person of a distinct kind: 'He is at once a cosmic traveller, a healer, a master of spirits, a psychopomp, an oracular mouthpiece' (Blacker 1975, p.209), and points out, like many before her, that the shaman alters his consciousness at will to communicate directly with the inhabitants of the supernatural world. Gerhard Reichel-Dolmatoff, a Colombian anthropologist who studied Colombian shamans, describes the shaman as an intellectual, a translator, possessing in the mind of his people the necessary esoteric knowledge and powers to use his contact with the supernatural powers for the benefit of society (Reichel-Dolmatoff 1975, p.216). The direct participation and long-term observations contributed to the final acceptance that shamans are mentally sound individuals, a professional group with skills and knowledge that enable them to help and heal within the community, which in turn brings them status and power.

In the 1980s and 1990s we encounter attempts to find common ground between scientific and indigenous knowledge. Richard Noll, an American clinical psychologist, sees the extensive use of mental imagery as applying to shamanism as well as psychology (Noll 1987, p.248). The medical doctor and anthropologist Roger Walsh suggested in 1990 that shamans are pioneers in exploring the as yet poorly understood capacities of the human mind, and Winkelman in his doctoral dissertation compares magico-religious practices in 47 societies, spanning 4000 years from 1750 BC to the present, pointing out that, prior to western influences, all of these used altered states of consciousness for religious and healing practices, but stresses that shamanic practices occur mainly in nomadic and hunting and gathering societies and that within such tribes the shaman plays many roles, such as healer, ritualist, mythologist, medium and master of spirits (Winkelman 1989).

DEFINING TRADITIONAL SHAMANISM

It can be said that traditional shamanism seems to be a path universally used in indigenous cultures to expand consciousness via entering altered states to connect with the essences or spirits of the whole and to work with those forces for the benefits, health and harmony of their communities and its members. Traditional shamans all over the world seem to be powerful, experienced and knowledgeable utilizers of such expanded states of consciousness, so-called 'masters of ecstasy'. They function as visionaries, divinatory practitioners, ritualists, mythologists, mediums, healers, dreamers, psychics, creators and manifestors. Due to their intense connection to 'All that is' and their vast knowledge and skills, they seem to be revered by their tribes, functioning as the guardians of the psychic and ecological equilibrium of the group and its members, achieving status and power, being able to form a bridge between the different worlds. One of these worlds is the world of normal, everyday consciousness, in which the world is experienced as consisting of matter, while the other worlds are experienced in states of expanded consciousness in which the world is experienced in the form of energies and spirits. Above all, they are interdependent with nature, their tribes and communities, working according to the needs and requirements of the community and spirit as well as living in both worlds, in the sense that they work 'part time' as shamans, while at other times they do the work they would be doing anyway, be it farming, hunting, gathering or building. This interdependence with the community is the trademark of shamans in comparison to other spiritual practitioners such as, for instance, priests or spiritual healers.

THE RECENT DEVELOPMENTS: CONTEMPORARY SHAMANIC APPROACHES

From about 1980 up to the present, our understanding of the nature of shamanism as well as our definitions have changed as indigenous cultures and traditional societies have become increasingly integrated, whilst mainstream society has begun to embrace and create new variations of shamanism. I want to mention a few influential voices to illustrate the variety of this development.

Anthropologists have studied the shamanic practices of city-dwelling ethnic healers, such as the curanderos of South America and the psychic surgeons in the Philippines. Two well-known researchers are Donald Joralemon and Douglas Sharon, who profiled 14 healers in their book *Sorcery and Shamanism: Curanderos and Clients in Northern Peru*, which was published in 1993. As a result, some of these urban healers have become quite famous and shamanic healing methods have been explored within medical settings, such as the Department of Integrative Medicine at the University of California.

Another recent development in the medical field has been the growth of ethno-medicine, the incorporation of traditional shamanic methods, especially the use of medicinal herbs, into modern medical practice. In many places with spiritual healing traditions, modern and traditional healing systems now exist side by side, with patients choosing to consult the local shaman for certain types of illnesses whilst using biomedical practitioners for more serious illnesses. Often, this is a mutually beneficial combination, as Julien Bastien describes in *Drum and Stethoscope* (1992), stating that when shamans and doctors collaborate a synergetic effect is produced which further promotes healing.

Western initiates have also begun bringing back what they learned from shamans, developing teachings for western audiences. One of these is Brant Secunda, who trained for 12 years with Don Jose Matsuwa, a tribal leader and shaman of the Huichol Indians, and founded, together with his teacher, The Dance of the Deer Foundation, Center for Shamanic Studies, running workshops and leading groups on Vision Quests and pilgrimages to places of power to learn the Huichol way (Secunda 2011). Joan Halifax, a well-known anthropologist and Zen Buddhist, who wrote the outstanding books *Shamanic Voices* (1979), mainly an account of shamans of the Americas, and *Shaman: The Wounded Healer* (1982), also began to include shamanism into her teachings, as did Michael Harner, who established the Foundation for Shamanic Studies to spread the teaching of his methods, designed for novices seeking to learn about shamanism and professionals interested in an in-depth training programme to learn about healing methods. His previously mentioned books, as well as his workshops, contributed to the growing expansion of teachings about shamanism in the West and produced a new generation of practitioners, such as Sandra Ingerman (1990), who brought shamanic journeying and soul retrieval to the forefront of techniques used in the field of therapy, and Tom Cowan (1993), who wrote extensively about Celtic shamanism. Along with others, Alberto Vivoldo later founded the Four Winds Society, which runs extensive training courses, especially in energy healing (Vivoldo 2010).

Arnold Mindell, physicist and developer of 'Dreambody Work', now known as process-orientated psychology, was influenced by and wrote extensively about shamanism, combining his experiences with traditional teachers in Japan, Africa and India with psychology, quantum physics and physiology (Mindell 1993, 2000, 2004) and, as already mentioned, transpersonal approaches of psychology incorporate shamanic world-views and teachings into their concepts to various degrees. John Perkins, one of the teachers I worked with, studied with the Shuar of the Amazons, the Quechua of the Andes and the Burgis of Indonesia, to name just a few. He contributed extensively to a new body of understanding, and to shamanic teaching and practitioners with his numerous books (Perkins 1990, 1994, 1997). He founded 'The Dream Change Coalition', which works extensively in the areas of conservation in the Amazon and education of businesses, and which brings together shamanic practitioners from different parts of the world. John Perkins has increasingly taken a critical political stance and became famous via his bestsellers *Confessions of an Economic Hit Man* (2006) and *Hoodwinked* (2009).

African shamanism has also come to the forefront. Luisah Teish published *Jambalaya: The Natural Woman's Book of Personal Charms and Practical Rituals* in 1991 and *Carnival of the Spirit* in 1994, introducing the world to the sacred traditions of the Yoruba in Africa, whilst the works of Malidoma Somé (1992, 1998), who also teaches extensively, has brought the world of the Dagara people of Burkina Faso, especially their initiation rites and ancestral teachings, to large audiences all over the world.

In the UK, shamanic workshops and later training courses were first offered by Leo Rutherford, a psychologist and the founder of Eagle's Wing College of Shamanic Medicine, who had learned from Joan Halifax as well as South and North American shamans and others, and elegantly and powerfully combines shamanism with his psychological insights (e.g. Rutherford 1997, 2008). Not long after that, the field of neo-shamanism began to grow steadily, in the UK and also in the rest of Europe. Today there are countless shamanic organizations and practitioners in the UK.

Along with their home-based teaching, most of the western shamanic practitioners and teachers began to take seekers to other parts of the world to experience shamanic practices, a movement that has by now, especially in the Amazon and the Andes, reached almost the level of mass tourism. It is not surprising that an increasing number of 'new shamans', who were nothing more than clever businessmen, appeared in South and North America, offering American and European tourists a variety of hallucinogens, ceremonies and teachings for mystical experiences. Although a good level of discernment is advised, the increasing demand for 'experiencing the real thing' shows the growing reawakening to the need for connection, for being more than we can be within the material world-view, and a deep longing of people in the so-called 'developed world' for spirituality, ecstasy, insight, expansion and a return to more nature-based roots.

DEFINING CONTEMPORARY SHAMANISM: A DEVELOPING, LIVING PRACTICE

Noticeably, shamanism has come a long way from its roots in traditional, indigenous cultures to the increasingly diverse applications we see in the modern world. It has become part of a progressively more urban and global world, gaining growing interest and acceptance from anthropologists, medical practitioners, psychologists and therapists. It has been integrated into the transpersonal schools of psychology, and has been adopted and adapted by the New Age and self-help movement for personal and spiritual development and by the ecological movement. In the process, it has become a blend of many elements and it is still growing and developing in multiple ways. To construct a single definition is therefore impossible.

Today we see psychologists and psychotherapists incorporate shamanic ideas, concepts and approaches into their practice. The workshops and training courses I have attended over the last 15 years, as well as the workshops and courses I have facilitated, have been increasingly attended by professionals. We also have many practitioners within the New Age and self-development movement who work shamanically, mainly with groups, employing a wide range of approaches and concepts, either relying on one tradition or experimenting, exploring and mixing a range of traditions originating from Africa, North and South America, Siberia or the Celtic realms. Sweat lodge ceremonies, Vision Quests, ceremonial work, journeying, shamanic energy healing, psychopomp work, trips to work with indigenous shamans, healing groups, drumming and drum making, equinox and solstice celebrations, Medicine Wheel teachings and many more are offered. The eco-movement has learned much from indigenous teachings, whilst some of the early western practitioners, such as John Perkins, whom I mentioned above, developed a more political approach, and political–spiritual activism, based partly on indigenous understanding, is coming to the forefront.

Generally speaking we can distinguish six branches of contemporary shamanism, which are in themselves intertwined, with the later types growing faster as the world becomes more urbanized and global and as shamanic practices are increasingly incorporated into transpersonal psycho-spiritual approaches of psychology and psychotherapy and mixed and matched with other teachings, techniques and tools:

1. Traditional shamanism, which still exists in rural, isolated communities, which are increasingly being impacted by economic and tourist influences from the modern world.

2. The use of traditional shamanic practices for healing in the different parts of the developing world and in ethnic communities in the western world.

3. The incorporation of elements of shamanism, such as using traditional medicine herbs, into modern medical practices.

4. The integration of indigenous teachings and techniques in humanistic and transpersonal schools of psychology and contemporary psychological, psychiatric and psychotherapeutic practice.

5. The adoption of shamanic journeying, trance, ceremonial and healing methods by those involved in the New Age, self-help and personal development movements.

6. The integration of indigenous knowledge generally and shamanic teachings and wisdom into the contemporary ecological movements as well as the political–spiritual activism movement.

There is much to learn from indigenous, traditional shamans, as well as from contemporary shamanic practitioners, who have adapted and expanded traditional methods and include contemporary therapeutic ways, political and ecological ideas as well as teachings and practices from other spiritual schools into their repertoire. However, it is also advised, as in all areas of life, to practise discernment. I will not delve deeply into the subject, but I would recommend you to read Mariana Caplan's book *Eyes Wide Open: Cultivating Discernment on the Spiritual Path* (2009), which provides profound insights, examples and analysis on the subject matter and outlines some of the pitfalls.

Nevertheless, I want to address a major criticism that is aimed at contemporary spiritual/shamanic movements, group facilitators, practitioners and teachers, namely that they 'mix and match' spiritual teachings, traditions and approaches. I am rather inclined to agree with Walsh (2010, p.25) who reminds us that we are fortunate because, for the first time in human history, we have all of the world's spiritual and religious traditions and practices available to us and are able to practise them without persecution, which not only makes us privileged to explore different teachings, disciplines and practices, but also makes it possible to identify what different traditions have in common, where they differ and which resonate with us and which do not. Above all it makes it possible for us to utilize the wisdom of spiritual traditions without succumbing to their 'superstition and fear aspects', which are part of many traditional spiritual and religious systems. Most importantly, it gives us a chance to develop our consciousness towards a level that is needed if we want to evolve or, maybe, even survive, without having to choose one religion or one system. The integration of different humanistic/spiritual systems is one of the positive signs of our 'zeitgeist', a sign that we begin to recognize the interdependence of 'the web of life' and begin to change our paradigm.

I will come back to the subject of integration in the last chapter, where I will show that, from a shamanic point of view, we are collectively at a point of our development where 'integration' rather than 'separation' is the way forward. To comprehend contemporary approaches to shamanism we need to understand that everything always evolves, or, in the words of Campbell, 'The old gods are dead or dying and people everywhere are searching, asking: What is the new mythology to be, the mythology of this unified earth as one harmonious being?' (Campbell 2002, p.xix).

Notes

1   There are scholars who differ: Ake Hultkrantz (1973) believes that the word 'saman' relates to another Tungus word, which would define the shaman as somebody who, with the help of spirits, attains ecstasy to create rapport with the supernatural on behalf of his group members. There are also claims that the word shaman came into modern language from Sanskrit; some ethno-linguists claim the word derives from the Chinese 'scha-man', while others claim that it derives from the Pali word 'schamana', a term used for a Buddhist monk. No matter where the word originated, it is now widely used to describe a range of indigenous and non-indigenous practices and it is certainly here to stay.

2   This is not to say that all indigenous practices were/are positive. Power can be misused and accounts of dark sorcery exist. Nevertheless, it is important to realize that some practices we hear about now, especially when it comes to witch doctors in certain parts of Africa, are based on modern-time greed and profiteering, rather than indigenous shamanic practices. Sadly, they feed into our preconceived notions and also tap into our natural scepticism when we are confronted with practices that seem strange.

3   Accounts come from all over the world and are too numerous to describe in the framework of this book. I therefore just describe some to give the reader an insight into the diversity. For a more comprehensive overview see Narby and Huxley (2001).

4   Castaneda's book, as well as the books he published subsequently, reached cult status despite sparking an intense debate over whether they were works of fiction or whether Carlos Castaneda was really apprenticed to an indigenous Mexican shaman called Don Juan, showing how hungry the young people of the 1970s were for the 'mystical'.

3 THE HEART OF THE MATTER

An Altered Consciousness and a Different Perception

THE SHAMANIC STATE OF PERCEPTION AND CONSCIOUSNESS

Shamans all over the world work in and with altered states of consciousness, and have been defined as masters of those states, as masters of ecstasy (Eliade 1964). These working realms of shamans are perceived as reality, accessed at will, explored and mastered in long, strenuous trainings and later utilized for healing, divination, blessing, creating and rebalancing (Peters and Price-Williams 1980). Whilst in an 'ecstatic state', the shaman experiences and sees the world within the laws of those realms, which are based on connected and interwoven energies, fields and essences and translated into spirit-beings, archetypal images and mystical stories. Unlike some of the spirit-possessed healers though, the shaman exhibits a 'dual state of consciousness' (Grof 1993; Walsh 2010). In simplified, contemporary terms, the shaman is simultaneously in command of all processes of a fully waking consciousness, such as speech, recall and awareness of his surroundings, as well as being in a deeply altered state. This, as I will show later, is by no means a given, if we look at the depth of state altering that takes place.

To reach the level of mastery that traditional shamans exhibit takes many years. Before the traditional shaman can call himself a shaman, and is equipped with his powers, he has been on an intense journey. He has fought with the demons, travelled to the

THE HEART OF THE MATTER

underworld, explored death and rebirth, mastered his mind and body and returned, after this period of training, instruction and initiation, to begin his work. In a way, we can say that traditional, indigenous shamans might have been the first individuals we know of who embarked on what Campbell (1968) described as the hero's journey, learning and cultivating through the different phases of that journey all of the above-mentioned practices and more. Shamans continue their journeys throughout life, healing themselves and others in the process, providing the connection with the forces that shape the world and all living beings, striving to restore balance and harmony for and within the tribe and to expand their consciousness.

The shaman's journey, like the hero's journey, begins with the call. Calls can take many forms; in the case of a future shaman it is usually a vision, a dream, a life-changing experience or, in some cases, the call is received before the shaman's birth. In whichever form the call arrives, it seems to be a frightening time, as the call is often accompanied by an initiation crisis, which today we might call a 'spiritual emergency'. Anthropologists who have explored shamanism in various cultures describe vividly the different, profound mental and physical disturbances during that initial crisis (for overview: Narby and Huxley 2001). Eliade, for instance, notes that attacks, hallucinations, prophetic dreams and profound changes of behaviour, such as seeking solitude or being absent minded, can last for weeks, months or even years (Eliade 1964, p.34).

After the initiation crisis, the training begins. The traditional shaman's lengthy training, which is often facilitated by an experienced teacher as well as by spirit teachers, requires discipline and perseverance. It always includes a time in solitude, fasting or an extreme change of diet, and a questioning for visions. Overcoming fears and anxieties and learning to control emotions play a major part. Some of the initiation rites demand overcoming the survival instinct. The novice shaman learns to work with dreams, visions and the spirits that inhabit 'All there is' and to understand the myths, rituals, teaching and cosmology of the culture. In the process of his training, the shaman enters extreme altered states of consciousness, he dismembers and remembers, goes through out-of-body experiences and almost always experiences the near death state and is reborn (Halifax 1982). He acquires spirit helpers in the form of power animals, guides, ancestral spirits and more, gets to know them intimately, and learns how to work with them. Walsh (2010, p.57) remarks that toughening the body, cultivating the mind, conquering cravings, facing fears and cultivating capacities such as concentration and endurance are essential for the shaman to emerge from his training with awareness of his 'essence', which we would now call the 'true self', as well as the essence of 'All there is', in its infinite forms of manifestation. He emerges with personal power and freedom, power over himself, control over spirits and freedom from fear, with a knowledge about 'this other reality', the individual and collective psyche and consciousness, which we can only begin to imagine.

WHAT ARE ALTERED STATES OF PERCEPTION?

A comprehension of what altered states are is important if we want to develop some understanding of shamanism, be it traditional or contemporary. It was always a mystery to me why we in the West, as a culture, have become so far removed from appreciating, exploring and utilizing altered states of consciousness. It seems that since the onset of the age of reason and enlightenment and with the development of science, we have neglected to explore the wider capacities of the human mind. In our hurry to demystify our knowledge of the workings of the universe, we have thrown the baby out with the bathwater, depriving ourselves of insights and knowledge that can only be accessed within such states. Or as Tim Read from the Royal College of Psychiatrists rightly remarks: 'Non-ordinary states of consciousness (NOSCs) have played an important role in shaping the cultural and spiritual life of our species... The insights derived from these states of mind have been valued by all cultures except our own western scientific culture' (Read 2006, p.1).

Altered states are quite natural and all humans are capable of experiencing them. In fact, we do it daily without paying much attention. Bourguignon (1973) maintains that the capacity to experience an altered state of consciousness is part of the psychobiological heritage of our species, and scholars such as Weil (1972) and Siegel (1989) go even further, telling us that there is a species-wide innate drive to experience altered states, an opinion I tend to agree with. Trance experiences are sought by many and on every level in society. Religious practices all over the world induce altered state experiences, while meditation and other spiritual practices have long ceased to be the domain of spiritual seekers and sages, turning into mainstream practices in various forms. Generations of young people have found ways and means to enjoy altered states, be it through mind-altering drugs, attending raves and festivals providing trance dance music, or by participating in high-endurance or high-risk endeavours. We feel nourished if we allow our brain to be for a while in an altered state, such as that produced by meditation, yoga or closing our eyes and drifting away whilst listening to a piece of music. We feel invigorated and excited by endurance and high-risk experiences. We feel connected with something deeper, wider or higher when we meditate or trance-dance or focus completely on a creative task.

I have never worked with any client in hypnosis sessions who didn't find the experience of an altered state positive, even if the hypnosis was basic. I cannot remember any hypnosis student who didn't love trance, even if it triggered strong emotions or brought to the surface previously dissociated material.[1] I have never met a participant in a group, be it shamanically orientated or otherwise, who didn't feel that another world opened for him or her, which was, if not ecstatic, certainly interesting and consciousness-expanding.

Not only do we seek altered state experiences, but the brain also alters our state profoundly in various situations and when we perform different tasks. Paul McCartney, for instance, stated that one of history's most famous songs, 'Yesterday', was composed in a dream, without any effort of the conscious mind (Turner 2005, p.83). He remembered it when he woke up, whilst still in the hypnopompic state, a state the brain exhibits between waking and sleeping. Artists will alter their state when they create, through complete focus and concentration and through activating those parts of the brain that are concerned with imagery and emotions. In fact, there is no creative act without a certain level of brain alteration.

Profound alteration also takes place when our brain activates our survival mechanisms. When we are in a life-threatening, potentially traumatizing situation, our brain will alter its state, automatically and autonomously, creating conditions that will provide us with the best possible chances to survive. It will produce the so-called 'fight or flight' response, getting us physically fit to run or to fight. To help us further, it will dissociate us from the perception of physical pain, numb our emotional perceptions and responses, especially those of fear and anxiety, and narrow our focus onto the one thing that matters in such a situation: survival. If we look at underlying mechanisms of emotionally distressing issues we clearly see 'dissociation' and 'repression' emerging as the forerunners. Most long-term trauma responses are of a dissociative nature. To achieve what we call dissociation, namely the non-integration of material into the normal, integrative functioning of the brain, the state needs to be altered and many psychological and psychosomatic symptoms are based on it.[2]

Altering our mind's state is in a way nothing more than producing different brain activities from the ones that dominate when we are awake and focused on perceiving and processing input from our environment. The altering of our brain functions can be mild and subtle, such as when we daydream or are involved in a creative activity, or they can very be profound, such as when we are in complete shock or have an NDE. States can be measured with electroencephalography (EEG), which gives us information about the amount of brain-wave cycles we produce per second. The Beta state is the normal, outwardly focused state of an adult, with brain waves oscillating between 14 and 30 cycles (Hz) per second. When we begin to relax, as in meditation or daydreaming, we exhibit brainwaves in the Alpha frequency, about 8–13 cycles per second. Theta waves become dominant in a deep meditative trance state, such as the one we experience just before falling asleep, and Delta waves, fewer than 4 cycles per second, are measured when we sleep. Lately, via fMRI scans, we can also observe which brain regions are active and which are less active when we alter our state with different means. Interesting research by Beauregard and O'Leary (2007) into brain plasticity shows us that people who are involved in meditation and other altered state practices over longer periods of time display activity alterations that seem to be permanent and even show permanent alterations in the structure of the brain. For instance, Buddhist monks, by focusing their thoughts on loving compassion for all living things, experienced 'permanent emotional improvement, by activating the left anterior portion of the brain – the portion most associated with joy' (Beauregard and O'Leary 2007, p.71), and the brain scans of 20 Buddhist meditators showed that the parts of the brain associated with attention, awareness of sensation, sensory stimuli and sensory processing were thicker in the meditators than in the controls (Beauregard and O'Leary 2007, p.74).

CHARACTERISTICS OF ALTERED STATES

There are certain characteristics of altered states that might be worth knowing as they explain some of the phenomena happening when we alter our state:

- narrowed focus of attention

- increased absorption and reduced distractibility

- inattention to environmental stimuli

- increased concentration on a particular aspect of an experience

- increased suggestibility

- reduction of voluntary activity (mental and physical)

- passive responsiveness

- relative effortlessness

- reduction of internal dialogue

- alteration of cognitive functions – facilitation of atypical modes of thinking

- a degree of physical relaxation or highly activated physical functioning

- altered sense of one's body – not being in one's body

- increased imaginal processing – surfacing of archetypal imagery

- alteration of memory processing – increased activity in the memory parts of the brain

- relative dominance of right hemispheric functioning.

Altered states are also interesting because they produce so-called 'altered state phenomena', which can occur spontaneously, but can also be induced, such as:

- catalepsy – a stiffness of muscles

- dissociation – a split in the normal integrative functions of the mind

- amnesia – memory loss or forgetting

- hyperamnesia – very vivid remembering

- analgesia – loss of sensation in a certain part of the body

- anaesthesia – complete numbness, pain relief in the body

- age regression – a very vivid remembering of past/childhood experiences

- age progression – a very vivid creation of an imagined future

- time distortion – slowing down or speeding up perceived time

- suggestibility – heightened openness to suggestions.

Looking at the above lists, which are by no means complete, it becomes obvious why it seems to be much easier and more beneficial to work therapeutically directly within altered states, especially if we want to access subconsciously held material, than to work with the brain in its normal state. Altered states vary and we have a certain amount of control over them, which increases with practice. Depending what we focus on we can, for example, slow down brain activity or we are able to increase activity in the parts of the brain which are involved in 'remembering' or which 'think in images', or we can decrease activity in the part of the brain that 'experiences pain' and so on and so forth.

When we use altered states directly in a therapeutic setting, we not only have direct access to dissociated, painful and frightening material, but we give clients a chance to expand their consciousness in the process. We help them to open a world that they rarely access. Whether we interpret this world as being solely the personal subconscious, or also the collective unconscious, or as existing outside our minds or inside our minds, is at this point irrelevant; what is important is that we give clients a chance to expand what they perceive as being their world. We may ask people who have been traumatized to recall events, to deal with the highly stressful emotions that can be released. Why do this without also giving them the benefit of experiencing what altered states can produce, such as deep relaxation, archetypal helping figures and the sense of being embedded into something bigger and larger, into something that caters for their soul? As long as we pay attention to proper integration and re-association and do not enforce the original dissociation, altered state experiences are beneficial to clients.

It is not surprising that we find many highly traumatized people consulting New Age practitioners and attending spiritual groups. For a long time, I believed that this first represents an escape from the emotional wounding into the realm of the spiritual, an avoidance of painful processes to heal the emotional damage, and second that it fits their mental capacities, as many trauma survivors are used to dissociating from traumatizing realities by accessing and activating certain states. After having spoken to and worked with a fair number of trauma survivors, I still think this reasoning is valid, but I also understand that many instinctively realize that the spiritual component is comforting, embeds the suffering they went through into a larger context and that some of the spiritual practices can release mental/emotional trauma on a much deeper level, provided they also cater for the cognitive integration of the material.[3]

WHAT WE ACCESS IN ALTERED STATES

The information we can access when we consciously and deliberately practise altering our states is wide ranging and complex, depending very much on our intent, the specific practice, the depth we reach, if we practise repeatedly, such as when we have a daily spiritual meditative practice, and, if we are skilled, which parts of the brain we deliberately activate. The following can therefore only provide an outline of different states, without claiming to be complete. The boundaries within altered state experiences are fluid. Thus, whilst the descriptions, classifications and maps we develop are necessary for our mind to make sense of such states, they are, in the end, just maps that represent the territory, but not the territory itself.

Personal subconscious, unconscious and collective unconscious

In psychological terms, we of course access personal material that lies buried and hidden on different levels of the subconscious and unconscious realm. This material can take various forms: memories and past experiences, images that accompany a thought process, associations to a theme, deeply held beliefs, strong emotions and so on. We access these because we activate, as described before, certain parts of our brains whilst calming down the activity in other parts. If we, for example, activate those parts of the brain that are concerned with memory storage and emotions – the hippocampus and the amygdala – we will experience strong emotions connected to certain memories. If the memory is dissociated, in the sense that it exists consciously only as an experience without emotional attachment, or if the emotionality exists in the form of an anxiety response, without a memory being attached to it, we can begin to re-associate the memory with the emotion and vice versa. If we go a bit further, we can access associations we have formed over time that are related to that memory/experience and those feelings. The next step, in therapeutic terms, would be to consciously integrate via reactivating our normal frontal lobes by, for example, questioning, understanding and putting the experiences we had in the altered states into a rational context.

If we subscribe to a wider view of consciousness we can also enter realms of the unconscious – for want of a better expression – that contain material and information that are not necessarily based on our personal experiences. Jung (1977) would define those realms as the collective unconscious, which holds material that has never been in consciousness and therefore has never been individually acquired. The content owes its existence to heredity, be it in the form of genetically transmitted knowledge or, if we want to go a step further, to the ability to plug into and access knowledge that exists outside the boundaries of our physical brain. According to Jung, the content of the collective unconscious includes images, potentials and predispositions inherited through our ancestral lines, such as fears, attractions and symbols. It is universal, pre-existent, similar in all individuals and shows itself to us in archetypal form. Archetypes are universal images that are likely to be recognized – with variations – almost anywhere in the world. Unlike memory images of past experience, archetypes are not fully developed pictures in the mind. They are rather 'complexes' that we translate into visualized images.

When we begin to work with archetypes, we can access the meaning we associate with them, which again is fairly universal. Jung outlined five main archetypes:

1. the Self, the regulating centre of the psyche and facilitator of individuation

2. the Shadow, the part that contains qualities with which the ego doesn't want to identify (e.g. anger, fear, brutality, sexual urges)

3. the Anima, the feminine image in a man's psyche

4. the Animus, the masculine image in a woman's psyche

5. the Persona, the image and qualities we present to the world, which acts like a mask.

There are many more archetypes. They appear all over the world in fairy tales, myths, legends and folklore. Well-known mythological archetypal motifs and figures include the child, the maiden, the hero, the mother, the crone, the wise old man, the wise old woman, the trickster, the mentor, the devil or monster, the redeemer, death and rebirth.

In shamanic terms, the realms of the personal unconscious as well as the collective unconscious are vital. The imagery of the contemporary shamanic journey, for example, has similar psychotherapeutic effects to those coming from Jung's notion of active imagination and other techniques, in that the imagery creates a situation whereby a dialogue is initiated by the client with archetypal material from his or her own unconscious. The view of most western therapists is that the internal dialogue with different figures that appear in the shamanic journey is a communication with archetypal material that facilitates individuation. The traditional shaman would dispute this, seeing the materials and events in the individual and collective unconscious as objective, real events – as a reality on a different level (Peters and Price-Williams 1980, pp.405–406). The traditional shaman would also be referring to some of those figures as 'spirits', experiencing and seeing them housed within the energetic field of 'All there is', rather than within the confines of the brain, a notion that could, as I will show later, be more accurate than we have previously assumed. It is interesting in this context that Jung frequently referred to the collective unconscious as the objective psyche. In other words, the appropriate attitude towards the inner images, events and dialogues is to treat them 'as-if-they-were-real' (Peters and Price-Williams 1980, p.406).

Already, when we reach the level of archetypal imagery, we understand how artificial the boundaries we draw can be. Many therapists, I am sure, have come across archetypal imagery when clients describe abusive experiences, especially sexually abusive ones, if they happened when they were very young. The monster that comes into the bedroom of the small child can be the monster based on a memory of a nightmare, the monster of a TV programme the child watched, an image for something entirely different or the description of the father who abused the child. The small child often stores terrifying experiences and experiences it cannot make sense of in archetypal form. The angel or fairy that comforts the child is an archetype, but it could be that the experience for which the child needs comforting was a very real one indeed.

EXTREME ALTERED STATES OF CONSCIOUSNESS: DISMEMBERMENT, VISIONS AND NEAR DEATH EXPERIENCES

Taking the altering of brain functions a step further, we enter a realm that is informed by altered states that seem beyond our normal state-altering capacity. The shamanic journey, the 'shaman's flight', as seen by Eliade (1964), Harner (1982) and others, leads him outside the body into the quantum realm of 'All there is'. As far as I can judge, shamans, especially traditional ones, certainly develop an amazing ability to alter their states in most profound ways. The closest we can come to imagine and describe those profoundly altered states are 'dismemberment experiences', 'visions' and 'NDEs'. Shamans, having gone through a rigorous training during which they seek to experience and familiarize themselves with such states, seem not only to control and work within such states, but are also able to re-experience them at will. They also seem to remember clearly the events that happen whilst they were in such altered states, which is not always the case when we enter very deep trance states. These deep trance states, and the knowledge and learning that come from exploring 'All there is' in this way, inform the shaman's way of seeing and defining the world and working within it. It is therefore important to briefly look at profoundly altered state experiences, such as dismemberments, visions and NDEs. I will do this taking my own experiences as well as research into account.

Dismemberment

I have been involved with 'altered state experiences' for most of my adult life. I began to seek them when relatively young, living in ashrams in India. I have practised Vipassana meditation and mindfulness on and off since, participated in countless spiritual groups, workshops and trainings over the years, been apprenticed to shamans in South and North America and trained in clinical hypnosis, which I taught for many years. I had altered state experiences that taught me the difference between an imagination and a vision, which is profound. I experienced states of sheer horror that showed me the depths of the human shadow and states of sheer bliss that produced enlightened insights. I went through an early, horrifying experience of dismemberment and also, much later, through an NDE. Both left me changed in more ways than one.

I had a rather frightening encounter in India in my mid-twenties. I participated in a seven-day Vipassana meditation group that consisted of meditating ten hours per day, observing our breath, and practising mindfulness. The meditations were only interrupted by the intake of rice and vegetables and meditative walks. After having refined my body and mind to a certain extent over the previous months by eating a restricted diet and partaking in various spiritual practices, I woke up one night and was immediately overtaken by an experience that felt extremely real and begun without warning. I started to shatter into many, many pieces, then I came together again; next, I was blown apart again, then came together again and so on. How long this went on for I do not know; it could have been for quite a while, as later, when I regained some control, dawn was setting in. I certainly remember how very frightened I was. I had difficulty in thinking rationally. It seemed as if my mind was not under my control. Whatever was happening, it was happening to my body without me being able to stop it. Parts of me flew at lightning speed through the universe, coming back without my being able to get a sense of being 're-assembled' in the way I should be. My legs were in the wrong place; parts of me were missing; I felt extremely cold, and then suddenly extremely hot.

I also couldn't communicate. I remember trying to sit up, but falling backwards and lying on my back, desperate to get up, but not being able to move any of my muscles. My body felt completely paralysed. Visually, I was still splitting into a thousand pieces and all I felt was fear. At one point I started to tremble. My heart was pounding and I knew somewhere in a dark corner of my mind that I experienced a panic attack (I had never had one before). I tried to move my arms, but they were shaking. I remember that I felt tears running down my face, which was the first indication that my face was actually where it should be, rather than ripped to pieces flying through space. I tried to breathe deeply and focused on regaining my voice, to wake somebody up, but it was to no avail. We were in dormitory-style accommodation and, after what seemed a long, long time and for reasons unexplained, the girl in the bed next to me seemed to sense that something was wrong. She came over and asked if I was OK. I shook my head, still trembling and unable to speak, but realized that I was reacting normally to her question. This realization, together with some rather soothing images of light whirls around me, seemed to bring me, slowly, back to 'normal' consciousness. The girl went to get the meditation leader, who sat with me for a while, stroking very gently down my right arm, explaining, talking to me, soothingly. The engagement of my 'left brain' finally took hold and I could begin to answer questions in a monosyllabic way. My heart rate slowed down and the experience of my body shattering stopped. I drank some sweet tea, felt somebody covering me with the sari that had fallen off the bed, and then I fell asleep. I woke up in the afternoon, weak and in physical pain, feeling as if all my muscles had been overstretched and subjected to unfamiliar exercise.

This was my first experience with an uncontrolled, deep altered state. At the time I had no knowledge of dismemberment experiences. I only knew that this wasn't a 'dream' in the classical sense, although at one point, when the experience started to lessen in intensity, it became more dreamlike, with curiously soothing light and vibrations swirling around. Nevertheless, at the time I couldn't put it into any context, except that something was different afterwards. I became more certain of myself, and although I became more aware of the fragility of the body and the power of the mind, I felt on the whole stronger after the experience and, quite importantly, less fearful, more focused and more appreciative of my life.

I would now classify this as a dismemberment experience, a symbolic transformation drama, which has been described in various mythological traditions, although my experience seems mild compared to most accounts. In Greek mythology, Dionysus was torn to pieces by the Titans whilst his heart was rescued by Athena, Goddess of Wisdom. The Egyptian enactment of this drama can be seen in the myth of Osiris, the pharaoh who was dismembered and supernaturally resurrected to conceive his son Horus. The Inuit Indians of the Arctic celebrate Takanakapsaluk, the dismembered goddess whose various disconnected parts gave form to all the creatures of the sea, and, in pre-Aztec religion, the earth itself was created out of the dismembered parts of the goddess Tlaltecuhtli.

Goodman (1988), a linguist and doctor of cultural anthropology, who taught at Denison University and is widely known for bringing 'ecstatic trance postures' to our awareness, notes that Siberian shamans regarded dismemberment as an essential phase of initiation. She also talks about the universality of this archetype and observed that those Westerners she worked with who had spontaneous dismemberment visions were consistently destined to become various kinds of healers. Kalweit (1988) explains that shamans have often been critically ill and suffered immensely for longer periods of time during which their bio-psychic process of transformation is taking place, a process that culminates in a dismemberment experience that represents a turning point of change towards a spiritual state of being.

Experiences of dismemberment trigger our primordial fears. At the deepest level, dismemberment dismantles our old identity; it strips away the unnecessary, the dispossessed and the dis-jointed and it forces us to examine the bare essence. Metzner (1998), Professor Emeritus at the California Institute of Integral Studies, reminds us that the cure for dismemberment is remembering who we really are. Our sense of who we are, our self-concept, changes profoundly after a dismemberment experience and, according to Metzner, transformational processes of this magnitude help us to transform our consciousness by helping us to synthesize the fragmented, separated parts of our psyche into a harmonious whole, regaining that original unity at the core of our being. As this is the task of the shaman, he experiences it himself. Joan Halifax talks in similar terms about the issue of seeing the shaman as a healed healer, a person who went through a personal transformation, retrieving the broken pieces of his or her body and psyche and integrating many planes of existence. It is this integration of the mind and body with the soul and spirit, the ordinary reality with the non-ordinary, the individual and the community and nature with the unseen, the historical and the mystical and the past with the future and the present, that is seen as a hallmark of indigenous traditional shamans (Halifax 1982).

Visions

My second experience with a profoundly altered state was during a Vision Quest. Here I encountered my first 'real' vision, something that went well beyond a visualization in an altered state. Visualizations, of course, lead to an altering of our state, but they are generally stronger when the person is already in an altered state and is then asked to visualize something. When a person is visually inclined and the altered state is deep, visualizations can be quite striking. If the person is not visually inclined, they feel more like a 'sensing' experience. No matter if they are memories, or visual journeys or archetypal images or symbols, visualizations seem to be under our control, in the sense that we can make them go away, change them or move on from them, and they are always influenced and set up by the original intent.

A vision is different. It appears suddenly, out of the blue, without warning, and it has a different quality. It is just there, and in its intensity it goes way beyond the visual. For me, it felt as if I were spellbound. There was no way I could have changed the vision, or moved on, or influenced it in any way or form. It was something that took over, rather than something that I 'saw'. It also had an insight attached to it that wasn't a thought or an image. The insight came in the form of an 'absolute knowing'. The vision changed my life. Whether the decision which was based on the vision was the right one or the wrong one, I will never know, but it felt that I had no choice but to act according to the insight the vision produced. I haven't had many visions, but I learned the difference between a vision and a visualization and I understood that we can experience much more than we dare to allow ourselves, and that those kinds of experiences have a profound impact on the way we see the world and ourselves within it.

When I had the privilege to learn from an Ecuadorian shaman, he told me about a vision that changed his life. He had the vision while meditating and communicating with a spirit at his 'power place', which was a lake at the bottom of one of the mountains he works with. In his vision, he saw himself teaching the people of the Eagle. In his view of the world, teaching the people of the Eagle meant people from North America. At the time of this vision he had never met anybody from North America, but he knew that when the time was right he would have to honour the vision and, as these things work in the connected world, a few years later people began to travel to see him and he began to teach them his healing practices. It is interesting how he treated the place where he experienced his vision. He pilgrimages there, uses the herbs and plants that grow there for healing and treats the water of the lake as sacred. He leaves offerings for the spirits of the place and told me that he often visualizes it and connects with the place of his vision when he works, especially when he works with non-indigenous people.

Visions are profound experiences. The most well-known shamanic vision, which I have already mentioned, is without doubt that of Black Elk, a Lakota. Neidhardt's book *Black Elk Speaks* (Neidhardt 1988), which was first published in 1932 and has been republished many times (with a new Kindle format being available now), is a revelation. I would recommend it wholeheartedly as it shows the profound insights and foresights which turned Black Elk into who he was, a great visionary, healer and remarkable man, but it also describes the consecutive visions of the medicine man and shaman Black Elk and the price he paid. He experienced his first vision at the age of four and during his second vision, at the age of about nine, he was sick for 12 days – unconscious and fighting death. In his vision, the six grandfathers, representing the West, South, North, East and the Sky and the Earth, appeared. He was given powers by each of them and was shown how the world works. He was shown much and he describes his 'strangeness' to his own people afterwards as well as his inability to put into words the images, feelings and words spoken to him, which he remembered well. There are also descriptions of other tribe members remembering the change in the nine-year-old boy, who became ill as a boy and emerged from his illness a grandfather. Like all great visionaries, Black Elk had to follow the visions; he had to suffer the pain and the greatness and knowledge that comes with such profound state changes and, as far as I can see, most of what he envisaged came true.

Near Death Experiences

We know from extensive literature (Kübler-Ross 1997; Moody 2001; Van Lommel 2010) that NDEs are transformative because they change our sense of who we are, our self-concept and in most cases also the concept we have of the world. We cannot understand shamanism without taking their 'dying and being reborn' into account. NDEs are the closest we can come to imagine their experiences and I will therefore briefly outline what we know about them.

The transformative effects of NDEs are well documented. They seem to change people's self-concept, their sense of identity and their view of the world. Shamans, who on the whole go through them deliberately, will always have a view of the world that is transcendent of normal, manifested reality. But not only shamans hold a different world-view: from Jung's account in his book *Memories, Dreams, Reflections* (1961), to the accounts collected by Kübler-Ross (1997) and Moody (2001), who compared 150 NDEs, there is a growing body of people who talk of the transcendental experiences of their consciousness travelling into realms that are beyond the boundaries of the body. They usually report travelling out of the body, into the light. Often they review their lives, feel ecstatic and peaceful and sometimes have spirit entities around them and, most importantly, NDEs are transformational with regard to world-view and attitudes.

Van Lommel, an eminent cardiologist at Rijnstate Hospital in Arnhem, is just one of the latest experts to shake our view of consciousness. In his highly acclaimed book *Consciousness beyond Life: The Science of the Near-death Experience* (2010), he confronts us with evidence that seems to confirm that consciousness is not encapsulated by the boundaries of the physical brain, citing that out of the 344 survivors of cardiac arrest 18 per cent (62 patients) had recollections of events that happened during the time when they were clinically dead. In a paper presented at the Royal College of

Psychiatrists he also cites other studies, such as an American study of 116 survivors, of which 10 per cent had memories stemming from the period of cardiac arrest (Van Lommel 2004, p.4). Most of the patients reported experiences which seem typical of NDEs, such as awareness of being dead, feeling very positive, moving through a tunnel, meeting with deceased relatives, being out of the body, meeting 'the light' and/or experiencing a life review. Van Lommel performed a longitudinal study – two and eight years after the NDE – designed to assess whether the 'transformation in attitude towards life and death following an NDE is the result of having an NDE or the result of cardiac arrest itself' (Van Lommel 2004, p.4). The results were as expected: after a period of consolidation, those patients who did have an NDE showed no fear of death; they strongly believed in an afterlife; and their insight into what is important in life had changed. Love and compassion for oneself, others and nature had become dominant and they showed clearly heightened intuitiveness (p.5). Van Lommel, like Raymond Moody and others before him, looks at all the suggested theories, especially those of a physiological and neuro-physiological nature, and comes to the conclusion that the 'unproven' assumption that consciousness and memory are localized in the brain should be discussed (p.7). He furthermore concludes (I will come back later to this) that there is a strong case for consciousness being, after death, experienced within another dimension. Or, in his own words, 'the conclusion that consciousness can be experienced independently of brain function might well induce a huge change in the scientific paradigm of western medicine' (p.18).

Before we can begin to appreciate shamanism we need to understand that the shamanic state of consciousness is informed by extreme altered state experiences of this type and that the major cognitive shifts that happen during dismemberment experiences, visions and, especially, NDEs lead to major shifts in how we see ourselves and the world around us. It also seems to become more obvious, as research continues, that brain functions can be altered permanently and that traditional shamans, as well as some contemporary shamanic practitioners, display the characteristics of seekers who practise spiritual approaches, as outlined before, such as caring for others, decreased materialism, lack of fear of death, profoundly different world-views, awakening to higher spiritual realities, control over states of mind and much more.

Notes

1 I have training and profound experience in clinical hypnosis and hypnotherapy, functioned as the course director for a large international hypnotherapy college that trains hypnotherapists to MA level, and I teach 'Introduction to Clinical Hypnosis' to medical students. I will therefore refrain from referencing all my statements about altered states.

2 It is certainly worth asking why we are just beginning to take altered states of consciousness seriously and why we don't utilize them in therapeutic and medical settings more frequently. We can easily attempt minor and, in some cases, even more major surgery under hypnosis, but prefer to administer a cocktail of drugs to achieve anaesthesia, and we now predominantly use, within our NHS, CBT, which keeps our patients firmly focused on the cognitive-behavioural level of the mind. This raises some interesting issues about our western approach to healing, which cannot be answered by citing the cost factor or the lack of available research, which can both be disputed.

3 I will come back to this subject in Chapters 4 and 5.

4 STRANGE WORLDS

The Shaman's Spirit Realms and the Quantum Realm

THE SHAMAN'S HOLISTIC VIEW OF THE WORLD: AN INTERCONNECTED WEB

The shamanic view of the world is mainly determined by the shifts and transformation in consciousness via their experiences and workings in those different realms and by their transformational rites and initiations as described in the previous chapter. It is furthermore based on the knowledge passed on to them by previous generations and by their teachers as well as in the intense connections they cultivate to the natural world. Shamans all over the world describe the universe as a living, interconnected web, energetic/vibrational in essence and evolving. This view seems to be increasingly confirmed by science, especially by quantum physics and higher mathematics, which I will show later on in more detail. Where they differ from contemporary science is that they define 'spirit' as being at the core of all living things, with consciousness underlying all of creation. They also differ from modern science in the sense that it is through their direct experience that they access those realms, employing various techniques to shift and alter their states of awareness profoundly, as described, to open the gates to, connect with and utilize all accessible realms of consciousness.

In the process of their journeying into what shamans would call parallel universes and different realms of consciousness, they have developed a rich, often enchanting, sometimes challenging and certainly exciting repertoire of techniques, methods and ways to experience those different planes of reality, thus having acquired a vast knowledge about the vibrating fields of those realms, which are translated into landscapes and maps, images and visions, myths and stories and figures of helpers and teachers. Because, in the world of shamans, there are no artificial boundaries between the 'seen' and the 'hidden', between the different planes of consciousness, and also not between the human brain and the rest of the universe, they have developed ways and means to work and create within those realms, bridging and flowing between normal consciousness and altered state consciousness, energy and matter and the mundane and the sacred.

The following laws they see operating within the cosmos are based on their observations of the energy fields.

Everything is made of vibrations/energy fields and is connected

The way one sees and interprets reality depends on the state of awareness and on conditioning, both of which influence perception, processing and the translation of perception. Because shamans explore and experience reality from different planes of consciousness, or states, they perceive the universe in the form of vibrations and energy fields, and they come to the only possible conclusion: the world is a living, vibrating being and therefore everything within it is interconnected. Vibrations are repetitive, wave-like patterns in physical systems in the atomic and subatomic realm. As far as we know from quantum physics, the universe is a field where everything has an inherent wave-like pattern. These patterns are called quantum waves, or probability waves, as the patterns are relatively stable. That relative stability determines how probable events are on an atomic level and, of course, on the level at which we, as human beings, experience the physical world.

All things contain a life force: spirit

Connected to the perception that everything vibrates and is energetically interlinked and interdependent is the notion that all things are alive, containing a life force, defined as spirit. All things means literally all things – humans, animals, rocks, plants, rivers, lakes, oceans, all elements and the solar system. Some suggest that the word essence or soul might better describe this life force. In shamanic terms, the word spirit – or consciousness – is appropriate, as spirit stands for a basic force that can manifest itself in different ways and forms, while soul is often used to describe what we in the western world consensually call 'alive', namely humans and animals. Spirit is the specific essence that makes a being what it is, a human a human and a tree a tree, but it also transcends this because it is a basic life force that exists throughout the universe, manifesting itself in different forms.

Everything is evolving and sacred

Closely connected to the above is the notion that the cosmos is a changing, evolving and conscious entity. It is alive, interconnected and, most importantly, shows purpose and meaning in an ever-evolving dance of creation. The shaman will therefore treat the entire universe and everything in it as sacred, infused by the same spirit, expressing itself in different ways. The expression 'all life is sacred', as well as the expression 'nothing should be done to harm the children', are just two examples of how this view of the world creates the desire to strive for 'living a life that honours the sacredness as well as continuity' of creation.

Everything is treated as being reality

From a shamanic perspective, everything is reality, whether it exists in the form of matter or in the form of energy, whether we can see it or experience it with our senses in ordinary waking consciousness, or not. Shamans, including indigenous contemporary ones, are masters of 'the ecstatic experience' and, on the whole, as far as I can see, not too concerned with questions of 'what is real and what is not real and what can be proven or not in a scientific sense'. In this the shaman is, in my experience, quite pragmatic. She or he will utilize whatever works and is very conscious that everything is influenced by our perception. So, for the shaman, parallel universes, layers of reality, infinite possibilities and various states are not puzzling; as long as they can be experienced on some level of consciousness or another, they are real and, as consciousness is not seen as being confined to the brain, but able to expand and travel, can access and interact with 'All there is', and 'All there is' is certainly real. For the shaman, there is no sense of a 'natural' versus 'supernatural' world; there is only that which we can 'see' and that which is 'hidden', the visible and the invisible being equally real.

THE SHAMANIC/SPIRITUAL WORLD-VIEW AND CONTEMPORARY SCIENCE

Our knowledge about the workings of the universe, our planet and ourselves as part of it is still developing. We usually hold on to a certain view of the world, to a certain paradigm, until we are confronted with enough evidence in the form of discoveries or events that are incompatible with our current views, forcing us to question or even change our frame of reference. One of the major shifts we have undergone in our view of the world led us from the 'mysterious combined with religious beliefs' to the 'materialistic combined with scientific proof'. We have increasingly utilized the means of science, mainly mechanical physics, biology and mathematics, to explore the universe. The resulting physical laws we discovered have served us very well indeed, creating much progress and wealth, as those laws apply to the world of matter. So far we saw no need to shift our paradigm. The discoveries of physics within the subatomic realm and the development in mathematics keep pushing at the edges of this paradigm and seem to bring back the question: were the mystics right all along in their world-views, shaped by altering their states through meditative and other practices, which led them to perceiving the 'invisible' realms? At this moment in time, we happily work with two sets of laws, the ones that work in the realm of the material world, in the form of mechanical physics, and the ones that work in the subatomic realm, in the form of quantum physics. But the search for a 'unified theory' is ongoing, and the results of some recent experiments, such as the ones at CERN, the Large Hadron Collider, might question some views, which have been so far defined as 'absolute truths' (Ereditato 2011).

We have certainly arrived at a point of scientific knowledge where we can state without doubt that what we experience in our waking state of normal awareness is only a part of the story. Physics shows undoubtedly that what we experience with our senses in our normal state of awareness is 'the manifested realm', but that underneath this realm the world looks and functions quite differently. Once we venture into the quantum realm, the underlying reality of our physical world is made up of energetic elements: electrons, protons, neutrons and photons, consisting of wave-like patterns of probabilities, which follow strange laws.

It seems that the quantum realm comes much closer to the description of the world shamans use, when in an altered state, describing the spirits, energies and the fields they encounter. A very interesting contribution came from the British anthropologist Graham Townsley in 1993. He had, unlike most other anthropologists, learned the language of the Yaminahua shamans. He explains that the central idea that dominates the whole field of Yaminahua shamanic knowledge is that of 'yoshi', which is spirit or animated essence. This concept, alien to western thinking, sees all things as being animated and given their particular qualities by 'yoshi'. Yoshis are energetic entities that are not static but that interact and influence each other and are difficult to 'track down'. I am not a physicist but, as far as I can judge, his descriptions of yoshi come very close to what we would now describe as the behaviour of electrons and quarks in the quantum realm: namely, existing as probabilities, difficult to track down, coming into existence through our observation, seemingly either connected over distances, or travelling through a medium we don't fully understand yet, and influencing each other. Townsley reiterates that shamans' knowledge and power stems from their knowledge about those entities, and their ability to communicate with them and to influence them, which they do mainly in the form of songs and sounds (Townsley 1993, pp.264–266). If shamans work within the quantum realm, this would explain why they can do what they say they can do. It would also explain the similarities we encounter in many different, completely independent indigenous cultures, and why their view of how the universe works, especially that consciousness (spirit energy/essence) underlies everything, seems increasingly less strange and exotic. The material world-view that has prevailed since Newton, namely that matter is primary, is being profoundly challenged by the findings and constructs of the subatomic realm. This makes counter-intuitive demands on us, challenging our common sense perception so that we may have to abandon the notion that matter comes before mind or consciousness (Powell 2001b).

The two major theories about consciousness also reflect this challenge. The 'productive theory' states that consciousness is a product of neural processes happening in the brain and that it therefore cannot exist without the brain. The 'transmissive theory' proposes that consciousness is inherent within the cosmos and is therefore transpersonal, independent of our brain and senses, but is mediated by them, suggesting that the brain may act as a filter or lens through which consciousness is filtered, adapted, focused and experienced (Crowley 2005; Read 2006). This 'transmissive theory' could account for such phenomena as encountering dead relatives, awareness of surroundings whilst being out of the body and holographic life reviews, all of which are typically described by those who have had NDEs. It could sufficiently explain such common human experiences as mothers knowing the precise moment their sons die on the battlefield, the information people we label as 'genius' seem to receive, or stories of repeatedly traumatized people speaking of 'leaving the body', and of course it could lead us closer to understanding the abilities of indigenous and other healers, of precognitions and so on, all of which cannot be explained within the productive theory of consciousness. Shamanism would most certainly subscribe to a 'transmissive theory', and the old, productive theory seems increasingly flawed and untenable when we take recent scientific findings into account.

THE REALM OF QUANTUM PHYSICS: QUANTUM REALITY, ZERO-POINT FIELDS, HOLOGRAMS, SUPER STRINGS AND CONSCIOUSNESS

Quantum objects and how they behave

Contemporary science, especially physics, in the form of quantum theory and quantum mechanics, shows us that the physical universe is a sea of energy and that all physical matter, at its fundamental level, is nothing more than a collection of electrical charges interacting with a background matrix of electromagnetic and other electric charges. Quantum theory suggests that all matter can exist as either waves of spread-out energy, so-called probability waves, which are in non-local space, where notions of time and distance don't matter, or as discrete particles located in space and time. In other words, the electron is no longer thought of as a particle, spinning around the nucleus of the atom, but is conceptualized as being 'virtual', spread out throughout space as a quantum wave, which only turns into a particle in our physical 'space-time' when observed. Therefore, whether the electron is experienced as a wave of probability or as a particle depends on the observer, as the very act of observation leads to a 'wave collapse', whereby the numerous possibilities collapse, concentrating the electron as a particle for a moment in time in a particular spot, for anyone to see (Rosenblum and Kuttner 2006, pp.72–77). This is clearly shown in quantum physics with the complementary aspect of light, which can behave like particles (photons), under certain experimental conditions, whilst in other experiments it behaves like waves.

It is now widely assumed that the underlying reality is a sea of infinite vibrating energies, where all possibilities exist. Within this field, everything interacts with everything in a non-local way. The laws of this quantum realm, of quantum objects, are baffling: the wave collapse, mentioned above, shows that an object cannot be considered to exist within space and time unless it is observed as a particle. A quantum object, such as an electron, can be in more than one place at the same time. A quantum object can simultaneously come into existence in one place and cease to exist in another without passing through the space in between. A quantum object, which comes into existence as a result of our observation of it, simultaneously influences the twin object associated with it instantly, no matter how far from each other they happen to be. The newest, and not yet completely proven, baffling results of the Large Hadron Collider experiments seem to point in the direction that subatomic particles have beaten the speed of light (which we assumed so far as being the absolute speed limit). This could, for instance, mean that they can travel, or send information, via a realm that is as yet unknown to science, a realm without distance (Ereditato 2011).

The quantum vacuum – zero-point field

Besides the baffling laws of the quantum objects described above, recent writers have focused on the zero-point field (ZPF) or quantum vacuum. Let's begin with the simple before moving on to the complex. Everything we see in this world is made of atoms. The overwhelming consensus is that the average atom is almost empty – we could say that it consists of 99.99 per cent of what we would call empty space, just as the void of deep space is empty. In the last few decades, physicists and mathematicians showed that this empty space is actually full of energy: full of the energy of the ZPF. The ZPF is seen as an empty space that carries energies that are present at a zero point, where classical forms of energy vanish (McTaggart 2001). This ZPF is a physical field with real physical effects. For example, the photons emitted by electrons' shifting orbits exchange energy with the ZPF, which in return keeps atoms stable and prevents the electrons collapsing into the atomic nuclei. The ZPF, as well as transmitting light, pressure, energy and sound, can also carry information. Laszlo (2004) writes about the rediscovery of the Akashic Field, which is described in ancient Hindu philosophy as the medium underlying the physical universe, out of which everything evolves and to which everything returns, holding the memory of everything.

> The quantum vacuum is conceived of as a frictionless medium so that waves of energy move without resistance and thus do not become extinguished. Laszlo refers to the

torsion wave theory, where the excitation of the ground state of the vacuum by charged particles cause torsion waves with magnetic impulses, which store information in the quantum vacuum much as magnetic impulses do on our computer disc. This leads to the emerging paradigm of a physical substrate for the collective unconscious, where there is a high-energy field that contains information encoded in a holographic way. (Read 2006, p.5)

This field may also be the substrate for David Bohm's implicate order (see below) and could be recognized as a universal field of nature.

Bohm's implicate order: the universe as a hologram

The insight into how holographic structures work led physicist and Nobel Prize winner David Bohm to an unexpected interpretation of the discovery that subatomic particles seem to influence each other at faster than light speed and over vast distances. Bohm suggests that the alleged distance between the subatomic particles that influence each other and stay in contact with each other is an illusion. He argues that, at some deeper level of reality, they are not separate entities (Bohm 1983). This would mean that the universe functions like a hologram. This theoretical construct might now be experimentally proven, if the already mentioned results of the experiments in the Large Hadron Collider are repeated.[1]

To understand why Bohm makes this startling assertion, one must first understand a little about holograms. A hologram is a three-dimensional photograph made with the aid of a laser. The object to be photographed is first bathed in the light of a laser beam. Then a second laser beam is bounced off the reflected light of the first and the resulting interference pattern (the area where the two laser beams commingle) is captured on film. When you develop the film you get an image that looks like a swirl of light and dark lines. But as soon as one illuminates the film with another laser beam, some quite mysterious things begin to happen:

1. A three-dimensional image of the original object appears.

2. If a hologram of say a tree is cut in half and then illuminated by a laser, each of the halves will still contain the entire image.

3. If the halves are divided again and again, each snippet of film will always contain a smaller but intact version of the original image.

4. Therefore, every part of a hologram, no matter how small, contains all the information possessed by the whole.

The quantum hologram was discovered and experimentally validated by Professor Walter Schempp whilst working with magnetic resonance imaging (MRI). 'He discovered that the phenomenon of emission/reabsorption of energy by all physical objects at the quantum level carries information about the history of that object. The mathematical formalism used by Schempp is the same formalism used in holography, thus the name quantum hologram' (Mitchell 2011, p.2).

The 'whole in every part' nature of a hologram provides us with an entirely new way of understanding organization and order. When we dissect it to study the parts, as western science has done for centuries to understand the world, we find that if something is holographically structured, we will not get the components of which it is constructed, but smaller wholes. Bohm called the above described underlying reality 'the implicate order' and suggested that it had holographic properties, in that accessing a part of it allows access to the whole, as those particles are not separate parts, but facets of a deeper and more underlying unity that is ultimately as holographic and indivisible as the previously mentioned tree (Bohm 1983).

Edgar Mitchell, former Apollo astronaut, founder and driving scientific visionary behind Quantrek, takes the subject further, also combining quantum physics, the ZPF and the concept of holographic structure. He writes: 'Recent research...suggests that we, and every physical object, has a resonant holographic image associated with our physical experience. It is called a quantum hologram. One can think of this as a halo, or "light body" made up of tiny quantum emissions from every molecule and cell in the body' (Mitchell 2011, p. 1). He continues to suggest that every structure has a hologram and resonates with the underlying infinite unstructured energy of the ZPF. 'This quantum mechanical type of resonance is an exchange of energy with the zero-point field such that the "phase change" (interference pattern) of quantum emission carries complete information about the history of the system' (p. 2). Quantum phenomena were for a long time seen as being irrelevant to macro structures, but according to thinkers such as Edgar Mitchell, the quantum hologram is the first energy phenomenon that directly links all macro-scale matter with the quantum world.

A holographic universe, in which the apparent separateness of subatomic particles is illusory, means that at a deeper level of reality all things in the universe are infinitely interconnected. The electrons in a carbon atom in the human brain would theoretically be connected to the subatomic particles that comprise every bird that flies, every heart that beats and every star that shimmers in the sky, and the field would contain all information – past, present and future. If the above is not confusing enough, we can go further and cite some theoretical constructs, such as string theory and super string theory, which aim to reconcile quantum mechanics and general relativity and gravity, attempting to create a theory of everything in a mathematically complete system. String theory mainly posits that the electrons and quarks within the atom are oscillating one (or two)-dimensional lines. The importance here is that string and super string theories require the existence of several (11 according to M-theory) space-time dimensions in the universe. According to string theory, not only is everything connected and contains all the information in holographic matter, but there are also multiple layers of parallel universes at work.

THE EMERGING SCIENTIFIC MODEL OF THE UNIVERSE

Bohm (1983), as described above, suggests an implicate and an explicate order, with the implicate order being able to unfold into the explicate order – the reality we experience with our senses –

whilst the implicate order itself is a unity that is not understandable within the laws of space and time. He raises the idea, which he shares with others (e.g. Mitchell 2011), that meaning is a primary organizing force of the implicate order; thus matter and meaning are inseparable. Bohm used the term *soma significance* to emphasize the unity between consciousness and matter.

An emerging model of the universe would therefore have three basic facets: soma/physical, energy and significance. Soma is the world we can perceive in our normal waking consciousness. It functions according to Newton's laws and is governed by the laws of time. The second facet is the quantum world of information and energy, where everything is connected with a constant interchange between the clusters of energy. The quantum world is like a web, and everything in the physical world, including ourselves, is clusters of energy in this web. The third element may be consciousness functioning as the organizing principle, collapsing the web of energy at the quantum level into the entities of our knowable world (Mitchell 2011).

This emerging model would also, according to Edgar Mitchell, explain why people all over the world and since ancient times seem to notice quantum exchanges while in deep meditation.

> The zero-point field resonates with each point in the universe but is outside space-time; it can only be described as infinite and eternal. When one shifts one's point of view from the samadhi to the existential state where existence and location in space-time is the more prominent reality, then the zero-point field appears to exist at each point in the macro scale universe. One can observe from the zero-point or from the macro scale world, but not both simultaneously. (Mitchell 2011, p.2)

One's experience depends entirely upon the point of view that awareness chooses to experience within the spectrum of consciousness. Or, in the words of Van Lommel, 'the physical aspect of our consciousness in the material world, which we experience as waking consciousness and which can be compared to the particle aspect of light, stems from the wave aspect of the "complete" and "endless" consciousness created by collapse of the wave function in non-local space' (Van Lommel 2010, p.266).

To bring these mind-boggling discoveries of physics, which are still in progress, on to a more understandable level, I will end this chapter with the words of Edgar Mitchell:

> Given what is now known, certain research in progress, and with well informed speculation as to what will be verified in the near future, I suggest that the common experiences can be understood by means of the quantum hologram and related quantum phenomena:
>
> - Nonlocal intuitive feelings about people, events and objects.
>
> - All forms of psychic information (a form of intuition).
>
> - The therapy of past life regression and with it the popular belief in reincarnation.
>
> - The basic nature of our conscious experience.
>
> (Mitchell 2011, p.3)

Much points in the direction that it is this underlying realm, which we have just begun to explore and uncover, that form the worlds which indigenous shamans, past and present and in degrees, access, describe and utilize for their work. If this is the case, they have much to teach us about those realms and how to work within them.

Note

1   The recent results of the experiments at CERN, home of the Large Hadron Collider, have confounded physicists because it appears that subatomic particles have travelled faster than the speed of light, which so far was thought to be the highest speed possible. If those results are repeated we will have to rethink our whole understanding of the universe, with Bohm's construct being one of the possible explanations, namely that there is a level of reality in which there is no distance involved.

5 THE SHAMAN AS THERAPIST AND HEALER

Towards Integration and Wholeness

CONCEPTS OF HEALING, THERAPY AND WHOLENESS

It would be nice to be able to supply a simple, unambiguous definition of what shamanic work is all about, but because shamanism is ultimately about wholeness – about healing in the classical sense of Old English 'hal', meaning whole – and has developed over time and in different regions, various approaches are used. Matters are further complicated as traditional, indigenous ways have been adjusted to contemporary needs. As this chapter progresses, this will become clearer and, later, when I describe some of the teachings, tools and techniques that we can transfer and apply in a therapeutic setting, the different strands will become apparent.

Wholeness

However, it can be stated unambiguously that whatever shamanic practitioners do, or attempt to achieve, is approached with the intention of working towards integration and wholeness. They work towards integrating the different aspects of the mind with each other and with the body, as well as the mind/body with the soul and spirit, and furthermore the individual with a wider community and the community with 'the whole and with spirit'. Even without taking their work on the level of community into account, their psychotherapeutic work has to reach beyond the mind, as the mind is identified with emotions, desires, thoughts, beliefs and actions and linked with the body, thus being ultimately concerned with the survival of the organism and issues of this world. Issues of the soul and spirit, in contrast, reach beyond, towards something that is sacred, eternal and underlies the physical manifestation.[1] In shamanic work, soul and spirit are therefore vital, and a transcendent integration, namely the transformation of the ego and the self into a universal structure of integration and wholeness, is often the aim of elaborate ceremonial and also energetic healing work.

In a spiritual sense, wholeness is about spirit seeking to manifest itself through us to its highest possible level. As I will explain in detail later in this chapter, we have an innate 'knowing' of this highest level, albeit very subconsciously, on a level that we can call soul. Health can therefore never be defined as purely physical, in the sense of a healthy body, or mental, in the sense of a sound mind, or even as the integration of a sound mind and a healthy body, but has to be defined as coming as close as possible to the highest level we can reach, to wholeness. What guides us, pushes us, steers us towards this is our 'soul'. Or, in other words, it is originally spirit that seeks to manifest itself through us, and it is our specific human essence, our soul, which impels and drives us towards growth, towards change, towards becoming all we can become. It is the shaman's task to help the individual and the community to stay in alignment with this desire of 'spirit' to manifest itself through us to the highest possibility, and the shaman's work is therefore mainly of a psycho-spiritual nature.[2]

World-view

All the pains that people suffer, no matter if they are mental/emotional, psychosomatic or existential, are defined within the paradigm of a world-view. As shown in the previous chapter, in the case of shamanism, the world-view is primarily defined by the interconnection of underlying energy fields (consciousness) and orientated towards the spiritual, whilst the pains people suffer are defined in our society within our contemporary materialistic paradigm, which is still largely mind/body orientated. As all practitioners know, a shared world-view with shared healing myths is essential in psychological healing. For example, the person who doesn't believe that exploring emotions, thought processes and belief systems and working towards changing those will help him will not consult a psychotherapist or counsellor. A woman who comes from a culture which puts the shame of and guilt for rape firmly on the victim might not be able to talk about the experience, no matter how often we explain to her that talking about it will help her. Somebody who thinks 'homeopathy' is a lot of nonsense will often find that homeopathic remedies won't work. Therapeutic practitioners know that we have to strive at the beginning of treatment to understand our clients' world before we can begin to assist them to change their view of it, should this be necessary. For instance, we might need to assist a client in changing underlying beliefs that create or reinforce his or her suffering, replacing them with beliefs that are beneficial. To achieve this, those maladaptive beliefs (world-views) have to be disputed, insight has to be gained and new beliefs have to be established. Shamans will, in a more indirect way, also attempt this change of world-view by changing the beliefs of their clients, mainly by providing experiences which shatter these beliefs, as they also know that their 'healing' will work better, and sometimes only, when the client's belief is shattered and thus changes. The experiences of Howard Charing, co-author of *Plant Spirit Shamanism* (Heaven and Charing 2006), reflect my own. He explains that all the traditional and indigenous shamans he has encountered share one unifying characteristic, namely that they will do whatever is required to help a person into well-being by catalysing in one way or another that person's inner belief system, so that they feel and know that they will get well. This change of belief is as important as the 'real' and tangible medicine work.

Transformation

Although shamanism and psychology/therapy share the intent of healing as they both seek to alleviate suffering which is mainly psychological, it is the humanist, the Jungian and the transpersonal sections of psychology that share common ground with shamanism, as they embrace a world-view that includes the spiritual and as they both work towards 'integrative wholeness'.[3] Within this world-view, the concept of 'curing', which focuses on symptom removal and underlies western medicine and many of the western psychological therapies, is too narrow. This doesn't mean that symptom removal is never advised or never necessary. Shamanic practitioners will also attempt it at times, although in shamanic terms this is mainly done energetically, as I will explain later. Nevertheless, as soon as we venture into the field of the human psyche, symptom removal always carries the danger of removing the messenger, rather than the cause. There is also the danger that removal of a symptom may provide the illusion of a cure, which is particularly evident when we use medication such as anti-depressants, or when we help addicts successfully withdraw, just to see them become users again after a brief period of time. Shamanic practitioners will therefore on the whole try to deal with symptoms via a transformation rather than a removal, or work with the underlying causes, which they see in more spiritual and energetic terms. A good example is the Gabonese healing ritual, which I will describe later in this chapter.

Development

The concept of wholeness always implies psycho-spiritual work towards development. Needless to say, apart from treating symptoms, contemporary therapy also helps the person to shift perceptions, change beliefs, change what can be changed and to come to terms with and accept losses or illnesses that can't be changed, contributing in both instances to growth and development. The difference here between western approaches and spiritual thinking is how far we expand the context, with shamanic practitioners utilizing the forces of 'the field' of soul and spirit also, addressing psychological issues as well as existential questions within a wider framework. Another concept which is important with regards to development is that of crisis. Shamanism understands that severe disturbance, crisis and 'breakdown' can be gateways to development, which, once successfully negotiated, lived and worked through, can result in greater psychological and spiritual well-being, and that we can in the process shed outdated, restricting and life-denying modes and enhance the spectrum of our lives. The shamanic initiation crisis is an extreme example of this. To see crisis as a transition period, a push of the psyche for further development, is a concept applied in shamanically orientated work. It is seen as a facet of the inbuilt human urge to individuate and to actualize and can be the outcome of the tension between the need and urge to grow and the holding on to the familiar, restricting and stagnating. 'The individuating psyche abhors stasis as nature abhors a vacuum... Rather than tolerate stagnation, the psyche may wilfully create crises that force development' (Perry 1986, pp.34, 35).

Integration

Psychological treatments are very helpful in a wide array of physical and psychosomatic diseases and illnesses and we know that many of the patients consulting medical practitioners need help with psychological problems. Walsh (2010, p.208) states that 50 per cent of patients consulting medical practitioners need psychological help and the same seems to apply to shamanic practitioners. A study of Taiwanese healers found that 90 per cent of their patients suffered from psychological disorders and almost half of the physical complaints were psychosomatic in nature (Kleinman and Sung 1979, p.7). Therefore, although the spiritual component is paramount, the 'world's most enduring general practitioners also draw from the gamut of physical, social and psychological therapies' (Walsh 2010, p.207). That indigenous shamans have developed a wide arsenal of such tools, especially, but not only, in the form of rituals, ceremonies and journeys, is not surprising, as besides purely physical ailments that were mainly treated with herbal medicine, 'soul loss', being de-spirited and existential anxieties, as well as taboos, superstitions and the fear of the unknown, played and still play a role in tribal cultures (Rogers 1982). Now, in the twenty-first century, contemporary shamanic practitioners, both traditional and western, will incorporate and utilize contemporary therapeutic approaches and techniques, as shamanism is a 'surviving approach' that has always adapted to changing times and developments and continues to do so.

I have experienced how vital such adaptations and integrations of different healing paradigms are when I worked in Africa in an area affected by years of horrendous war. After 20 years of war, the traumas inflicted in the form of killings, mutilations, abductions, living in camps, abuse, rape, loss and starvation were multiple, heartbreaking and beyond what we, living in war-free countries, can comprehend. It had become obvious to many agencies, governmental and non-governmental, that the highly traumatized people, starved of hope and full of underlying fear, rage, sadness and despair, needed 'psycho-social support'. This psycho-social support was partly provided by psychiatrists, specially trained social workers, psychologists and other trauma therapists, who were in competition with indigenous healers, but above all with several church initiatives, some of which were highly fundamentalist in nature. Unfortunately, two very different world-views provided many misunderstandings. The indigenous healers provided traditional rituals and ceremonies, mainly aimed at the reintegration of individuals, especially former child soldiers, into the community and at forgiveness from the community being given to these former soldiers and other forced combatants. This integration is vital as a basis for all mental/emotional healing in traditional cultures because, unlike western cultures, African people define themselves very much via their tribes and communities. Without reintegration into a community there can be no complete recovery. Providing a vital service, the traditional healers nevertheless knew little about traumatization and its emotional/mental and psychosomatic consequences. The western social workers and therapists understood to a good extent the underlying trauma-related issues of the dissociated, depressed, suicidal, raging, violent and/or mentally very disturbed clients, but could do very little to help them to cope with their existential fears or with the rejection from their communities, let alone provide a wider spiritual framework. To cut a very long story short, it was in the end the churches which seemed to be the most effective in drawing people in, providing community, a spiritual home, hope and pastoral counselling of an often dubious, fundamentalist nature.

Another example, which might explain why I am passionate about the inclusion of different healing paradigms, in order to enable us to address the whole spectrum of the person, stems from my experience working for a brief period in Sri Lanka after the 2004 tsunami. Astonishingly, Sri Lanka had no trained professionals, as all psychological/pastoral care was traditionally provided by monks within the spiritual communities of Buddhism. There was a distinct non-comprehension that traumatic experiences might need to be addressed on the level of the mental/emotional and not only on the communal/spiritual. Having said this, my time in Sri Lanka also showed me how important it is for emotional and mental recovery to be embedded in a spiritual system and community when existential crisis strikes.

This need to integrate the spiritual and the therapeutic also applies to contemporary western therapeutic approaches to enable us to address the whole spectrum of the person. The depressive, hopeless client, the angry, helpless survivor of abuse, the person who feels that her world is ending because of the breakdown of her long-standing marriage, the mother who loses a child, the husband who loses a wife and/or the addict who is convinced that living is impossible without the substance he takes all need a wider framework within which to recover and grow from this place of hurt and suffering. The western therapist can address maladaptive thoughts, behaviours and the underlying beliefs. She can help with emotional release and, if appropriate, with trauma techniques, ego-state work and reintegration of dissociated parts, but within this narrow context she is not able to offer the patient a field of exploration that might help them to put themselves and their experiences into a larger context and touch their own soul. To stay on the level of mind doesn't make sense in the light of the suffering that has been endured and doesn't help the client to feel embedded in something that is bigger than her or him. This is where spiritual approaches are desperately needed, and where shamanic tools and teachings can help, as they, as Powell and MacKenna put it so beautifully, enable 'the wisdom of the soul to enrich the limitations of the mind' (Powell and MacKenna 2009, p.4).

WHAT DO SHAMANS DO AND HOW?

Shamanism uses a compendium of ceremonies, stories, maps, teaching tools, techniques, rhythms, sounds, movements and understanding and knowledge about the underlying workings of life, collected over many millennia in different parts of the world, to help us to expand our consciousness, to experience our soul, our connection with spirit and as being an embedded part of the whole and of being whole ourselves. So let's be a bit more specific, looking into what shamans actually do and try to achieve.[4]

Although the shaman is much more a man or woman of the soul and spirit than of the body, physical healing is an aspect of his or her work. Generally speaking, the shaman focuses on addressing what underlies the physical malaise. Direct physical healing can be energy healing, where the shaman works directly with the energy body of a person. Shamans also use herbs and plant medicine for physical healing. It can be healing that is done within the realm of 'spirit', the quantum realm, where the shaman influences the forces before they manifest in matter or summons and uses forces that can help with the healing of the physical. Physical healing can also consist of extraction of a spirit attachment or dealing with a 'psychic attack' that has already manifested in physical form.[5]

Shamanic healing can also be healing of the soul of the person and more often than not this is the focus. The retrieval of soul parts, the extraction of spirit intrusions and/or the aligning of the person's soul with its spirit intent are all forms of therapeutic healing that work towards 'wholeness'.

Shamanic work also creates fields where clients and participants of groups or community members have a direct, intense holistic experience that produces the desired connections, shifts and transformations – for example, as I will show later, when we use ceremony and ritual. An ancestral ceremony, a sweat lodge ceremony or a general healing ritual can be a prolonged affair of immense focus, beauty and joy, involving profoundly altered physical and emotional states, often of high energy levels. A ceremony such as a sweat lodge ceremony will take a whole day and night, or even longer, with the psychological preparation, the physical building of the lodge, the creating of the fire and the actual 'being in the lodge', as well as the 'telling of the story' and integration of different strands afterwards, all being part of the transformative experience.

Shamanic ceremonies and other tools and techniques are applied with the aim of transformation, in the sense that they aim, as I have already stated, for our world-view to change. When our view of the world begins to change from a material one to a more spiritually connected one, when what we believe to be reality changes, we view ourselves and our environment in a different, more integrated light. This changing of the world-view usually reaches much deeper than the change of a belief. It seems that the experiences in profound altered states of fields and vibrations, of emotions and mental and physical processes, change something within participants on an almost cellular level, bringing about a transformation and reconnection with forces and ideas that we 'have forgotten'. The NDE is an extreme example of the changes that can be achieved via a profound change of a client's world-view stemming from an intense experience.

General spiritual practices, such as meditation, communing with nature, blessings, giving thanks, sharing and many more, are a major part of shamanism. Again, these aim, in various ways, for a shift in consciousness from a separation consciousness to a consciousness of connection and with this to a higher state of consciousness. On top of these we also have approaches that will bring spirit into our conscious awareness in the form of communicating with and acquiring spirit helpers and guides, but also in developing an awareness of hunches, intuitions, coincidences, signs and so on.

Shamanism, especially the more contemporary variety, also provides more directly accessible teachings about and tools for personal development and therapy of the mental/emotional, such as working with the shadow, with detrimental emotional states and for the connection of the emotional and mental with the spiritual aspect of the person. Examples include the adaptation of the Medicine Wheel, journeying with 'therapeutic intents' and ceremonial work for therapeutic purposes and meditative and other spiritual practices.

Shamanic work is about psycho-spiritual development and about achieving the highest possible integration of all aspects of the self in alliance with what spirit tries to express through us. In general terms, shamanism talks about dark and light 'arrows' we can aim at 'targets'. The dark arrows are attachment, dependency, judgement, comparison, expectation, neediness and ego self-importance. They keep us stuck. Light arrows are illumination, introspection, trust, wisdom, seeking balance, open-hearted communication, will, intent and focus. They move us on. Within the idea of psycho-spiritual development, emphasis is furthermore placed on purpose and meaning. Thus the shamanic practitioner helps clients to quest for visions, to access purpose and deeper levels of themselves, which help to reveal 'our tasks in life'.

Last, but not least, the shamanic practitioner is also concerned with dying, with the dead and with the deceased. Although, like energy healing, this will not be part of this book, it is worth mentioning at this point that the shaman also functions as a psychopomp, helping spirits of deceased people who have ended up 'stuck' on the earth plane to move over to the plane of spirit, where they should be.

A HOLISTIC TRANSFORMATIONAL EXPERIENCE: THE GABONESE HEALING RITUAL

The Gabonese healing and initiation ritual is used here to illustrate the above and to show how indigenous shamanism will, quite often, aim towards a holistic, transformational experience. It demonstrates the transformative power of an initiation and healing ritual that creates profound altered-state experiences and addresses all levels – the mental/emotional, physical and spiritual – in the process. I am also using this ritual as it has become quite well known in the treatment of addiction and has been observed and analysed by western researchers, who have come up with some interesting interpretations of the process. Although some western researchers try to 'de-spiritualize' the process, their findings with regard to the changing brain functions are informative. They help us not only to appreciate the extensive knowledge of the human psyche and mind that traditional healers and shamans can possess, but also the extensive healing capacity of different states of our brains, once we can begin to allow ourselves to utilize them.

In the Gabonese healing ritual the person to be initiated consumes the root bark of the Iboga shrub, containing a substance called Ibogaine, which has a hallucinogenic component.[6] The indigenous healers see Iboga as a plant spirit that teaches humans. The consumption of Ibogaine is ritualized, with doses being given in a controlled way and effects that last for 6–15 hours. The ritual is accompanied by music with a steady rhythm of 5–6 Hz, with sounds being different for women and men. During the treatment, initiates experience various levels of brain alterations, have visions and relive childhood experiences. Overall, the Gabonese healers expect the process to produce a recall of childhood experiences, a connection with spirit and, generally, a death and rebirth experience, as well as profound mental/emotional and spiritual healing in the form of a transformation. A healer accompanies the initiate, or the person who needs healing, in many cases now westerners who are addicted to strong substances, such as heroin, crack cocaine and others, throughout the process.

A most interesting study, which analyses the neuro-physiological aspects of what is happening during the ritual, is by Strubelt, a psychologist, and Maas, a medical doctor (Strubelt and Maas 2008). They come to the overall conclusion that the work done by the Gabonese healers, with the help of the plant medicine and the steady rhythm of the music, produces the typical elements of a profoundly altered state that seems to come close to, or is, an NDE, characterized by 'a life review, out-of-body experience and floating over various landscapes, an encounter with deceased, gliding through a tunnel into an ulterior world, and an encounter with a divine entity – finally the arrival at a point of no return, which is not to be surpassed by the living, and then the return to life' (Strubelt and Maas 2008, p.2). Furthermore, the expected outcomes, again supported by the countless research papers and reports studied by the authors, also show striking similarities to the outcomes of NDEs, which, as I have shown, are well researched: acceptance of responsibility and reduction of dependencies, increase in spirituality and reduced fear of death, as well as a new love for people and environment, are unanimously observed as effects of the encounter with death (Bonenfant 2006; Strubelt and Maas 2008, pp.5–9).

Neuro-physiologically Strubelt and Maas see the following happen:

1. Taking Ibogaine induces a protective reaction against prospective oxygen deprivation in the brain, a mechanism that seems to happen when the brain anticipates death and when people go through NDEs.

2. The rhythm of the music that is used during the initiation corresponds with the theta rhythm of the brain, a frequency of 4–8 Hz, therefore slowing brain activity down to a relatively deep altered state.

3. The interesting connection is that theta rhythms are naturally generated in the hippocampus and develop within the first years of life, becoming dominant at the age of about six or seven, serving the formation of episodic memory and the encoding of new information in the hippocampus. The authors conclude that the recall of memories is highly likely to be facilitated by the same EEG frequencies that were present during memory formation. 'We hypothesize that the phase of dominance of the theta rhythms is responsible for the episodic life review in near-death experiences' (Strubelt and Maas 2008, p.6). In modern psychological terms we are looking at state-dependent memory being deliberately activated, enabling the recall of – and confrontation with – childhood memories, which are psychotherapeutically guided by the healers.

4. At one point during the Gabonese healing experience the brain activity slows down to delta waves (0.5–4 Hz), which are usually only observed in humans during sleep,

but dominate the EEG of reptiles when in a waking state and also the EEG of newborn babies, who are not able to memorize information about space and time. The authors offer this as an explanation for the special perception of time and space in NDEs. They furthermore conclude that if we measure delta wave patterns in humans whilst awake, the brain must have shifted to evolutionarily older structures, which are more resistant to the lack of oxygen than the neuro-cognitive networks of mammals (Strubelt and Maas 2008, p.8).

5. An interesting anomaly occurs with the intake of Ibogaine as well as partly in NDEs. Whilst in delta-wave state, we usually lose the function of speech and especially the function of memory. Nevertheless, during the Ibogaine 'night of vision', functions of speech and memory are intact, which also seems to be the case during some NDEs, at least as far as the function of memory is concerned, as people can recall them. In the initiation ceremonies of the Gabonese, the maintenance of those cortical functions is considered to be therapeutically very important. The healers demand constant verbal communication from the initiate about the observed matters and their possible meanings and request target-orientated activities afterwards. 'Only a remembered vision is considered successful. Therewith new spiritual contents of the unconsciousness as well as knowledge of interior processes are opened to the consciousness, and conditions are prepared to transfer them into long-term memory' (Strubelt and Maas 2008, p.8). This new spiritual content applies especially to the death and rebirth experience. In modern terms, the client processes consciously whilst being in a state that, under normal circumstances, would allow no conscious processing, and at the same time expands his/her consciousness.

6. Another interesting observation is the activation of the 'old vagal' system. Mammals, including humans, have two vagal branches, an evolutionarily older one and a second

newer branch, originating in the nucleus ambiguus. As far as we know, humans only use the older one during birth, or sometimes in life-threatening situations. The NDE consists not only of images but also strong emotions that are experienced as being exceptional: 'the exceptional vagal stimulation during near-death experience might explain that the situation is perceived as completely new and beyond comparison with other "real" experiences – one dies and is re-born' (Strubelt and Maas 2008, p.9). This might furthermore explain why very strong, painful experiences, such as intense trauma, can be recalled during this controlled NDE and later during the aftercare stage, and seem to be transformed. The extreme calmness produced by the vagal dominance gets associated with the memories and would, in modern terms, help to desensitize them. But not only would it desensitize them, it would also create a state that people will have access to in future, especially those who suffer from sympathetic over-reaction, such as most trauma survivors, people who suffer from depression, people who are drug dependent and so on. Mash, Kovera and Pablo (2000) were, for example, able to demonstrate an improvement in depression sufferers, using a self-rating depression scale.

7. The 'night of vision' is followed by a period of isolation of the initiate. 'Hereby he is continuously accompanied by healers and other initiated persons in the processing of the experiences' (Strubelt and Maas 2008, p.10). The researchers suggest that we are looking at a hippocampal neurogenesis during that period of aftercare. The hippocampus is a major player in the consolidation of information from short-term to long-term memory and it seems that the focus on integrating the experiences of the night of vision increases cell production in the hippocampus, which could in turn again contribute to the consolidation of the personality change. In psychological terms, we are seeing a conscious integration of the material.

The transformative power of such profound altered state experiences should not be underestimated. This is not only a solving of problems, or a change of beliefs, but a transformation via a transcendental experience. The world of visions, of archetypal imagery, of helping 'spirits' and of an NDE, combined with the cognitive integration of old, often painful, material stemming from childhood as well as the questioning of deeply held dysfunctional beliefs, whilst being in a physiologically highly relaxed state and held in a ceremonial way by experienced healers, as well as the time spent afterwards in integrating the experiences, is transformative. The transformation comes about through the therapeutic integrative work on every level, the altered and the normal cognitive state, which is combined with an expansion of consciousness. It is this healing and transformative expansion of consciousness that we shy away from, a potential that is, in the words of the authors, 'neglected in Western psychotherapy' (Strubelt and Maas 2008, p.12).[7]

TOOLS AND HELPERS IN SHAMANISM

Indigenous and contemporary practitioners use various means, approaches, tools and techniques, as well as 'helping' energies, in their work. Whilst I will return to describe some of those and their applications within a contemporary therapeutic environment in more detail in Part III, I want to provide a brief overview of the basic means and tools that are used and introduce the concept of 'spirit helpers'. It is important to recognize, although I am using the word 'helpers', that the shaman couldn't do the work he or she does without working with such energies. In that sense they are vital forces within the working realm of the shaman, seen often as wiser and more knowledgeable than humans.

All basic approaches in shamanic work will produce an altered state of perception and awareness and create an energy field that is beneficial for the work to follow, but they are also in themselves 'shamanic tools'. To clarify, let me start with an example. The counsellor, within the therapeutic relationship with the client, uses certain skills in specific ways to achieve a desired outcome, such as empathic listening, positive regard, questioning maladaptive thoughts and beliefs, enquiring about emotional contents and more. Besides achieving what they directly try to achieve, such strategies also result in the development of a therapeutic alliance, a relationship between the counsellor and the client that is based on trust, consistency and feelings of being listened to and understood. This relationship is in itself therapeutic, with some suggesting that it is this specific relationship that is the most beneficial part of the therapy, rather than the strategies and techniques employed.

Shamanic work runs along similar lines. The means shamans use produce specifically designed states in the shaman, the client and the group that are first in themselves 'healing and therapeutic' and are second also tools and techniques that are applied to achieve certain outcomes. For example, the monotonous beat of a drum used for journeying produces an altered state required for the journey, but even without journeying the drumbeats are in themselves 'healing', as they have a relaxing effect, stimulate the imagination, remind us of the heartbeat and can also be used for healing itself, as drumbeats can be adjusted to change vibrations in the energy body. In more complexity, the same can be said for ritual or ceremonial work. The ceremonial work leads the participants into a realm of community, focus, beauty, spirit and intent, creating an energy field that is in itself profoundly moving, cleansing, balancing, energizing and healing. The specific function of the ceremony, for example letting go of something, calling something in or giving thanks, is the second level. Ceremony, as already indicated before when looking at the Ibogaine healing, can 'create a whole brain experience that awakens the curiosity of the neocortex, satisfies the need for safety of our more primitive limbic brain, and makes ecstatic states accessed by the frontal lobes of the higher brain possible' (Vivoldo 2010, p.90). This happens regardless of the specific aim or function of the ceremony or the ritual. Both basic energy levels, as well as the intent of the ceremony, work together to provide the holistic, transformational experience.

Shamanic means and tools

Here I will briefly describe the main means to produce certain states that are used in contemporary shamanism: ceremony and ritual, the creation of vibrating fields via drumming, sound and movement and tuning into nature as well as the main helpers. These descriptions are by no means complete. There are variations that will be discussed in more detail later, as well as means, such as the use of hallucinogenic plants, which are not included in this book as they are either not transferable or need profound training. The techniques that are used within the created states, such as journeying, soul retrieval, ceremonial healing and more, are discussed in Part III. The following therefore only provides an overview of the main vehicles and helpers.

CEREMONY AND RITUAL

Ceremony and ritual form one of the foundations of all shamanically orientated work and will be discussed in depth later in the book. Rituals and ceremonies connect us with the powers of the universe, with the divine and with deeper levels of ourselves and are used in all traditions to connect with the sacred, to become aware of the different energies in and around us and to work on the level of soul. In this sense ritual is a vehicle to make us aware of – and integrate – aspects of our multi-dimensional selves, forming a bridge between ordinary realms and the realms of the unseen. Traditionally, ceremonial work is used for healing, for rites of passage, for blessings, initiations, dedications and cleansing, for the shaman's flight and journeys, for giving something back to the earth, for expressing gratitude and for quests and meaning and purpose.

Having participated in indigenous rituals and used ceremonial means with groups and clients, I can only agree with Walsh (2010, p.210), who cautiously proposes that, at their best, shamanic healing rituals probably induce the full panoply of healing responses simultaneously:

- cultural therapy: they heal and create community

- socio-therapy: they repair relationships, harmonize social structures and stabilize society

- psychosomatic therapy: they diminish disease and its complications

- gene therapy: they modulate gene expression

- psychotherapy: they heal the subjective dis-ease of illness

- spiritual therapy: they relieve a sense of alienation and estrangement from the universe, create a sense of connection and alignment with the sacred and foster a transpersonal/ transegoic sense of identity.

VIBRATIONS AND SOUND

The main vehicles used to enter altered states and to call in spirit are the creation of vibrations through drumming, singing, chanting and/or humming. There are many different types of drums used within shamanic work, for example djembe drums in Africa, frame drums and pow-wow drums in North and South America, and tablas in India. 'The drum is the Great Spirit's favourite instrument. That's why we were all given a heartbeat' (Mano, Navajo Elder) expresses the meaning of the drum. Looking at it from a more western point of view we discover that the drums are played in certain ways, depending on the wavelength the drummer wants to produce and on the general intent. In the classic 'shamanic journey drumming' the beat is adjusted to the theta wavelength of the brain; in fire ceremonies the basic drumbeat is often adjusted to the rhythm of the heart. The monotonous rhythms of the drumbeats or chants are kept up for hours, or even nights, or they are just used to create the desired energy field or altered state consciousness. I have experienced shamans in South America using their voices to call in spirit, varying the sounds and rhythms depending upon the spirits they want to call, an experience that is quite mind-boggling in its intensity and its creation of various states. In the Ibogaine ritual, the sounds and drumbeats used are also adjusted to the delta wavelength of the brain and to the sex of the client.

MOVEMENT, DANCE AND TRANCE-DANCE

Long, ongoing movement in the form of dance is another means to, first, enter an altered state of consciousness and, second, also to raise the vibrations of the body and to travel beyond the limits of it. Movement and dance is also used to embody whatever needs or wants to be embodied, such as spirit essences of animals or other spirits, and to embody and experience on a cellular level desirable changes and outcomes. Shamans can and will dance through the night to achieve a state where their whole body and mind are vibrating on a very high level, so enabling them to be 'one' with energy fields which are inaccessible in a normal waking state and/or to 'flee the body'. The dance of the dervishes is one that is familiar to many and we have probably all seen indigenous ceremonial dancers from Africa. Movement can also be highly ritualized, creating intended fields through the vibrations of the movements.

TUNING INTO NATURE

Shamans see and perceive everything in nature as the manifested form of spirit and will therefore communicate with it regularly and learn from it constantly, treating all life as being sacred and honouring all creation deeply. The shaman will regularly tune into nature to learn and embody, but also to retreat, which is necessary to recharge energies and to re-ground. 'How do you know that this plant can be used to lower fever?' a shaman from South America was once asked by an American scientist. The shaman looked puzzled and answered: 'Easy, the plant told us so.' The tuning into nature spirits and melting with those vibrations is often done in silence and over a period of time through long walks or meditative practices, by observing a plant, tuning into its vibrations, until the watching becomes 'seeing' and 'hearing' and 'knowing'. Many ceremonies and rituals, such as initiation rituals or Vision Quests, are not only performed in nature but also include a tuning into it.

SHAMANIC HELPERS

Indigenous as well as contemporary practitioners will always state that they work with helping spirits. Those helpers can take the form of spirits or objects, and in most cases shamanic practitioners use both. The main helpers for shamans are power animal spirits, spirit guides, spirits of ancestors, nature spirits, the spirits of the sky and the earth, as well as the spirits of the elements of fire, water, air, earth, metal and of the four directions. Helping spirits are real in non-ordinary reality and are difficult to describe. They are essences/ beings with wisdom, knowledge and power, willing to protect, help, guide and teach the living. Shamanic practitioners use them as sources of power, teachings and wisdom, which they draw upon in their life and work. Spirit helpers are difficult to describe as they are energetic in nature. We give them forms through the way we 'see and experience' them. Spirit helpers are called in via special calls, often in the form of quite humble power songs, and can either be used during the shamanic journey, healing work and ceremonial work or they can be embodied. The working relationship with spirit helpers is developed over periods of time and maintained by continuous practice. The shaman is chosen by spirits but also calls for them and stalks them. The shaman learns increasingly about the qualities of the different spirits and how to use the specific qualities for specific tasks. He or she develops through their teachings and learns how the underlying energetic world works and impacts on humans. The relationship is interdependent and mutual: 'the shaman has learned to surrender to the wisdom of the helping spirits and they in turn allow the shaman to focus their help to create desired human results' (Pratt 2007a, p.201).

POWER ANIMALS

Power animals are helping spirits in the form of animals. They usually vibrate on a different level to that of, for example, spirit guides. One could say that they relate to the lower chakras, the old brain, the vibrations of animals on the planet earth. Power animals are very strong energies. When we are in touch with an animal spirit, we are strong, powerful and more likely to be in touch with nature

– our own as well as the natural world around us – and therefore less disconnected. Power animals are guardian spirits that protect and guard the shaman, in the physical as well as spiritual world. In shamanic work they are guardian spirits, used mainly, but not only, in lower world journeys and utilized for healing, guidance, creativity and soul retrieval. The relationship with the power animal is central in many indigenous cultures, and for the shaman is a strong reciprocal relationship as the shaman knows that there is no power of healing without the spirits of animals, plants and nature generally. Animal spirits, as Christina Pratt (2007a, p.25) points out, are neither lifted to the status of deities nor are they lowered to the status of a psychological metaphor. They are seen as manifestations of a natural power that is stronger and often wiser than human beings.

SPIRIT GUIDES

Not all schools of contemporary shamanism talk about 'spirit guides' in distinction to ancestral spirits, animal spirits and other spirits, as described and given form to the energies/essences of the non-material, parallel, invisible worlds. But as I have introduced the distinction between the upper and the lower world, one can say that spirit guides are often seen as the spirits of the upper world. As beings of the upper world they are of a different vibration, having a mostly ethereal, cosmic quality and often a humanoid form. Their gifts are more of a universal wisdom quality; they are the ones who can help us to see the 'bigger picture', and often guide and answer questions around subjects like soul, sense, purpose and meaning.

SPIRITS OF ANCESTORS

The spirits of ancestors are very important in shamanic work. In many cultures it is believed that the deceased ancestor returns to the world in spirit form to assist the living. Ancestral spirits can also be named the ancient ones, the old ones, the grandmothers and grandfathers, depending on the culture. Ancestors have knowledge of the land, and it is believed that they come back and stay in and around the land and the people they are connected to. On the whole it is the task and duty of the ancestors to hold the memories and the learning/wisdom of humankind, back to the beginning, and because they have left the living they also know about things 'otherworldly'. By being connected to – and by honouring, consulting and working with – the ancestral spirits, the shaman draws on the collective wisdom of the ones that came before and translates their teachings and advice into appropriate, contemporary means for the benefit of the living.

SPIRITS OF NATURE

Everything in nature has certain 'essence qualities' or spirit, which the shaman respects, connects with, learns about and from, and uses when working. A nature spirit is the spiritual/essence aspect of any form that can be found in nature, such as plants, trees, water, sky and stones. The spirits of nature are believed to dwell in those physical forms, and the spirit/essence of a stone is different from the spirit of a crystal, which is different from the spirit of a tree, which is different from the spirit of a flower. How nature spirits are seen and worked with varies between cultures. Generally speaking their qualities are used purposefully: the shaman might, for example, use a stone for pulling out energy from the body during healing, the tree for recharging, a certain plant spirit for healing, always aware that all 'essence or spirit' also resonates within a human.

POWER OBJECTS

The power object is a physical object in which powerful essence resides. It can be a natural object in which the power of the spirit essence is utilized or it can be created and energized – loaded up with power. The sacred pipe, for example, is created by hand from 'sacred stones' and then increasingly charged via ritual and ritualistic use, with clear intents, but it also has already 'sacred essence' as it was given to humans by spirit. The sacred essence of the pipe is based on the beautiful story of White Buffalo Calf Women who brought the sacred pipe to the Lakota during a time of famine and taught them many rituals. Power objects can be created for specific uses and then destroyed or they may be created for long-term use. Most practitioners will create certain objects for long-term use. For instance, I have crafted the feather bundle which I use as well as my medicine shield and my drums and for about 12 years have been working with the same two stones that were energized for me originally by a Brazilian shaman. Power objects, which can be also shown to the seeker in dreams and visions, can be then searched and found and energized – given power – with power rituals, purpose and intent, and utilized for specific purposes such as healing, calling spirit and cleansing. Other objects include those that are handed down from generation to generation, being already powerful, or are found at certain places that have power. Power objects must be maintained, treated well, cleansed and re-energized if necessary, and generally related to in a caring, respectful and nurturing way.

Notes

1 See Chapter 6.
2 This concept will be explained in more detail in Chapter 6.
3 See Chapter 1.
4 I will give examples in Part III.
5 Physical healing and energy approaches that focus on physical healing are not part of this book as it focuses on mental/emotional interventions.
6 Ibogaine is now widely and successfully used – albeit in some countries illegally – to help people with drug addiction. A team of psychiatrist researchers from three medical schools, Kenneth R. Alper, Howard S. Lotsof and Charles D. Kaplan (2008), write in their article about the growing medical subculture of Ibogaine, seeing it as a vast uncontrolled experiment with all its benefits and dangers.
7 It is in this context interesting that western research, as well as some western clinics, try to take the hallucinogenic as well as the spiritual experience out of the treatment with Ibogaine. Strubelt and Maas (2008) state that private clinics in several industrial countries underestimate the importance of the spiritual experience within Ibogaine therapies against drug addiction. Although drug addicts often report elements of NDEs after the intake of Ibogaine, these are neglected by the pharmacological research, or are considered as being disturbing and without influence on the success of the therapeutic process, and it is not surprising to me that pharmacology tries to eliminate the hallucinogenic content of Ibogaine (see also Alper 2001). It is really quite telling how very afraid we are of brain activities we cannot control and how little we know how to hold and handle experiences which are out of the ordinary.

6 | THE SHAMAN'S WORKING REALMS

Maps of Interconnected Human Reality

When we begin to work with concepts as invisible and complex as the underlying essence field, holographic universes, parallel universes or, to put it in more spiritual terms, 'All there is', 'spirits or essences' and 'souls', we need to create maps, models and constructs that our thinking minds can work with and make sense of. It is crucial to understand that all these forces and essences are energetic in nature and therefore that any model or map we construct is just that, helpful to provide an overview, a structured description, a sense of the territory and a tool to work with, but neither the precise territory nor the totality of reality itself. The second difficulty we are presented with is that, on the whole, shamanic maps put the human within a wider field. Thus maps about individual consciousness are relatively crude, or have been developed first to teach about layers of 'the whole' and only later, mainly influenced by contemporary practitioners, adapted to the human mind and human development. In older traditions the human mind is only a vehicle to access those layers of consciousness. We must also appreciate that shamanism is an evolving system and that many contemporary practitioners now adapt such maps to more contemporary views and knowledge.

I will introduce here three major concepts that can be adapted to work therapeutically with people, be it individually or as groups: the 'cosmic spirit worlds', the idea of 'soul and spirit' as major driving forces of human existence, and the Medicine Wheel as a comprehensive map and tool, that includes all aspects. Later, in Part III, I will describe how to utilize those concepts within the therapeutic context.

THE COSMIC SPIRIT WORLDS: LOWER, UPPER AND MIDDLE WORLDS

In shamanism, where everything is spirit in essence, we distinguish three levels of 'cosmic spirit worlds', which are non-linear, timeless and infinite: the lower, upper and middle worlds. These worlds are also not separate, but connected. There are numerous levels within each of these worlds and their descriptions vary, depending on culture, but also bear remarkable similarities and parallels. I will use the most widely known descriptions and definitions, which contemporary practitioners in the West use, and which on the whole are based on Eliade's and Harner's observations and teachings, as well as teachings of contemporary practitioners, such as Ingerman, Wesselman and others (Eliade 1964; Harner 1982; Ingerman and Wesselman 2010).

Generally speaking, the three levels create distinctions between earth and underworld/lower world, sky and upper world, and the here and now worlds of our everyday reality. The lower and upper worlds are transcendent realities, so-called non-ordinary realities, which we are not trained to see when we are in our normal waking state of consciousness, but which can be accessed in altered states. The middle world is twofold: it consists of the energetic aspects (dream aspects) of the everyday world we live in, and its visible, physical aspects in the form of the worlds we experience daily with our five senses. Besides understanding that the boundaries between those worlds are more or less artificial constructs, as those universes are seen as being interconnected, it is also essential to realize that all three worlds are of equal importance, forming together the description of 'the whole'. Some practitioners use the worlds to describe what we would see as the layers of the mind, for instance likening the lower and upper worlds to Jung's idea of the collective unconscious, as the images we encounter in those worlds are of a similar quality and form, especially the archetypical images and their meanings. Nevertheless, in strict shamanic terms the worlds exist separately from the individual mind, although they influence it and the mind influences them, and they are accessible through the mind when the state is altered.

This book is not the place to enter into the debate about how much of what we experience when accessing these worlds is shaped by our cultural and belief systems and how much is actual reality. Personally I have come to the conclusion that cultural concepts and beliefs will influence the interpretations of those energies and realms and it seems quite obvious to me that powerful shamans also influenced their cosmology and cultures through their interpretations of their experiences. In fact I am convinced that, as this whole book argues indirectly, all descriptions and interpretations of experiences are coloured by the medium. For example, I have issues with the concept of angels, which might well be based on my rejection of the more fundamentalist teachings of Christianity. In my journeys angels seem to be suspiciously rare, indeed almost absent, despite encountering guides of different shapes and forms, whilst I know people working in the spiritual field who seem to encounter angels often. How we experience those energies, and especially how our mind translates them into images and figures, be they archetypal ones or others, seems to depend partly on our beliefs and preferences. Having said that, it is also my experience that the qualities and attributes of certain energies are very similar, whether I call them guides or a colleague calls them angels.

The lower world

The lower world is pictured as a landscape, taking different forms, such as mountains, trees, deserts, forests, rivers, oceans, valleys, jungles or combinations of these. It is shaped by the 'dreaming' or 'non-ordinary' reality of all things that make up what we call nature. The lower world is home to the spirits of animals, trees, plants and rocks, as well as human-like spirits that are connected to the mystery of the earth (Ingerman and Wesselman 2010, p.31). The stories of the lower world are myths and fairy tales, mostly involving an encounter with a dark force. The lower world is accessed via a journey through an imagined opening or portal into the earth. The access can take the form of a tunnel, the roots of trees, a hole in the ground or a cave or well that leads downwards into the earth.

The lower world – and that is a most interesting aspect for therapists – is also the world where we find what Jung called the shadows. Frightening, devious, evil or monstrous beings can populate the lower world of the shaman's clients, be it individuals or the community. As I said before, for example, if we work with people who have suffered abuse in their childhood or other severe traumatization, or those who suffer from anxiety disorders, addictions or borderline personality disorders, we can easily come across such beings in the form of monsters, reptiles and threatening and violent male or female and archetypal figures representing violence, shame, guilt, rage, anger and fear, to name just a few. Split-off soul parts, a concept that is quite similar to psychology's concept of dissociation, will also often reside in the lower world and are retrieved and integrated by the shaman for the client.

Indigenous shamans who work regularly in the lower world have extensive knowledge of it, and accept wholeheartedly the idea of soul loss as well as the shadow side of existence, in the individual as well as the collective. Dark forces exist in every culture: potentially debilitating and destructive negative feelings, such as anger, hate and jealousy, damaging behaviours, inhuman treatment of 'the other', selfishness, greed and violence are just a few we experience daily within our society. Unlike indigenous shamans, we increasingly shy away from addressing those forces, their highly energetic/emotional charges and at times devastating consequences.[1] Dr Allen Holmquist, a therapist working shamanically, remarks:

> a case can be made that the only difference between the horrors of the underworld found in aboriginal societies and the horrors of the modern western world is the massive scale to which westerners have taken the problems and the fact that we have externalized and projected the evil spirits onto other people, races, countries and religions rather than accepting them as part of human nature. Native people

owned the whole of creation, positive and negative, good and evil, as it existed within themselves, within their culture and within all of creation. (Holmquist 2007, p.287)

The knowing that we receive when we access the lower worlds via the shamanic journey, which I will describe in Chapter 10, is more instinctual than intellectual; it unfolds like a film and appears in different forms, such as images, sudden insights and emotional reactions, or, and this is an important aspect in all worlds, it can be shown to us by spirit helpers. The spirit helpers in the lower world mainly take the form of power animals, but we also find other guides entering the lower world. The journey to the lower world, together with the integrations, will always resolve the issue in one form or another or, alternatively, it will function as a diagnostic tool, forming the basis for further interventions or therapeutic processes.

The upper world

The upper world feels and appears quite different from the lower world. After passing a transition space, which often looks and feels like a dense cloud, one enters an etheric realm of many layers. The lighting is bright; colours are usually pastel, light and somehow fuzzy. Crystal structures, cloudlike realms and an airy feeling as well as cosmic beings can be encountered. Sandra Ingerman remarks that the upper worlds are 'formed by the dreaming of the higher gods and goddesses, the ancestors, the ascended masters, the compassionate angelic forces that are willing to be of service to us – most often as teachers and guides' (Ingerman and Wesselman 2010, p.31).

The upper world is traditionally accessed via tree branches, ropes or ladders that reach upwards, mountains, maybe flying animals that take you up into the sky, rainbows, smoke and anything else one can think of. Some access the upper world via the lower world. The journey usually starts with a visualization in nature and then, like the lower world journey, unfolds as a process. The upward travel can lead via stars and planets – which are still in the middle world – and there is usually some kind of transition stage before one reaches the lofty grounds of the upper world.

The upper world is inhabited by helping spirits in humanoid forms; formless, cloudlike spirit beings; some nature spirits and some power animals also populate those realms. In the upper world we retrieve information, seek guidance and wisdom. The information, guidance and wisdom that we receive in the upper world is, in contrast to the lower world, not instinctual, but rather has philosophical and wise qualities in the sense that it is knowledge that seems to reach beyond 'what we know'. In the upper world we find our higher spirit guides and teachers and are able to connect with our ancestors in spirit forms. Some contemporary shamanic teachers also recommend we look for our own 'higher self' within those realms, reconnecting with our transpersonal aspect, which is sometimes also called the over-soul in accordance with the thoughts of essayist Ralph Waldo Emerson: that immortal aspect of ourselves that has lived many lives and will live many lives in future and can be a source of intuition, inspiration and guidance, communicating with us through dreams, visions and ideas (Gilman 2011).

The middle world

The middle world is the 'non-ordinary, spirit aspect' (energetic fields) of the physical universe we live in, in which the mental, emotional and spiritual energies flow in patterns that are accessible to the shaman when in an altered state. This is the everyday physical reality, but also the parallel energetic universe of our realm, with all its beauty, trickery, strangeness as well as horror, and it is furthermore seen as populated by spirits of humans who have not completed their journey after death. The middle world is accessed by the shaman entering an altered state and 'leaving the body', floating through the realm. The middle world journeys are mainly used to communicate with nature spirits – such as the spirits of trees, plants, rocks, the sun, moon and other entities of our realm – or the worlds of spirit people, such as devas, fairies or elves.

The middle world is where psychic phenomena happen, spirit extractions are performed, synchronicities observed, hunches and omens received and thought forms happen. Telepathy is believed to be possible and it is the world where psychics and energy healers work as diseases or illnesses manifest themselves there before moving into the physical. In a healing ritual the shaman most often travels to the middle world to gather facts about people, animals and plants which are significant to the condition of the person in need. This is the world where cures are sought before one gets physically ill by extractions or cleansing of the energy fields of the body.

The middle world is difficult to traverse and beginners are usually discouraged from doing so because it is assumed that energy fields and spirits in the middle world can be negative, detrimental and outright evil, especially, but not only, because deceased humans who haven't made their way over to higher planes are trapped in this middle world.

Boundaries between the worlds

The boundaries between the worlds are fluid and, in my experience, whilst the maps are constructs which help to traverse the worlds, they are not helpful when taken too literally. The easiest way to explain this might be via a journey of a friend, who is himself involved in shamanic work, but who asked me one day to facilitate a journey for him.

CASE EXAMPLE: CROSSING THE BOUNDARIES BETWEEN THE WORLDS

After 30 years of marriage he was suddenly confronted with his wife having an affair. But it wasn't the affair that caused the incredible pain, it was the sudden negating of 30 years of his life and also the fact that his wife blamed him, wouldn't communicate with him and rejected his attempts at seeking relationship counselling.

He was in a desperate place. He had sunk into depression, experienced panic attacks, couldn't sleep and had lost a lot of weight during a relatively short period of time. He suggested that he journey into the lower or upper world to find out what he could do to help himself. It was within minutes that I realized that we must be looking at a case of 're-traumatization' as his journey turned from a lower world journey into a middle world journey and back into a lower world journey, with the boundaries being quite fluid. He saw himself as a small child being pushed into a deep well without water. As he hit the ground of the well his bones shattered. He lay there, helplessly, being shot at with arrows, becoming more and more wounded, whilst beasts of the lower world circled him. I suggested calling for his spirit helpers, who had disappeared, and in therapist fashion asked him to visualize his adult self to appear as well. By this time he was literally on the floor, in physical pain, sobbing.

To cut a long story short, his power animal appeared almost immediately after the call and took him out of the well. He then saw his adult self together with his power animal attending to his injuries and, as this unfolded, he suddenly remembered himself being a child during his parents' divorce. It turned out that, as some children do, he had taken the blame, feeling that it was his fault that his parents split up. It confirmed what I had already suspected, namely that the shock of his wife's affair, together with the blame she laid solely on him, whilst openly seeing another man, had regressed him into the vulnerable state of a small child. It was after this session that he began to 'get back into his adult self' and began to deal with what was happening in his relationship without making himself helplessly ill.

SPIRITS, HUMAN SPIRIT AND SOUL

Another distinction we need to look at is the one between spirits, the human spirit and the soul. The fundamental connection between ancient spiritual practices is the assumption that there is a kind of field that underlies creation, a power, energy, essence or consciousness that initiates, energizes and sustains all of creation, the universe in its many manifested forms and appearances, and that it is to this field of essence to which everything returns. This basic energetic building block of existence is viewed as being shared by all of life, with the various manifested life forms emerging from it, vibrating on different levels. It is this innate energy life form of 'All there is' that is called 'spirit' or 'great spirit'. Spirit is neither good nor bad, neither holy nor evil. It just *is*, manifesting itself in different forms within a universe that is harmonious, in the sense that it works in an inter-relational flow, that it creates and recreates itself and manifests itself without limits in time and space, ever expanding. In that sense we are all 'spirit' as we possess this innate life force, manifesting/ expressing itself through everything, and thus also through us in a physical world.

Therefore the shamanic view of the human being suggests that, like everything else, we are essentially spirit in manifested form, with the manifested form being our body/mind. As, within this theory, humans are just one such form, albeit a complex one, our lives are expressions of a 'spiritual intent' that works towards 'becoming'. This intent is contained within our spirit essence, which is more than our DNA. It can be seen as a potential that seeks to manifest itself to the fullest. I personally have struggled with the concept of 'becoming' and have concluded that becoming ultimately means to develop to our highest level of possibilities and ultimately to our highest possible level of consciousness.[2]

Spirit

If we are spirit in manifested form, it is vital to define 'spirit'. Spirit consists of frequency, of that which moves, vibrates. In shamanic terms if one refers to the spirit of a particular plant, a specific star, a person, an animal or any object, one talks about its unique patterns of frequency, its unique vibrations and, most importantly, the information these unique patterns carry. Every living being vibrates at a certain frequency at a certain moment in time. Vibrations are not static: they can and will change and, of course, what we define as a 'living being' depends on our viewpoint. The answer to the question of whether a stone is a living being depends on whether you view it from a matter perspective or a 'frequency and matter perspective'. If you do the latter, then the stone is alive, vibrating at a certain level. Whether you experience it in its solid form, made from particles, or in its energetic form, consisting of vibrations, depends on your intent and of course whether your state of consciousness is altered or not.

When we talk about 'spirit' in the above sense, we could replace it with the word consciousness, which is a more contemporary term for, as far as I can see, the same field that underlies everything. Let's do that to help us understand. So, in the beginning there was this consciousness. It is perceived in all spiritual systems as whole, undivided, as the source of all creation. This Wholeness, this state without division, this One-ness, this God-mind, this Great Spirit created all the aspects of creation. In scientific terms we might call the beginning of this act of creation the 'big bang'. In spiritual terms we talk about creation from the source. The source can only create if it divides, or, as Deepak Chopra says, 'Out of itself, One-ness creates the many' (Chopra, Ford and Williamson 2010, p.88). If we look at nature we can see that out of a single cell-division all life evolved. All the different aspects of creation are already, in the form of possibilities, inherent in this One-ness. Deepak Chopra presents a map that might be useful. He says that this source is like a small dot, something that is smaller than the smallest particle we have ever discovered, but its manifestation, the source or God as the manifest universe, is larger than anything else and is ever expanding. If we see the human as also being created from that source, the basic energy is that source, and it is whole.

We never lose the connection to this source, to this consciousness, completely, but we get attached to and lost in our 'created world', the world of the physical body, of our emotions and thoughts, our beliefs and the world that we, as a species, create around us – our work, our families, our societies, our laws and rules and so on – because we only experience this manifested world with our senses. If we want to experience the energetic levels of creation, and ultimately the consciousness of One-ness, we need to alter our mental states and return to the source. As far as I can see, this is the aim of most spiritual practices.

Spirits

Spirits are not to be confused with the 'Great Spirit'/'God-mind'/One-ness, described above. Spirits, from a shamanic point of view, are entities in the unseen world, which are felt/experienced as being intelligent and non-material, separate from the ego or self and residing outside the mind. They provide the shaman with information, power, wisdom and energy that the shaman cannot access by himself alone (Walsh 2010, p.143). On the whole, spirits are neutral. Nevertheless, they can either be harmful or helpful in relation to human well-being. The interaction with helpful spirits creates greater harmony, improves well-being and is a source of wisdom and power. Interaction with non-helpful spirits, such as the spirit of a dead person who hasn't passed over properly to the land of the dead, or a spirit who intrudes, using the host's body, can be harmful to a person's well-being.

An in-depth debate over whether spirits reside outside, as independent entities, or whether we create them in our minds as symbolic or metaphoric representations of aspects of the self, is too far reaching for this book. Nevertheless, it is beneficial to examine the subject briefly. All indigenous traditions and all the teachers coming from indigenous traditions that I have worked with, such as Malidoma Somé from Africa, Don Esteban, a Yachak from Ecuador, Victor Sanchez from Mexico, Ipupiara Makunaiman, a Brazilian shaman, and others, refer to spirits as entities that live separate from – and outside of – the human mind. Some of them, such as ancestor spirits, have a tendency to stay around the places they lived in and the people they are connected to, and are contacted, consulted and honoured and so are the helping spirits, with which the shaman works. Other spirits are further removed and are only contacted when needed for help, advice, information, guidance and wisdom or when they are honoured for different reasons, and, as mentioned above, some are 'troublesome spirits' that need the shaman's doctoring to eject or release from the community or the individual.

The wide field of psychology does not dispute the capacity of the mind to enter states in which we come across images, personalities, symbolism and metaphors that come close to the shamanic view of 'spirits', but it interprets them in several different ways. A more traditional viewpoint is that such experiences are hallucinations or that we are dealing with dissociated 'ego-states' or 'sub-personalities'. Jungian and transpersonal psychologists might view them as belonging to the transcendent aspects of the psyche, producing entities such as the 'higher self', the 'transpersonal witness', the 'inner guiding helper' and the 'inner wisdom teacher'. These seem to be far beyond our normal 'imaginational fantasies', transcending the normal state of consciousness, and can arise spontaneously, and if they do, they often have life-changing effects. Jung and others reported that they were advised by inner guides who arose unbidden. Jung, for instance, writes about Philemon, a figure who provided him with superior insight. 'Philemon and other figures of my fantasies brought home to me the crucial insight that there are things in the psyche which I do not produce, but which produce themselves and have their own life... Philemon represented superior insight... At times he seemed to me quite as real as if he were a living personality' (Jung 1961, p.183).

There are countless reports of profoundly transformational healing experiences described that involve such guides. Walsh (2010, p.146) describes the experience of one of Achterberg's patients. A woman who suffered from chronic pelvis pain, in one of her imaginations, was led by a coyote guide called Wildwood to witness her own horrifying rape and murder by a gang of hostile tribal Indians. At the instant of her death she 'woke up', felt that she was back in the body and her pain was completely and permanently gone. She attributed the experience to a past life.[3]

CASE EXAMPLE: TRANSFORMATIONAL HEALING EXPERIENCE

In my own practice I have, with astonishment at first, witnessed similar curative and unexplainable experiences. One of the first was with a male client who suffered from chronic lower back pain. The client was not working in an environment that we would normally associate with lower back pain. He exercised, was slim, on the whole quite agile and, according to the medical examinations, there was no detectable physiological cause. He had travelled medical, physiotherapeutic, osteopathic and homeopathic avenues without much success. The pain in his lower back always recurred after some time. I worked with hypnosis at the time and, after everything else seemed to fail to produce a lasting effect, introduced him to the idea of an envisaged guide, which was at first alien to him, but, as desperation can also produce open-mindedness, he was more than willing to attempt a 'shamanic journey'.[4]

The only rather vague, open-ended and fairly non-directive instruction for the journey was that he would meet his guide and follow the guide to wherever he was to take him, because the guide would show him something that would be very important with regards to his backache. After finding the guide as a visual image and some travelling with the guide, my client saw himself in a scene of war, being stabbed repeatedly in the back with a sword and, as he tried to crawl away, with a dagger that stayed jammed. He experienced himself lying there, unable to crawl away, an experience that was painful and led to an abreaction in the form of trembling and crying. Suddenly, just before he gave into the knowledge of dying, the guide appeared again, reached down and pulled the dagger out. When I saw him a week later, he was pain free, and when he contacted me six months later it was to report that the pain hadn't reoccurred.

In shamanism, the guide would be seen as a spirit with healing powers guiding the client to an experience that was, in energetic terms, very real, manifesting physically as pain in his body. The guide's actions brought about the energetic removal of the dagger. In contemporary therapeutic terms we could speculate if it was the idea of a past life that produced the dissociation and with it the images and focus necessary to explain his backache and, as it was explained, it lost its power and strength. Or we could speculate that the power of the belief enabled him to 'let it go', or that the abreaction of tension during the experience resulted in the relief from the pain. Whatever we use as an explanation, in the end it is only a constructed, unverifiable explanation, and which one we prefer depends upon our belief system.

On the whole, our assumptions about how the world works, our general views about spirituality, our religious and other beliefs, and especially our personal experiences, will determine whether we interpret spirits as entities, existing outside and independent of the human mind, or as constructs of the human mind, or as a mixture of both, as we have no proof that all sources of, for instance, inner wisdom or spontaneous healing come from the same realm. Nor can we say for certain whether we can access everything that is available to us without developing much further as a species. We do know that spiritual practices lead us to experience the world in more energetic form, changes what we perceive to be real, expands our world and puts us into a context that can only make us more whole. Nevertheless, the mysterious, spiritual and psychological do not necessarily rely on clear-cut answers and I personally like the 'shamanic approach', which pays less attention to being right or wrong but rather to what works and what doesn't.

Soul

Closely connected to spirit and spirits is the concept of soul. Spirit and soul are at times used interchangeably because their subtle shades of meaning vary from culture to culture. Both terms reference an invisible force, but the term soul often refers to something immaterial and independent of the body, that is specifically within human beings, whilst spirit is, as explained above, a force more generalized, inhabiting all of nature. For example, Carl Jung defines the soul as 'the living thing in Man, that which lives of itself and causes life' (Jung 1959, p.26).

In many indigenous cultures 'soul' is used to describe this force within the human whilst he is alive and, when the soul returns into the pool of consciousness after death, it is described as being a 'spirit'. For example, a shaman's grandmother's life force is referred to as her soul whilst she is living. Once she is dead her soul passes on into the spirit world and is referred to generally as 'spirit'. Were her spirit to return to help the shaman, it would be a helping ancestral spirit (Pratt 2007b, p.456).

Soul, in many traditional cultures, is an immortal/energetic life force within the human being with the function to guide the mind/body consciousness, that which we humans call 'I', towards – and on – the path which is most aligned with the desire and wish of 'spirit' to express itself through us in its purest or highest form (Grigori 2002). Or, in other words, it is originally spirit that seeks to manifest itself through us, and it is our specific human essence, our soul, which impels and drives us towards growth, towards change, towards becoming. For instance it is our soul that provides us with a kind of inner voice, a moral compass and direction. It is our soul that we hear as this 'little voice inside' reminding us that there is more we can become, and it is our soul that suffers when we don't nourish it by integrating a spiritual component into our lives and striving to give our lives meaning and purpose.

So, as humans in a shamanic-spiritual view, we are a part of an ongoing relational flow of creation. We consist of a life force that we can call spirit and a soul, which consists of this life force field contained within the physical body, together with imprints we carry in the form of individual and collective experiences or Karma. Spirit, as an essence, contains all the life force possibilities, whilst it is our soul that drives us towards becoming all we can be and can be altered by our individual and collective experiences during every lifetime.

In the world of traditional shamanism it is assumed that it is mainly the loss of soul that causes emotional, physical and mental disease as well as a diminishing of vital life energy, and it is the returning of the soul, or parts of the soul, to the client which is one of the shaman's main tasks. This concept has been adapted and is widely used in contemporary shamanic practice. Soul loss usually describes the splitting off of parts of the soul, a description that shows remarkable similarities to what contemporary psychology calls 'dissociation'. Like the psychological concept of 'dissociation', the shamanic concept of 'soul loss' recognizes the capacity of human beings to split off parts of their psyche in response to trauma and/ or adverse circumstances, but whilst contemporary thinking would locate 'dissociated parts' within the mind, the shaman assumes that soul loss is a spiritual illness and that dissociated parts can 'flee the body' and hide somewhere outside, in the case of soul loss mainly in the lower, sometimes in the upper, world. The other difference is that although shamans have always known that the original activation of dissociative devices requires an altered state of consciousness in contrast to contemporary thinking, they assume that certain parts cannot be retrieved by the affected person as those parts are located in worlds inaccessible by the client. Therefore they journey into those other realms to retrieve lost soul parts, to bring them back for the individual and for the community and to reintegrate them.[5]

LIFE IN CIRCLES AND SPIRALS: THE MEDICINE WHEEL

Another, more complex map is the Medicine Wheel. It is widely used by indigenous peoples of the North Americas and has been adopted by many contemporary practitioners. For me it is a most inspiring map of life and a therapeutic tool, starting with the elegantly simple and leading to the profoundly complex. Medicine doesn't mean something that medicates, but is a term used in those indigenous traditions to describe the inherent, mysterious power that exists in anything. Everybody and everything possesses medicine, a unique power and quality, which, in humans, for example, consists of a combination of talents, gifts, learning and wisdom.

The Medicine Wheel is a map of life, a way of understanding the cycles and spirals of life as well as the energies that create and influence them. It is also a ceremonial tool, and a teaching tool that teaches about the interconnectedness of all life and about the human within it. It illustrates and connects, just as the mandalas of the East, the microcosm within the macrocosm. In many forms and ways it is now widely used as a tool for personal exploration, growth and transformation, as well as for processes of a more psychotherapeutic nature. The structure of a wheel is based on the assumption, which most indigenous and other spiritual approaches share, that life moves in circles and cycles and that linear aspects, with beginnings and endings and straightforward cause and effect lines, are created by perceptions that depend on our point of reference, rather than being reality.

The origins of the Medicine Wheel are not entirely clear. Wheels or circle-like structures as magical, sacred constructs and as ways of organizing and passing on of understanding, knowledge and information about the world and life have been used by indigenous people all over the world. The mandalas in the East, the Neolithic stone circles of Europe, the circles in Australian Aboriginal and Maori traditions which are symbols of the never-ending journey of discovery and rediscovery, the South American Mayan and Aztec circles and the wheels/sacred hoops we find in Northern America and Canada are just some of the many circles that speak of this view of the world.

Storm (1997), who is credited with introducing the Medicine Wheel to the West, claims that Medicine Wheel teachings have their origin in the Mayan culture, or even earlier, and were only later, through generations of migration, brought to the North American tribes. It is certain that by the time of the European colonization of the Americas the Medicine Wheel was an established tradition within the majority of tribes, having become part of their own sacred understandings, teachings and practices and adapted to their own cultures. The first one to be discovered, according to the Royal Alberta Museum, was the Big Horn Wheel near Sheridan in Wyoming. This massive stone structure, consisting of a central circle of piled rocks, surrounded by a huge circle of stones with rays of stones travelling out from the core and its surrounding circle, so that the whole structure looks like a 'bicycle wheel' when seen from above, was named Medicine Wheel by European Americans after its discovery.[6]

The basic Medicine Wheel

The basic formation of the Medicine Wheel is a circle representing and incorporating the powers of the four directions and the interrelatedness of all life, the centre being the 'sacred mysteries' or 'the children's fire' or 'all that ever was and all that ever will be'. The four directions correspond with the four elements, the four seasons, the four races, the four aspects of the human and the four stages of life. The basic wheel connects the directions in a circular fashion and also connects them via the spirals that extend from the centre. However, this basic wheel is just the beginning of more complex wheels and teachings, with most practitioners using at least eight directions around the wheel. Every direction of every wheel can again be represented as a wheel. Thus, theoretically at least, we end up with an infinite amount of interconnected wheels.

Wheels are applied to a wide variety of subjects, from the workings of the universe, the workings of nature, the workings of communities and the working of humans within the whole. There are wheels about human aspects such as the body, beliefs, behaviours, emotions, creativity and spirituality; about development, ego-centric as well as soul-centric; and many more. Harley SwiftDeer Reagan, the founder of the Deer Tribe Metis Medicine Society, who claims to be a Medicine Wheel shield carrier, reports that his first teaching shield contains 144 Medicine Wheels. Leo Rutherford's highly accessible book *The View through the Medicine Wheel* (2008) gives an in-depth description of numerous wheels and how to use them in practice, from the personal and the communal to the universal, providing a rich source for practitioners and therapists. Plotkin (2008) offers a new, insightful approach in his book *Nature and the Human Soul*, using the wheel to describe the eight stages of human development, personal, social and spiritual, defining the tasks at each stage to become 'who we can be', based on the hero's journey and spiritual development.

Wheel interpretations, such as the concrete teachings of the different directions, differ slightly from tribe to tribe and there also are different adaptations by contemporary shamanic practitioners. I have been taught a combination of the Hopi and Mayan wheel and will use this one for the purpose of this book.

The directions of the wheel

Nature provided the template for the design of the wheel, based on the four compass directions, the four seasons and the daily cycle of the sun, seen from a Northern Hemispheric perspective, with the centre being 'the children's fire', that which always was and always will be. Wheels were later adapted to include the four aspects of the human: the physical, mental, emotional and spiritual. I will include here the human aspects within the basic four-direction wheel – the East, West, South and North – to provide an overview, and also add the four moving directions in the form of the Southeast, Southwest, Northwest and Northeast. When we include the human aspects we place the self into the centre, split into the 'I' as well as the 'soul' or 'higher self', depending on what we use the wheel for.

Four directions	East	South	West	North
Four seasons	Spring	Summer	Autumn	Winter
Four elements	Fire	Water	Earth	Air
Four races	Yellow	Red	Black	White
Four aspects of the human	Spiritual	Emotional	Physical	Mental
Four stages of life	Birth/death	Developing: child and youth	Adulthood/intro-spection	Wisdom/elder
Four more directions	**Southeast** Ancestors; Self-concept	**Southwest** Dream	**Northwest** Karma/laws	**Northeast** Design of energy

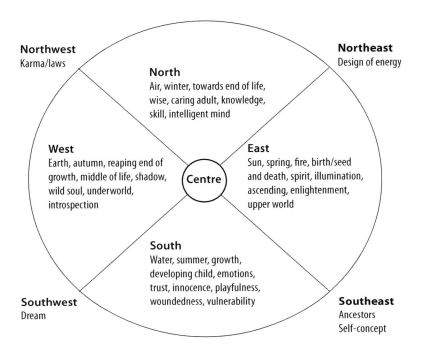

Enlarged Medicine Wheel

Basic nature and human wheel: four directions

This basic wheel teaches us about the fundamental cycles of life, how the different aspects are connected, develop and evolve. Within the human wheel each direction consists of a 'light' aspect and a 'shadow' aspect, and each direction suggests specific growth work, ego-centric as well as soul-centric. The following provides a very brief description of the directions and how they are interconnected. A more detailed description, including the light and shadow aspects, as well as how to work with the wheel in a therapeutic setting, will follow in Chapter 15.

THE EAST

The East is where it all begins and ends and begins again. The season is spring, where seeds are planted. It is where the sun rises, lighting the world after the darkness of the night. It is the place of spirit and therefore associated with illumination, creativity, 'enlightenment' and with the upper world. It is also the place where we come back to at the end of our lives.

THE SOUTH

The South is the place of warmth as the sun reaches its highest point. It is the time of growth and of flowering of plants, animals and humans. It is the place of water, the place of flowing. In the South we encounter our emotional self: the growing child, with its beauty, innocence, playfulness and wonder, but also its wounding, which lives in the South. The South is, in psychological terms, associated with the 'inner child'. The South asks us to look at our emotional wounds and to rediscover our magical child.

THE WEST

The West is the place of sunset, of dusk, of the transition from light to dark. It is autumn, the end of the growing season. It is the place of earth, of the physical, of manifestation. The West is a transition place. It is not quite dark, but also not light. For humans it is the place of 'shadow' of the under world. The West is where we introspect, go deep and confront our demons, all that the ego doesn't want to acknowledge as part of our self.

THE NORTH

The North is cold and dark. It is the time of night, the place of winter, where growing has stopped. It takes skill and endurance and knowledge to thrive in the North and the North is therefore linked with competence, skill, knowledge and wisdom. In human terms the North is the place of the mental, of the adult. Our thought processes, our beliefs and our philosophies are represented in the North. The North asks us to 'stop the world' in the sense of stopping our thought processes so that we can examine them and our philosophies and beliefs.

The enlarged human wheel: eight directions

If we want to understand the developmental aspects of the wheel we need to add the four moving directions, Southeast, Southwest, Northwest and Northeast.

THE SOUTHEAST

The Southeast is the place of the ancestors and of self-concept. It is the place that symbolizes our talents and gifts, the legacies we bring with us through our ancestors, our DNA, our cosmologies, our beliefs, our mythologies and our early imprints.

THE SOUTHWEST

The Southwest is the place of the dream. It is the place that symbolizes the underlying dream of the manifested life that we create. The dream is usually based on our learning, our beliefs and on how we process our experiences.

THE NORTHWEST

The Northwest is the place of rules, laws and Karma. The power of the Northwest is the acceptance of 'Karma' and learning from our life's lessons.

THE NORTHEAST

The Northeast is the place of the design and choreography of energy, our life's energy. The power of the Northeast is that we can choose how to choreograph and design our lives from an energy point of view.

The circle as a developmental map

When we go around the wheel we have a developmental map. We start in the East, the immaterial, being in spirit form. We are born, a spirit in a body. Then we travel through the Southeast and South bringing with us our DNA, our ancestral lineage, our cultural teachings and our emotional and mental imprints and learning from our upbringings. The beliefs we adopt, the abilities we develop and the thought and processing patterns we hold stem from that time, forming the 'mostly unconscious' basis of the Southwest, namely the dream we hold. We manifest and live the dream in the West. The West is the physical manifestation of our inner world, our inner dream, and comprises our professions, our family, our activities, our contributions, in other words our whole way of life.

The West is the place where light turns into dark. Up until this time, most of us live fairly unquestioning lives. At some point during our travels in the West we reach, in one form or another, a 'crisis'. Here, people call it 'midlife crisis', but the crisis can come much earlier or, for some, much later. I like to call it the 'wake-up call'. No matter what we name it, it is a time where we are called to question, to introspect and to become conscious, as something in us realizes that we are not satisfied, that we have been living a life that is not quite right or is out of balance. If we follow the calling in the West, we will go 'into the cave'. We will introspect, painful as it might be. When we have done this, we begin to move towards the Northwest. The Northwest symbolizes the patterns, the rules and laws we live by. Some call it Karma. Those patterns and rules and laws are mainly determined by our journey so far, but after we have gone through the introspection phase in the West, we will change them. We will work on creating rules that support the balance, harmony and creativity of our own choice and the life we want to lead. Only if we do that will we be able to become the 'wise adult' in the North, changing our design of energy in the Northeast to focusing on what really matters to us, and, arriving in the East, reaping an inner state and an outer life that is in alignment with our soul's direction and spirit's desire to manifest itself to the highest potential through us.

Needless to say, each change we make in any of the directions of the wheel will also influence the other directions. So when we work in the South, healing some of our childhood wounds, we will change some of our maladaptive beliefs and how we think about things in the North, and, vice versa, if we change our thought processes and beliefs in the North, our emotional self in the South will change.

The diagonals as determining and balancing opposites

The directions on the wheel are not only connected via the circle, but also connect diagonally.

North and South: The personal axis of the wheel. The intelligent, thinking, skilful, leading adult needs the emotional, playful, delighted and wondrous child, and vice versa, to achieve balance. The emotional South, disconnected from the wise mental adult in the North, can be irresponsible and self-indulgent, whilst the North can become hard and judgemental without the emotional self from the South.

East and West: The spiritual axis of the wheel. The East is illumination, ascent, inspiration, spirit. The West is physical, shadow, introspection, descent and soul. According to Medicine Wheel teachings, without the descent into the West we cannot be whole; we will be at the mercy of our shadow and cannot embody the spiritual of the East. It is the ignoring of the West in spiritual systems which has left our world, although full of people who proclaim to be spiritual, in the grip of the shadow. Without the West the East can just be 'directionless spiritual energy', whilst achievements in the West can be greedy and meaningless without the spiritual of the East.

Southeast and Northwest: The laws and rules, the Karma, of the Northwest are determined by what we bring into the world via our genes, our culture and our early childhood experiences in the Southeast. Once we change the rules and laws that do not serve us we will also influence/change the Southeast and, of course, vice versa.

Southwest and Northeast: Our dream of life directly influences the design of energy and vice versa. If our 'dream' is disjointed and fragmented, or not our personal dream at all, our energy will not have the focus needed to achieve our goal, or we will give up or self-sabotage. Our general design of energy will also influence our dream, especially the manifestation of it.

Notes

1   I will come back to soul retrieval and shadow in Part III. I personally believe that on every level of society we shy away from acknowledging the shadow, not only projecting it onto other people, other nations and other religions, but also take away from ourselves a chance to be aware of it and transform it whenever possible.

2   This corresponds with Maslow's concept of self-actualization.

3   If we participate in a past life workshop or use past life techniques ourselves with clients we come across quite profound experiences that feel and look as if they were past life recalls. This can of course rarely be verified and, from a spiritual/ therapeutic point of view, the true nature of such experiences is not important as long as the experience is therapeutic. Such experiences could be experiences which our brains create for us because we address a certain issue; they could be recalls of other people's lives because we plug into the collective unconscious by altering our states; they could be symbolic for or mimic a painful experience we had in childhood but have dissociated; or it could be that we experience something that is prevalent in the collective unconscious field, such as war or rape or other forms of violence and powerlessness.

4   The shamanic journey will be described in detail in Part III.

5   Soul Retrieval will be described in Part III.

6   Some indigenous tribes also use the term 'sacred hoop' when talking about a Medicine Wheel, but it is the term 'Medicine Wheel' that has been widely used to describe all structures that were discovered after the Big Horn Wheel. About two-thirds (46) of all known indigenous Medicine Wheels in the North Americas are in Alberta, Canada, which seems to suggest that Alberta was a central meeting place for many Plains tribes who followed Medicine Wheel ceremonies.

PART III

Practical Applications

INCORPORATING ELEMENTS OF SHAMANISM INTO THERAPEUTIC WORK

Spirituality links the deeply personal with the universal… The psychology of spirituality in its purest essence involves recapturing an appreciation of wholeness, of indivisibility, and concerns reconciling this with the apparent disjunctions of material reality, of time and space.

Larry Culliford (2011)

7 A SENSE OF THE SACRED

Clients, Space and Objects

Two basic concepts that we can transfer into the therapeutic realm for the benefit of the people we work with, and for ourselves, are that the outer and the inner are connected and that every living being is 'spirit' in its essence, with an innate drive to unfold itself to its highest possible level. Those concepts, which influence all shamanically orientated work, ask us to treat our clients as being 'spirits in a body', sacred at their core, and to understand that the space we work in is 'alive' and can therefore either be detrimental or enhancing to the client's quest to express him or herself to the highest possible level. Within this concept we are asked to treat the space also as being 'sacred' in the sense that we infuse it, to the best of our ability, with a positive, balanced energy.

When we talk about concepts such as consciousness, essence or spirit underlying all of creation and begin to comprehend that we are all part of a whole that is expressing itself, the question of how we treat everything within this 'whole' becomes essential. Just as Buddhists try to see the Buddha nature in everybody, shamanic practitioners are asked to see spirit and sacredness at the core of all living beings.[1] When we work as therapists, we connect with another human being's emotions, thoughts, behaviours and sensations. We encounter his longings, his passions, his hurts, his disappointments, his anger, his love, his light and his shadow, his dreams, his beauty and his darkness. We work with a human being who longs for connection, meaning, purpose, sense and self-realization. As all life is in essence spirit revealing itself in different forms, with an innate drive to express this to the highest level possible, the ancient healer will strive to be aware of this essence field of possibilities that wants to reveal itself to the highest level possible. It is astonishing how our whole way of working changes when we keep this idea of a sacred essence field firmly embedded in our minds, as it leads us beyond the symptoms, beyond the obvious and the outer and connects us with the 'inner' of the client. This is easy to forget when we work in a more clinical way, focusing mainly on symptom alleviation and within a contemporary set-up that puts limits on the time we can spend with a person, or when we work with clients whom we find difficult, who are stuck in loops of negativity, or who provoke feelings of uncertainty or even incompetence in us.

The shaman knows that the outer is influenced by the inner and that the inner influences the outer and that, within this interplay, his or her state of mind and intent influence the person he or she works with. So, with the idea of the sacredness of all life embedded in his or her consciousness, the shamanic practitioner works in a way that gives the client the feeling of being sacred, of being a spirit in a body, of being much more than the symptoms they present with. It is vital that we make a distinction between sacred and holy. Shamans do not strive for holiness in the sense of saintliness or goodness. They strive to develop respect for all life, because it is an expression of spirit. They also strive to treat all life as sacred because they know about the interconnectedness of it and recognize that if they treat another living being with disrespect this will affect the interconnected web and ultimately also themselves.

SPACE AND OBJECTS

A similar concept applies to space and how we treat it, especially the space we work in. Shamans understand fully that energy is without boundaries and that the space we work in influences – albeit in a subtle way – our therapeutic work. If the energy in the room supports the idea of sacredness, the person in the room will find it easier to resonate with the sacredness of his/her own being. Space, like everything else, has power. It either supports you or it works against you. We all know this instinctively. When we enter a place we either feel good and welcome in it or we feel uncomfortable. Shamans create 'sacred space' for their work by preparing it via cleansing, by their intent and by calling in helping forces. Guided by the same ideas, they also take care of the objects they use.

There are many ways in which to cleanse a space. The most common one is to use smoke by burning sage – either loose sage, which is burned in a shell or a bowl, or bound sage, which forms a bundle. The smoke is spread throughout the room with a feather. Make sure you 'smoke-out' the corners of the room. If you find the smell of sage too pungent, you may use an incense of your choice or, if you want to spend more money, buy a selection of natural sprays. What we use doesn't really matter. What is important from a shamanic point of view is our intent. State it out loud and hold the intent throughout; for example, 'I am cleansing the space so that all the work which will be done here will be beneficial to my clients and to me.' There are no rules with regard to time and intensity. You will sense when the space seems clear and clean.

If the energy in the room feels rather heavy, you can use a Tibetan bell, which produces a high frequency sound, to 'lighten and lift' the feel of the room. If the field does not seem grounded enough, use a drum or some other instrument that will produce a low vibration. I usually circle the space with the instrument a few times, moving either clockwise or anti-clockwise, until it feels 'right' to me. Again, keep a positive, clearly formulated intent in mind while you do this.

I am aware that the furniture, objects and pictures in the room also contribute to the energy of the room and I personally prefer a clear, uncluttered space where most of the objects are either functional, beautiful (to my eyes) or have meaning. I have worked in clinics where the energy was unfavourable to deeper work, as it didn't support a 'holding environment'. Not long ago, I attended a meditation day in a centre and was taken aback by the 'feel of the place', which was cold and unwelcoming, and therefore not supporting people meditating. I have also seen consulting rooms that were cluttered with angels and fairies and crystals, leading to a feeling of overload and chaos. When we open our minds to the subtle energies that work upon us, we begin to pay attention to what we want the room to do. If our overall intent is clarity, focus, harmony and sacredness, we will create a space that expresses those intents.

I care for and look after the objects I have in my room and use for work as they carry 'energy'. I use a small altar, on which are objects that represent the elements and my two spirit helpers. The centrepiece is a circle of people, holding hands. This circle also functions as the 'children's fire', as it can hold a small candle in the middle. Also on the altar are the objects I sometimes use, which are a feather, a drum, a stone, a crystal and a Tibetan bell. I make sure that they are placed in a fashion that creates a harmonious picture. I also smudge the altar and cleanse the objects regularly, but not religiously. What matters is to have a connection with the objects you use for work, rather than having rules. A colleague who 'is into crystals' told me that I must cleanse them in salt water on a regular basis and then dry them in the sunshine. The moment I hear 'must', the sceptic in me awakens. I personally do not accept hard and fast rules because it is important to learn to trust your instincts, which should be based upon your intent. I am inclined to 'feel out' if my objects need cleansing, so I pay attention to how it feels to be around them, to hold them and to work with them. If they feel wrong, then I cleanse them.

I am aware that objects such as crystals or feathers have traditional meanings, but that doesn't mean I have to comply with those meanings. I am not an indigenous shaman and I must take the freedom and the responsibility to empower and utilize objects adjusted to the work I do. Crystals, for example, are widely used by shamans as divination tools. A shaman might, for instance, look in a crystal to identify the illness of the person they are helping. Crystals are widely associated with sky spirits and initiation and/or with guardian spirits and spirits that move between the worlds. If used for initiation, the crystals are implanted in the shaman's body by spirit or by another shaman. The crystals' recurrent structural patterns are associated with the shape of the universe and the cycles and patterns of nature. Crystals are alive, in shamanic terms, and therefore need to be fed. Some cultures have special 'food' for crystals, but in the final analysis it is the energy that you transmit through your intent and its vibrations that feeds the crystal. I personally don't get on with crystals – I am not into divination – and I therefore don't use them. I do use feathers, though, which are also traditional power objects that link the shaman with the power of the sacred bird spirits, because one of my power animals is a bird. Particularly in South America, in the Amazon, we see the most exquisite feather crowns being used during ceremonial work, connecting the shaman with bird spirits and facilitating his shapeshifting into – or embodiment of – the power of the birds.

The phrase 'must do this or that' is in sharp contrast to a little encounter I had with a shaman from Brazil whilst participating in a training course led by John Perkins (Perkins 1990, 1994, 1997). We were instructed to 'go out and find a stone you can use when you work with clients'. I found myself walking along, holding the intent of finding a stone that would be beneficial in my work with clients in my mind. After a while a black, oval, smooth stone caught my attention. I picked it up and it fitted perfectly into my hand. It felt 'right', but of course I doubted that it would be 'right' as it was black. Being more kinaesthetic than visual I have always known that I need to trust how things 'feel' rather than 'look'. I therefore took the stone with me after asking it if that was OK.

When I entered the group facilities again, I bumped into the Brazilian shaman. I silently held out my stone to him and he took it. He held it for a while and then started to gently rub it while humming a monotonous tune. He closed his eyes for a few minutes, continuing the rubbing and humming, and then suddenly he opened them, stared at me and said, 'This is a female stone.' 'How do you know?' I enquired, expecting, of course, some deep and mystical explanation. 'Well,' he said, 'a male stone could not be that smooth.' The moment he finished this sentence, we both started to laugh. We both knew that I had learned something profound and transferable: don't read something complex and mystical into something that is just simple and easy. He could have said anything – 'This is a water stone' or 'This is a fire stone' or whatever else came to mind. For reasons unexplained he chose to call it a 'female stone'. I didn't even enquire about whether he had energized my stone by humming and rubbing it, or whether he thought it was the 'right' stone or anything else. I fully understood that the stone was a stone and that the energy of the stone would be determined by my intent, by the way I used it, thought about it, interpreted its function, treated it, cleansed it and so on. I have used this specific stone ever since, for the last 12 years or so, as my 'soul retrieval stone'.

GROUPS AND SACRED SPACE

What is happening in a group can be influenced by the space you create. If your space is harmonious and balanced, it will contribute to a harmonious and balanced holding environment; if your space is unbalanced and 'messy', in an energetic sense, it will enhance those qualities within the group. But not only will it influence the group, it will, albeit subtly, influence the work you try to do with a group. I personally like to keep the space clean, clear and balanced, with light sources adjusted to what I want to achieve.

A space used by groups often becomes messy, cluttered and energetically confusing in no time at all. To keep this to a minimum, I instruct people to leave everything they don't need outside the group room and provide a space for those things. I also make sure that the circle is re-established after each break, that the clutter that has built up is removed and that the candle that I use as a centrepiece on the altar is always lit. In shamanic groups, we smudge people before they enter the group room. We do this, theoretically, to cleanse the energy field, or aura, around the person. Some sage is either burned in a bowl or a sage bundle is used and the smoke is distributed in a certain fashion around the body with a feather. I usually pick two participants to do this for their fellow group members, telling them to hold an intention of cleansing and blessing and welcoming in their minds whilst smudging the person. This has an astonishing effect. It sets a certain tone for the group as something changes in people's state whilst being smudged. It is as if people leave 'the world outside' and begin to enter into their own inner sacred space. When some heavy emotional work has been taking place in a group, I also make sure that the space is smudged again during a break and that it is aired. In addition, I might walk around with a Tibetan bell or some other thing that produces a high frequency sound, to 'lighten' the energy.

I also like to have an altar somewhere in the room, preferably in a corner. I use a small, easily transportable table, covered with a fairly neutral cloth. I represent the four elements – fire, water, air and earth – with a candle, a little bowl of water, a feather and either a flower or some small green branches in a small vase. I also have a representation of 'All there is'. I like the idea of every group member being represented on the altar and usually ask people to bring a small object they like with them. Representing each member on the altar is done ceremonially, preferably on the first morning of the group. This, together with the smudging before people walk into the group room, creates a special, sacred space and bond between people, which is, in a subtle way, quite strong. In shamanic groups, one would make sure that the altar as well as all other objects were attended to during the running of the group: for example, the candle would always be alight, the water replaced if necessary and the objects on the altar laid out in a way that 'feels right'. I often encounter people who, after participating in a group, begin to pay more attention to the energies in their own space at home with beneficial outcomes. One participant for instance told me that she finally got round to cleansing the house properly after a workshop and that her children remarked about how much nicer the home felt when they arrived back from school.

At this point it might be helpful to tell you the story of a group in which I was participating quite a few years ago. I had attended a one-year ceremonial training, run by a female shamanic ceremonialist, for women who worked as therapists. The group had formed a strong bond over the year and we decided to meet up twice per year for a long weekend in a residential centre in the Lake District to continue the work by ourselves. We would agree on an intent for ourselves a few weeks before the meetings, planning via email who would be taking responsibility for what and deciding on a rough schedule, and it seemed that all of us genuinely looked forward to getting together. This went very well until, during our third meeting, something became incredibly stuck. We didn't work productively; our energy levels were low; the usual enthusiasm seemed to have left us; our ceremonies seemed sloppy and half-hearted; some came back in late from the lunch break; and two women started arguing about 'small stuff' like who would do the washing up.

Being a group of therapists, we tried to address what was going on in the evening group meeting. Instead of creating a ceremony, or dancing or sitting around a fire, or any of our other usual evening activities, we sat down in a circle and 'addressed the issue'. Being a 'shamanically orientated group' we decided on a 'pow-wow' format, letting the talking stick go round as often as necessary to give every woman a chance to speak until everything she had to say was expressed. Lots was expressed that resonated, but nothing seemed to hit the spot properly, until somebody said, 'Do you realize that we didn't represent "water" on the altar?' Indeed, for reasons unexplained, the altar we had created, as always, on the first day, didn't include a representation of water. Water, a symbol for the emotions, for flow, for the child, was not represented. In normal circumstances, this wouldn't be seen as anything influential. In shamanic terms, it became suddenly clear that we had created 'emotional stuckness'. We decided to rectify this and to leave the rest up to spirit. Ceremonially, we put a bowl of water from the well in the garden onto the altar. Immediately afterwards, somebody suggested a 'dancing and drumming session', which of course cleared the emotional tension.

If you want to go a step further you will also pay attention to the 'energy field' that is built up over time when groups work. I generally ask people to go around the circle in one direction – it doesn't matter which – when they come back in or when we do something that asks people to come to the middle of the circle or to address other participants by walking around. I find that it builds up a field that is clean and consistent, making it much easier for people in groups to work on whatever they are addressing.

If you work with space, just use what feels right. Questions such as 'Does this space support harmony?', 'Does it provide a holding environment?', 'Does it feel as if I respect the people who work in this space?' or 'Does it honour the idea of sacredness?' will provide you with immediate insights.

Remembering the sacredness at the core of all living things, remembering that the outer influences the inner and vice versa, and thus caring for both, can make a subtle but beneficial difference in the way we work, teaching us and the people we work with a more respectful way of being. Writing this reminds me of a story I read. A small tribe in South America walked the same path to their hunting ground for many, many years. Then, one day, they decided to change this habit. Asked why, the chief explained that some of the flowers and plants that had grown along the path seemed to 'mind' humans walking past them. The western enquirer was astonished, asking the obvious: 'How do you know that they mind?' 'Well,' said the chief, 'it's simple; they told me.' 'How did they tell you?' The answer: 'They don't grow as well as they did before.' This is the kind of respect we could develop if we treat everything as 'being sacred', creating the best possible circumstances in which to honour the right to live and to grow.

Note

1   This is usually where we encounter the question of 'evil', to use a Christian expression. If we take the concept all the way we have to see the murderer, abuser, torturer as part of the whole, expressing extreme manifestations of the shadow, the dark side that is within each of us and, as energy fields, also surrounds us. This doesn't mean that we have to condone the behaviours. It just means that we have to understand that collectively we express both the dark and the light, and that our collective task is to 'develop', in the sense that we have to strive for the 'light' to be stronger than the 'dark', but that the dark exists for various reasons: violent, degrading, neglected and/or abusive experiences as a child (upbringing), poverty, transference, energies that are picked up, spirit intrusions and many more. Consciousness and its development is a most interesting subject and I have touched upon it in Chapter 1. The debate about whether we collectively develop towards a 'higher' consciousness, which should in the long run eliminate more of the 'dark' and enhance the 'light', is ongoing, with some supporting this view, whilst others point out that it doesn't look as if human consciousness has developed much and some even saying that we are currently in a 'dark' phase and that development is not progressive.

8 | GIVING IT FORM

Embodying and Bridging 'Intent' into Matter

A concept which I have already touched upon when talking about objects in the previous chapter is 'embodiment', especially the 'embodiment of energy in an object'. The concept of embodiment is used in shamanic work in many forms, but here I will focus on the bridging of intent into matter, which can be utilized within every therapeutic, counselling and coaching environment. As a concept it is generally based on the idea that we can embody various forms of energy either within ourselves or in objects or places. This chapter will focus on embodying energy into an object to be utilized as a bridging and integrative technique in any therapeutic environment and I will, in the following chapters, sometimes suggest that therapists utilize it whenever they feel that bridging and integration are needed and appropriate.

Before I come back to this form of embodiment, I want to briefly look at the wider context of the concept of embodiment, which is generally based on the interchange between the physical and the energetical, enclosing and expressing a force or an essence with, and through, a body. It is, after all, the body through which we experience life.

Traditional shamans are very physical beings. They rarely work without involving the body. They know that the strongest transformational effects are produced if we have a holistic experience, which includes the mental/emotional, the physical and the spiritual and, as far as I can see, they know more about the need of shifting energies on the cellular level than they put into words. They therefore prefer, for example, to 'move themselves into a trance' by trance dancing or whirling or conducting journeys, which are expressed physically, rather than 'sitting still', meditating. Shamanic practitioners, traditional and contemporary, as mentioned earlier, also don't shy away from eliciting emotions and facilitating their expression. One of the ways to elicit and express emotions is via moving energy through the body such as when we facilitate trance dance, work with trance postures, involve the body through dance and movement in a journey, or work in a way that can be described as play-acting, which can be observed during the high-drama performances indigenous shamans and healers often display.

The idea of 'embodiment' in shamanic terms stems, as far as we know, from the embodiment of the spirit, the spirit-possession. In spirit possession the healer goes into a deep trance state and lends his or her body to a spirit, who can then work through the healer's body and mind. When spirit possession happens the shaman/healer is not able to speak with his or her own voice and from his or her own mind and often has no recall after the possession. This is in contrast to the shaman who enters a deeply altered state but is still able to narrate consciously to observers and has perfect recall. The idea of embodiment also stems from a form of journeying that involves embodying a certain spirit – such as the spirit of a bird, for instance, if the shaman needs to fly – and it always leads to a deep trance state. Shamans embody the plant if they want to find out about its medicinal qualities, they embody the lion or jaguar or bear if they want the qualities or essences of those animals within their own body and psyche, and there is also a whole school of trance postures of animals and other entities, which are held for considerable periods of time to 'embody' their spirits and to connect with their essences. Ultimately, with practice of embodiment and focus, we can experience something like the essence quality of everything within ourselves, as we can 'become' it.

Embodiment in this, more classical, sense is an important part of contemporary shamanic work. The aim is to become the power animal, the mineral, the plant, the tree, the goddess or the god, the spirit guide, and whatever else you can think of. The character is embodied via imitating the movements, the voice, the habits and the behaviours. It is a strange sensation when we suddenly realize, after play-acting for a while, that we begin to feel and behave like the lion or the bear, the mouse or the goddess, the warrior or the wise woman, and realize that we perceive ourselves as bigger or smaller, feel more powerful or more agile, speak differently, sense things we normally don't sense and develop a perception and awareness we normally don't have. Such practices will further help to connect the seeker with 'All there is'. They will also make us understand on the level of experience that we are 'all of this' to a certain degree, that we can shift our mental state and our physicality to be and feel like a bear or a deer or a bird, which enriches us by showing us different facets of ourselves, whilst helping us communicate with – and understand – whatever we embody on a deeper level.[1]

Dance also plays a role in embodiment. The shaman dances the serpent or the bird or the mammal or any being whose power he wants to embody and utilize. Shamanic journeying, which I will describe in Chapter 10, can also be done via dance. Instead of journeying using the imagination, one dances the journey after having stated the intent. Needless to say that the journey becomes a mixture of images, physical sensations, movements and emotions, an altogether more holistic experience. The dimension of physicality is added whenever possible to, for instance, visualizations, journeying and ceremonial work, aiming for holistic experiences that include the mind, body, soul and spirit as explained in Chapter 5.

Those therapists who work with psychodrama, dramatherapy or with Gestalt approaches will easily be able to imagine the dramatic and beneficial effects of a complete experience. When we for instance embody the child, the parent or sub-personalities of ourselves during sessions of psychodrama, dramatherapy or family constellations therapy we begin literally to feel like the child, the parent or the part we embody. Our gestures change, our movements adjust, our way of talking and expressing changes and we feel like having slipped into the skin of somebody else. We 'become' the child or the parent to some extent and we begin to understand on a level that reaches beyond the cognitive.

Depending on how far you can incorporate embodiment within your practice I would advise every therapist not to shy away from it. We know from work with hypnosis that if we can turn a visualization, for example for goal setting and achieving in sports performance, into a 'hallucination' involving all the senses, the brain will code this as an experience and interpret it as if it were already a 'reality', establishing very quickly the belief that 'it can be done'. This takes much longer if we work with visual imagination and/or positive thoughts alone.

EMBODYING ENERGY IN AN OBJECT FOR THERAPEUTIC PURPOSES

A form of embodiment I really want to suggest here to every therapist and coach is that of creating or crafting an object – or any other piece of art – to form a container for energy, or connect with a certain energy, or to bridge the worlds, which in my experience enhances the therapeutic work we do. In all shamanic work, creating objects or paintings that hold the energy that needs holding, or to utilize crafted objects to form a bridge between the worlds, is seen as vital. An object or a piece of art is more than a symbol; it is seen as a container of the energy, the very spirit and intent of whatever the object or painting is about. Let's say we create a ceremony. The sweat lodge that is constructed, the altar that is created, the sand painting that is crafted or the labyrinth that is formed are not 'symbolic'. They are seen as holding the very energy of the spirit of the ceremony, creating a bridge between the worlds, a bridge the spirit can use. When I arrived in Ecuador, for example, the shamans had created three sacred hoops that held the energy of the mountains they worked with, and on the first evening they utilized the hoops for a 'welcome' ceremony. An example which most readers might be familiar with is the mandala sand paintings of Buddhist monks. If you have ever watched one being created you will know that the focus, intent and the prayers that are mumbled whilst the sand painting is created are what matters, not the actual outcome. In fact the monks destroy most sand paintings the moment they are finished. It is not about the piece, it's about the intent, the focus, the energy and the sacred.

Let's say a client needs to let go of something. In shamanic work we would certainly craft an object that symbolizes what needs to be let go, for example anxiety, anger, procrastination, guilt, blame, shame, and then burn it. But not only would it symbolize what needs to be 'let go', it would contain to a certain extent the energy of it because it would be created with intent, with complete focus and with 'the help of spirit', who would be called in and utilized. The same applies if a client wants to increase a certain aspect/quality of his or her personality such as, for example, confidence or focus or self-discipline or strength or creativity. We would advise the client to craft something that represents the desired aspect, keep it and work with it. Whenever the client journeys and discovers something, or brings back a part of him or herself, or finds the root cause of a hurt, or receives advice from a guide, we encourage bridging this into concrete reality by creating a tangible piece of art with focus, intent and the help of spirit. Needless to say that such work also facilitates integration.

We can also ask clients to find an object somewhere, holding the intent in mind, whilst searching for it. If you decide to use objects for clients in the sense that you ask them to find objects that represent something for them, it is advised that you let the client bring the object with them to the next session. Cleanse it – symbolically or with smudge – and ask your client to hold the object for a while, putting the intent into the object. The best way to do this is aloud, while closing the eyes and stating the intent 'This necklace will remind me that…' or 'This beautiful stone will help me to…' Advise the client to repeat this a few times at home and then treat the object in the way outlined above. It will, over time, become quite powerful, as it will be connected in the client's mind with the positive intent.

If you already work with writing, advising clients to write or to journal, I would strongly recommend incorporating crafting or painting as well, as the areas of the brain involved in writing are different from the parts that are involved in creating a piece of visual art. Language always involves 'thinking' to a certain degree, which is valuable as it processes things cognitively, but we get a more 'holistic' integration if we also involve those parts that get activated within a creative visual process.

I personally prefer clients to craft an object, rather than searching for one. When we bridge something into concrete material reality through crafting an object or painting a picture or, if somebody is inclined that way, through composing a piece of music or a song, we will give it the focus, time and energy it deserves. Crafting objects in shamanic work is a very focused affair. The intent is repeatedly stated and preferably held throughout. 'I want to let go of the anxiety because I know now that I had reasons to be anxious as a child but, as I am a grown up now, I have many resources' or 'I deserve to have more joy in my life and will therefore from now on allow myself to see the positive and beautiful that I have created in my life.' Needless to say that the resulting objects that have such underlying intents will often be quite beautiful. Besides holding the intent whilst crafting, the client is encouraged to go into a creative trance whilst working on the object. Sometimes gentle music and/or a mystical story accompanies the crafting, if it's done within the shamanic group or individual session. The third component of this kind of bridging is the help of spirit guides and spirit in general. The help of spirit is called in beforehand, and every once in a while during the creative process one should again call in the help of spirit, of forces beyond the mind. If all of the above is observed during the process of creating, the object, in shamanic terms, carries power in energetic form: it carries the intent, it expresses the client's own energy in form, and it carries spirit.

As a counsellor or therapist who works within stricter time limitations, you might want to consider giving this as homework between sessions. I have seen the most astonishing creations by clients who would have told me that they are not artistically inclined.

WORKING WITH OBJECTS AND GROUPS

This is also true for groups. Any object, painting or craft that is constructed by the group, expressing whatever needs to be expressed and holding the energy of that within the group room, is beneficial.

Acts of creation bring the group together, sharpen the focus of the group and load up the room with that energy. I personally consider this beforehand and ask participants to bring certain materials. The art here is to keep it simple so that people don't feel 'overloaded' and to take some responsibility by having material present. I keep feathers, balls of wool, different fabrics, leather strings, colours, crayons and a variety of pieces, ranging from broken bits of fashion jewellery to interesting pieces of bark, stones, shells and other bits I pick up in a box. I smudge the pieces before they go into the box, give thanks for them to nobody in particular and then forget about my box until I need it.

I like to observe participants when they work together as it gives me insight, but I never ever use what I have observed directly by addressing specific participants. In shamanic terms, to create something as a group is a sacred, creative act. Spirit is present and expresses itself through the people who create – so who am I to criticize or praise? I find it fascinating to see that the objects that are created, with different participants contributing in different ways, are always beautiful, harmonious and much more complex and expressive than expected.

It is vital to honour whatever a group has created. If individual pieces have been crafted they need to be brought together for the duration of the group. A dedicated space in the form of a table in a corner can be used. I usually form a circle, before a scheduled break. We either sing or hum or drum and each participant puts his or her piece individually on the table, saying a few words if that feels appropriate. If the piece is a collective piece I will smudge it and dedicate a special place in the room, asking a few participants to put it there, whilst the rest of us again sing or hum or drum. After crafting something it is always advised to take a break. In shamanic terms: when something is completed one walks away from it and lets it do its magic without interfering.

If the group crafts something that 'needs to be let go' it's a different matter. Those objects or the whole piece need to be 'let go' ceremonially, preferably in fire or, if that's not possible, buried in the earth. Under no circumstances should they go into 'the garbage'. Letting go is an act of love. Whatever needs to be let go has served the person at one point in their lives and therefore it has to be treated with respect.

A quite well-known group facilitator of shamanic workshops told me a similar story. The group had crafted objects representing a 'shadow figure' after a shamanic journey, with the aim of working with these representations ceremonially later on with the help of a fire ceremony. As is often the case, the shadow journey resulted in a long session, working through distressing emotions, which took up the rest of the afternoon. The group decided not to attempt a fire ceremony that night because of heavy rain. The objects, representing the shadows of 34 people, stayed in the room overnight. This friend told me that almost every group participant complained about sleep problems, the heavy energy in the group room, about feeling unwell and so on. A trained psychologist and psychotherapist colleague, who has been facilitating developmental workshops for over 30 years, found that nothing that happened in the group during the morning session could lift the energy, until he suddenly remembered that the 'shadow objects' were still laid out on a table in the corner of the room. He decided simply to go ahead with the fire ceremony that had been cancelled the evening before. The objects were ceremonially 'given away' by burning them, and the group energy changed completely.

I will in the chapters that follow sometimes refer to integrative work and remind you that 'embodiment' in the way I have just described is one of the tools that can be used beneficially.

Note

1   People who regularly meditate, for instance, will be familiar with the idea if they have experienced the feeling of pulsating like a single cell, when in a deep trance state, which has been likened to the essence of a single cell creature, such as an amoeba.

9 A PLACE OF POWER AND SANCTUARY FOR THE CLIENT

Shamans of many cultures have a special place in nature, often the place in which they were initiated or where they experienced their calling or had a strong encounter with a spirit power. Contemporary shamanism has adopted the idea of 'the special place', as has the world of therapy, in various forms. From an indigenous shamanic point of view, the power place is somewhere in nature that exhibits special powers for the shaman, but it can also be an imagined place in the mind as in shamanic terms there is no distinction between the different layers of reality: the place in the mind also exists in the world and vice versa.

The place of power is more than a sanctuary. It is a place in nature where we feel at home, where we feel that forces, which we do not fully understand, support us in our quest. For us individually, the place of power is sacred. Ancient sites for instance seem to have a strong effect on many people, positively and negatively. Feeling physically uncomfortable when spending some time in Cathar country in the South of France or in concentration camps like Auschwitz or in the Cambodian killing fields seems natural for most people, whilst spending times at sacred sites, such as Stonehenge, Mayan temples in South America or ancient Buddhist sites in India or Sri Lanka, seems for most people an enhancing experience. How much our minds create the feelings is a question of debate, but on a more mundane level, we all know that certain places, for no reason whatsoever, seem to support us, whilst others don't.

The power place, created in the mind, is a place of personal power where you journey from and to which one returns, where one communicates with power animals and guides, visits when in need of guidance or wants to recharge. In traditional thinking, where the place also exists in manifest reality, it is a place for regular pilgrimages to renew the connection and to honour it. Above all, especially in the indigenous traditions of the Americas, the place of power is the place to which the 'warriors' return when they die. It is a place of their choosing in which to fight the last battle and enter the spirit world when leaving the body for the last time. It is a sacred place.

Most professionals working within the field of therapy and counselling are familiar with the idea of the power place in the form of 'the sanctuary' or 'the special place'. By introducing the sanctuary early on in the therapeutic process you give the client access to:

- a place of safety

- a place of connection with the earth and with the light

- a place of meeting power animals and spirit guides

- a place from which to journey (e.g. shamanic journeys, past life regression or going back to childhood)

- a place to come back to after the work has been completed

- a place to utilize whenever a quick 'change of state' is needed

- a visualized safe space to utilize for deeper, perhaps emotionally challenging and painful therapeutic work.

The power place/sanctuary in contemporary therapy is first and foremost an imaginatively created place, which exists in the client's mind, is associated in the brain with the qualities it represents and can be accessed at any given moment. The power place/sanctuary can be created from scratch or be based on a memory of an actual place, or both. Generally, the sanctuary should be a place that feels safe, peaceful, relaxing, gently powerful and familiar and it should be also open to change and adaptable. For most clients, although they may live in urban settings, the sanctuary is represented by a nature scene, containing the main elements of nature, such as water in the form of a river or the sea, earth (plants) in the form of a meadow or forests, fire represented by warm sunlight and air by the sky. Nevertheless, some clients choose it to be a place inside, such as a specific room, and it can even be a place inside the body if that is the only place of safety a client can imagine. Some people's sanctuaries feel like fortresses, whilst others feel airy and spacious. The client's sanctuary can change during the therapeutic process, either completely or in parts. How the sanctuary looks and where it is situated is not important as long as it helps the client to access a state of peace, safety, tranquillity and gentle power. It creates a state of 'being' that is removed from the buzzing marketplace, be this in the client's real life, in terms of work or family, or in the client's mind, in the form of stressful thoughts, images or feelings.

HOW TO CREATE THE PLACE WITH THE CLIENT

When creating a power place/sanctuary together with the client, it is vital to recognize that the place only works its magic if the client creates it. I have experienced therapists who had preconceived notions about how such a place should look, where it should be and what it should contain. Yes, for many people being at the seaside or near water would be part of their sanctuary, and yes, many clients' sanctuaries are somewhere in nature, but to achieve the full potential of a mental power place/sanctuary, it needs to be the client's, not the therapist's. Who knows, your client might feel unsafe around water or might not like that place on top of a hill, as heights can produce associations with danger in the brain.

When creating the sanctuary, I explain the concept beforehand and just use a simple trance-induction, as described below. The client is encouraged to imagine, in his or her own way, walking down a staircase or a mountain path or whatever else is appropriate. I usually count them down, suggesting that by the count of zero they will arrive at a place, which can be inside or outside, which can be a place they remember, or a place they have never visited before. I encourage my client to be 'curious' about the place, to 'just let it come to mind' in whatever form it wants to appear and to signal me when they are there. I then ask for a description of the place whilst the client is still in an altered state, with his or her eyes closed.

The description helps the client to explore the place; it helps me to get to know the client a bit better, and it also gives me the chance to check if there is anything in the place that might have negative connotations. One of my clients was very surprised to find that the place that came to mind was her former school playground. School years are remembered by many people with mixed emotions, so in a case of this nature it would be wise to ask some questions to ascertain that the client feels relaxed, safe and positive while visualizing their 'safe' place. This also applies to places that feel somehow potentially dangerous.

I always encourage clients to explore the place, finding out if it is complete, and encourage them to add or remove parts until the place looks and feels 'perfect'. Once this is achieved, I will suggest they find a spot within the place that feels comfortable yet powerful and imagine that they sit or lie down in that spot for a while, to soak up the positive energy of the place. Depending on client and place, I might give some suggestions of peacefulness, calmness and relaxation as well as of this being a place of personal power and will. Before 'awakening', I suggest that whenever there is a need for a change of state the client can just visualize being in the sanctuary and begin to feel more relaxed, calm and peaceful and also more powerful.

During this first 'sanctuary/power place session', I avoid attempting any therapeutic work that might provoke negative memories or emotions in the sanctuary. My aim is to establish an image in the client's mind that is associated with feelings of calm, personal power, safety and peacefulness. To use the sanctuary too early in the therapeutic process for work that might be highly emotionally charged will contaminate the positive associations.

Once the sanctuary is established properly as an image, with comfortable feelings associated, it can be utilized during sessions for therapeutic purposes, but also outside sessions, when clients need to access a state that is connected with calmness, relaxation, safety, power and so on.

In some of the following chapters, I will suggest that you utilize the sanctuary for the shamanic journey and other approaches that will be described, especially if you cannot establish a trance state by working with vibrations produced by drumming or a drumming CD.[1]

I recommend that you use the following trance-script to establish the power place and to lead the client to the power place before you attempt using some of the later outlined techniques that work best when the client is in an altered state. If you are uncomfortable with using a trance-induction, centring the client through some breathing exercises, eye closure and the imagination exercises suggested in the following chapters is not ideal, but certainly sufficient.

TRANCE-SCRIPT TO ESTABLISH THE PLACE OF POWER/SANCTUARY

The first part of the script induces physical and mental relaxation; the second part establishes the power place; and the third part is a 'waking up' script to ensure that your client comes fully back to normal consciousness after the sanctuary is established.

Trance-scripts work best if your voice is congruent with the message you try to convey. In the first part, this message is about relaxation. Therefore speak slowly; take slight breaks whenever you see 'dots' in the script; and keep your voice soft and gentle. The second part is about establishing the place, and therefore it is beneficial to have a slight change of voice, employing a more 'exciting and uplifting' tone. After the client has found and established the place of power in his or her own mind and after you have explored it together with the client and changed what he or she wanted to change, you must employ a 'waking up' script to 'break the trance and bring the brain back to normal functioning'. The 'waking up' script should convey the message 'wake up and come back'; thus your tone of voice should be uplifting.

THE SCRIPT

Ask your client to make herself comfortable and close her eyes; gently ask them to focus on their breathing, relaxing the breathing on the exhale. Encourage your client to gently breathe in and out a few times, making the exhalation phase slightly longer than the inhalation.

Then continue in the following way:

As you sit there, just breathing gently, with not a care in the world, just taking some time out for yourself…relaxing…effortlessly and in your own way…in your own time…I would like you to become aware of your head…and as you shift your attention to the top of your head, to your face, to all the small muscles around your eyes…they will begin to relax…quite effortlessly…and maybe you can become aware of your jaws…and just imagine that you let them relax…also let your teeth part a little bit…relaxing your jaws…

And gently bring you awareness into your shoulders…letting yourself sink deeper into the chair…as you let your shoulders relax… ever so gently…without trying to achieve anything specific…it will just happen as you pay attention to the parts of your body I mention…and with your shoulders now relaxed, let yourself feel your arms relaxing… the right one…and the left one…all the way down to your fingertips… all the way down…both arms now beginning to relax…

Gently shift your attention to your chest and stomach…allowing the muscles in your chest and stomach to smoothen…to relax… to go a bit more limp…and as you do that…you might want to feel supported by the chair…becoming aware of the support of the chair on your back…and let your back muscles relax…all the way…from the top of your spine to the bottom of your spine…and becoming aware of your breathing now…taking a few gentle breaths now…enjoying the relaxation you have achieved so far…

And next time you exhale…bring your attention to the lower part of your body…let it just sink deeper and deeper into the chair… nothing to achieve…just relaxing your body…gently…and you might find that your mind calms as your body relaxes…thoughts come and go…but they are just thoughts that drift in and out of your conscious awareness…

Take another breath and as you exhale begin to shift your awareness onto your legs…the right one and the left one…until you end up becoming aware of your feet…and as you do that…you will find that your legs begin to feel soft and…your feet…all the toes… whilst standing firmly on the ground…even your feet can relax…those small muscles…

And as you sit there, listening to my voice, with not a care in the world, just enjoying the calm space…the relaxation you have achieved so far in your body…I would like you to imagine…as easily as you can…effortlessly…in your own way…that you are standing on top of a staircase…the staircase is well lit and it has a handrail…just stand there for a moment…wondering…whilst feeling more and more calm…

In a moment you will hear me count from 10 to 1…and when you hear me count down from 10 to 1, I would like you to imagine that you gently and safely walk down the staircase. This staircase will lead you to your own sanctuary, a special place of peace and tranquillity…a place you feel well in…a place that gives you a feeling of gentle power…a place that can help you to feel safe and nurtured, calm yet powerful… and you don't need to know yet how this place will look or where it will be…just be curious and let yourself be surprised…so, ready…

Ten…nine…walking down, gently, slowly…being curious… eight…seven…six…in case you have drifted away just come back to imagining that you are walking down a staircase…every step bringing you closer to that magical place…five…four…you can see or sense or feel that you are coming to the end of the staircase…relaxing deeper as you take another step down…three…and another one…two…you might already get a sense of your special place as you step down one more step…one…and as you now step off the staircase and into your special place…just take some time to explore it…look around…find out what's in your special place…where it is…how it feels…and… when you are ready…with your eyes closed…just tell me a bit about it…

Let your client tell you about the place and then encourage them to spend some time in the place and to change what needs changing. Instruct the client also to find a spot, their special power spot, which is a space within the place that feels just right, nourishing, safe and gently powerful. Get confirmation and a description and then suggest that the client spends a few minutes there, soaking up the energy until they hear you speak again.

SCRIPT FOR BRINGING CLIENT BACK TO
NORMAL WAKING CONSCIOUSNESS

In a moment I will ask you to leave your place of sanctuary and power and to come back into normal waking awareness. I will count from 1 to 10, suggesting that you walk up the stairs or drift up from your place, and that by the time I reach 10 you will be back fully in the here and now, opening your eyes, feeling refreshed and recharged. Before I count and before you come back, I would like you to know that you can visit this special place any time when you need a rest, or when you need to recharge your batteries, or when you are in need of a change of mood or whenever you 'feel like it'. It is always there for you. In fact, you might be astonished to learn that you can make yourself feel better simply by bringing this place to the forefront of your inner eye, to the forefront of your imagination, to your conscious awareness whenever you need to.

So, ready…one…two…three…walking up the staircase…coming back to normal waking awareness…four…five…six…coming back… feeling refreshed and recharged…a sense of peacefulness…seven… eight…begin to open your eyes…nine…ten…open your eyes…wide awake…fully back…

Once you have set up the client's place in his or her mind you can use this script as a trance-induction for journeying and some of the other work if you cannot use a CD that produces vibrations, such as a drumming CD. If you use it as a trance-induction for journeying just use the script leading the client back into the special place, shortening it as you see fit, and then begin the journey from there. Use the 'waking up' script after the journey – or any other work – is completed to bring the client fully back into a normal waking state of perception.

Note
1 You can purchase a drumming CD via my website www.christamackinnon.com or utilize any other drumming CDs designed for shamanic journeying.

10 THE SHAMANIC JOURNEY AS A THERAPEUTIC TOOL

The shamanic journey is a fundamental ceremony/technique in indigenous, traditional shamanism and has been adapted by contemporary practitioners. The literature about the shamanic journey used by contemporary shamanic practitioners is vast and I will therefore keep this description brief, focusing on examples of how to use it in a therapeutic setting.[1]

The shamanic journey is a process-orientated technique used to travel into the different worlds – the lower, upper and middle worlds – which I have outlined in Chapter 6. As discussed earlier in detail, it's a matter of dispute how we define those worlds: we can define them either as being different levels of consciousness within the mind, or as existing independently and outside the human mind, but nevertheless accessible through the mind in an altered state and, needless to say, influencing the human mind. In indigenous traditions, they are seen as existing independently of the human mind. In the main, they are called 'parallel worlds' or 'spirit worlds' in many indigenous traditions of the Americas, 'dreamtime' in Australian Aboriginal traditions and 'other worlds' in Celtic traditions.

Journeying is used by many different practitioners, including therapists and psychologists, some of whom might define the field we access when we journey as being the 'personal unconscious'. Having observed a vast amount of journeys of participants in groups and individual clients, and used the technique myself extensively, I would agree with Gagan who observes that the ancient themes of being and healing that can get activated during the shamanic journey point beyond the personal unconscious, as people seem to access material and images that 'may represent an archetype derived from the accumulated experiences of humankind' (Gagan 1998, p.64). Jung for example maintained that if we could peel away the layers we would eventually arrive at the stage of the amoeba. 'Just as the body has its evolutionary history and shows clear traces of the various evolutionary stages, so does the psyche' (Jung 1967, p.29).

> The notion of a collective sharing is akin to the holistic concept that all of life is connected. The subjective experience of moving into a dimension of consciousness outside the personal self – of the soul travelling along a web of interconnectedness to parallel realities – is within the bounds of the feasible, according to transpersonal psychologists, Jungian theoreticians, and generations of mystics. (Gagan 1998, p.65)

With regards to the shamanic journey, no matter what our personal view, it is more beneficial to define the worlds according to indigenous and contemporary shamanic views, as the structure of the journey has been created and tested within the framework of the three worlds, the lower, upper and middle. The realms of those worlds are accessed via the journey and traditionally utilized for diagnosis, to find out the source of the problem and the path of the resolution, such as which ritual or ceremony to perform, which herbs to use, which spirits to get involved or which soul parts to bring back. The journey is furthermore used for divination as well as for different forms of psycho-doctoring and healing.

Therapists are familiar with creative and guided visualization, and the shamanic journey begins as a visualization, but, in my experience and in the experience of many clients, it leads us deeper and is more profound. The second difference is the assistance of spirit helpers. In shamanic journeys, the client travels together with spirit helpers, in the form of power animals or guides or other spirits, or a combination of those, and the first journey in contemporary shamanism is often used to connect with such helpers. The vehicles we use throughout shamanic journeying to lead the brain into an altered state are drums, rattles or any sounds that produce the vibration of the theta state of the brain. For therapists and coaches who cannot work directly with a drum or rattle, or a drumming CD, it is advised to use a trance-induction that leads the client to their power place, such as the one I have provided in the previous chapter, and begin the journey from there.[2]

Most contemporary shamanic practitioners seem to have adopted Sandra Ingerman's suggestion of a time limit of 20 minutes for the journey, and most CDs that utilize drumming to accompany the shamanic journey and produce the required altered state are also 20 to 30 minutes long (Ingerman 2004). When I use journeying in the consulting room with clients, I will not always use a drum or rattle, but treat the journey like I would treat any process-orientated work. When I treat it like a process, I found it more beneficial to let the journey run for as long as it takes to come to a natural end, usually in the form of an adequate insight, solution, shift of belief or other conclusion. The journey is an unfolding process, the client's process, and thus much of the therapist's work during the journey is to listen to the narrative without interrupting and only sometimes, if necessary, to prompt or remind the client to repeat the intent and to ask their power animals and spirit guides for help.

Everybody can journey, just as everybody can sing, dance, draw or go through a cognitive process. Some people take to it easily and seem to be immediately proficient at it, others need a bit of practice, but everybody can journey to a certain degree. Clients who are more visual seem to journey more easily in the beginning, as they can utilize their visualization skills to start the journey. It is therefore important, as in guided visualizations, to explain to clients who are more kinaesthetic or auditory that they can also intuit what's happening, hear what's going on and/or develop a feel for the changing images, messages and events during the journey. Clients who can let a process happen, rather than analyse or question the surfacing material, have a further advantage, and I would advise you to explain this beforehand to your clients and ask them to 'just let the journey unfold as it wants to unfold' and to narrate it to you.

The traditionally initiated shaman travels out of the body whilst journeying, as I have explained in previous chapters, and they also have the ability to journey as somebody/something else, for instance as an animal. For most clients and workshop participants, it feels in the beginning more like a very intense altered state and a visualization. I personally have journeyed countless times when practising soul retrieval for individual clients as well as in groups and found that I can't be always sure if I am still in, or if I am out of, my body. Most times I am certainly not aware of my body and I have experienced journeys where I would definitely say that I am still in my body; on other occasions, I was clearly out of my body. More often than not, I ceased to hear the sound of the drums, was in worlds that were completely unfamiliar to me, but made sense to my clients, felt literally sick and, as group participants recounted afterwards, looked very white and experienced time distortion to a degree which was unfamiliar to me with other trance states. But I have also worked with clients whose journey wasn't much more than a visualization, which is perfectly adequate, as the process itself and the outcome are significant.

No two journeys are ever the same. The content and context of journeys can be complex and multi-layered. Nevertheless they are usually coherent and the content is consistent with the purpose/intent of the journey. It is vital not to interpret for the client, but to trust that the client knows the meaning of what unfolds. It's also important to let the journey come to a natural ending, even if this takes longer than expected, so it is not only empowering for the client but can have a transformational quality.

UTILIZING JOURNEYING IN A THERAPEUTIC ENVIRONMENT

Contemporary practitioners use the shamanic journey for many different reasons. You can use it to connect with power animals, spirit guides and spirits in general. One can journey to find something one needs to let go off, retrieve split-off parts and soul parts in general, reveal the root cause of an issue or problem, discover solutions, receive advice, untangle emotional webs, heal emotional wounding, find out about relationships and much more. We can also journey to receive learning about a range of things, such as our task in this world, our shadows, our spiritual selves, our connection with our ancestors, our essence qualities and so on.

It's most essential that you use your professional judgement to decide for which clients journeying is appropriate and at which stage of the therapeutic process you want to introduce it. I personally do not use journeying with clients who've survived trauma, present with PTSD and/or suffer from dissociative disorders in the early stages of therapy. I also advise against the use of journeying when, for example, a diagnosis of bipolar disorder or psychosis is present. Journeying, especially when accompanied by a drumming CD, produces a profoundly altered state, which could theoretically be harmful, reinforcing dissociative tendencies and/or triggering psychotic episodes.[3] If you work with a journey, it will take the whole session, as it is advisable to spend time afterwards to integrate the material from the journey with different means.

The structure of a shamanic journey

A journey is always conducted in the same way: the intent is clearly defined, a starting place from which to travel is visualized, a designation of the world to which the client wants to journey is stated (upper or lower world) and the help of a power animal and/or guide is requested. Once this is set up, both the client and the therapist are asked to trust the process completely, rather than trying to interfere, direct or interpret.

As a general rule of thumb, journeys of a 'psychological nature' lead into the lower world. Journeys that connect with spiritual/higher self states or ask for guidance from those realms usually lead to the upper world.

PREPARATION

1. Define, together with your client, a precise intent such as:

    *   I am going to journey to connect with my power animal.

    *   I am going to journey to get advice about [*insert appropriately*].

- I am going to journey to help me decide about my relationship.

- I am going to journey to find the root cause of my [*insert appropriately; for example, self-sabotage, depressive tendency, anxiety*] and what would help me to overcome it.

- I am going to journey to retrieve my creative part.

- I am going to journey to find out what I need to let go to achieve [*insert appropriately*].

- I am going to journey into the upper world to find/learn about my essence.

- I am going to journey to the upper world to find my place of One-ness.

2. Tell your client to narrate the journey to you and to trust the process, even if there are times when she seems to travel 'all over the place'. Also tell your client to ask her power animal and/or spirit guide to help with the journey.

THE JOURNEY

1. Use the trance-induction, leading your client to her sanctuary/power place (see Chapter 9), or use a drumming CD.

2. In the special place, instruct your client to find a way to travel into the earth (for lower world journeys) or to travel upwards (for upper world journeys). Ask for confirmation that she has found a way to do that and instruct her to state her intent at least three or four times, preferably aloud: 'I am going to journey into the lower world to [*intent*] and I ask my power animal and spirit guide to help me.'

3. Instruct your client to use her imagination to travel 'down' and just be guided by the images, feelings and/or sensations.

Instruct your client to let the journey unfold, just as though she were travelling or watching a film.

4. Ask your client to narrate the journey to you – where she is, what is going on, what is happening next. If you want to ask questions during the journey, keep them open ended, non-directive and neutral. If at all necessary I tend to ask, 'What is happening now?'

5. Let the process take over. Detach from any expectations with regards to the process or the outcome. Remind yourself and your client – if necessary – to trust the process.

6. If your client gets stuck, is all over the place or experiences very strong feelings, ask her to state her intent again, to ask for help, to ask her power animal or guide to show her the way and so on. Do not interrupt the journey.

7. When the journey has come to its conclusion (don't worry – you and your client will know), instruct your client to bring back whatever she needs/wants to bring back and count from 10 to 1, telling your client that whilst you are counting she will come back to her special place, and then back to the 'here and now' in your consulting room. Ask her to thank her power animal and guide for their help as she travels back to normal waking reality and then, after counting, ask her to open her eyes. If you use a drumming CD there will be a 'coming back beat' which is distinctly different from the 'trance beat'.

8. After this, process what has been happening during the journey with the means you usually employ: talk about the journey if necessary; find an affirmation if appropriate; make something that symbolizes whatever needs letting go and burn it; and instruct your client to write the journey down as homework and to reflect upon it.

9. If you have called in spirit and created a sacred space, don't forget to thank spirit afterwards.

JOURNEYS TO CONNECT WITH A POWER ANIMAL

If you intend to utilize journeying as a therapeutic technique and you want to assist your client to connect with the different spiritual layers, I would advise you to help him or her first to connect with a power animal. Power animals are wonderful creatures. As I have described, they are instinctual forces and have thus certain qualities, each of them providing a specific kind of medicine, which, let me assure you, will be exactly the one the client needs. Power animals can change over time, but most people will keep one for long periods. To have a power animal is exciting, will enrich your client's life and can be very helpful in various ways: to reconnect with their instinctual forces, to connect with nature, to make decisions and to help with difficult, emotional and stressful situations during any journey or indeed any therapeutic work. Above all, the power animal provides a positive, nurturing and helping internal attachment figure (Gagan 1998).

Because the power animal provides this figure, it is in itself a healing force. Power animals are nurturing, loving, cherishing creatures. They seem to provide a bonding experience for the client, especially those clients who go through early attachment difficulties, lack early attachment or are deprived of mental, emotional or physical nurturing in early life. The power animal holds the journeyer safe and secure; it nurtures through positive regard, reflecting the emotions and inner states of the client in a holding, generous and supporting way, which many people, particularly those who have had insufficient nurturing, have rarely experienced. The power animal, especially over repeated journeys, becomes like a devoted wise parent to the client, always ready to hold, guide, help, take action on behalf of the client, reflect back, criticize gently and constructively and play, praise and encourage creativity and adventure.

The intent for the journey to connect with the power animal is: 'I am journeying into the lower world to connect with my power animal.'

Proceed with the journey as outlined above. In most cases, people will end up in a landscape, either their power place or another place in nature, where they will meet the animal. Tell your client to walk away from the animal two or three times and, if the same animal shows up, then to ask it: 'Are you my power animal?' It is advisable to have just one or two power animals, rather than collecting a zoo. Tell your client to spend time with the power animal, to get to know its qualities and to connect with it. It's important that clients understand that all power animals are equal. A mouse is equal to a lion, although they have very different qualities. At the end of the journey, ask your client to find a way to bring the power animal back with them into 'normal waking reality'.

The power animal often either has qualities the client needs to incorporate more into his or her life or qualities that need to come more to the forefront. Discuss the qualities of the power animal and associations your client has with that specific animal. It is astonishing how much the client will learn about him or herself.

Once your client has made contact with the power animal, you should incorporate it as a helping spirit into all shamanically orientated work. It can also be used when needing guidance, especially when it comes to splits between the head and the heart, the instinctual and the rational. What the power animal advises reflects the instinctual. Power animals are also fantastic helpers when it comes to emotionally charged states, inner child work, ego-state work, regressions and soul retrieval. The power animal can be brought into the therapeutic work as a helping spirit at any time.

CASE EXAMPLE: HARRY

Harry is a client who presented with low confidence and an inability to take a stand and/or make decisions. He felt stuck in his career and unable to address uncomfortable issues in his marriage. Harry had very few social contacts; he concentrated on his professional life, which wasn't progressing the way he had envisaged, and he felt quite detached from his own two small children. His wife was a devoted mother and Harry talked to me about feelings of envy and jealousy towards the children, which he didn't dare to address within the marriage.

Harry was the youngest of five children, the next sibling being eight years older. His own perception was that he was an unwanted child. 'I am the child that arrived at a time when all that my mother wanted was peace and quiet and all my father wanted was to play golf.' His mother was 46 years old at his birth.

Harry understood the connection between the adjustments he made as a child – namely, to be as 'invisible and unobtrusive' as possible – and the behaviours he now exhibited in his private as well as professional life. He also knew that he didn't hold himself in high esteem and connected this with the rejection he had felt as a child as far back as he could remember. We worked on the whole with ego-states and inner child approaches and in parallel utilized CBT-hypnosis techniques to enhance his confidence, rehearse assertiveness and communication skills and work on behavioural changes.

For Harry, who visualized well, altered state experiences were a revelation. His shyness and his tendencies to over-explain and justify himself, displayed in normal waking consciousness, fell away and he proved to be quite daring and outspoken when in trance. When I, for example, asked him in one of the early sessions to visualize his family in a symbolic way, he saw himself as a little black dot, surrounded by big red dots with wide open mouths, saying, 'They are killing me with their anger,' after which he began to cry inconsolably, saying, 'They almost managed, you know, I don't know who I am at all.'

Without going deeper into the case of Harry, I want to share his first journey with you, as it shows the ability of the power animal to function as a positive, nurturing attachment figure.

Harry's journey to connect with his power animal

HARRY: I am going down through a kind of gorge. It's very narrow and quite difficult to navigate. Ah, I am in an open space now. There is a river. There are mountains on my right. The river runs along the mountains. I am standing in a meadow. There are trees on the other side of the river. I am walking towards the river. There is a crossing. I am crossing the river. It's warm, the water is warm, and shallow. The air is quite fresh… [silence] I am seeing a big bear. He is dark brown. He is coming towards me. He is a big bear, but I am not worried. He looks friendly [long silence]. The bear walked away, after looking at me for a while. I am walking in the other direction. Shall I state my intent?

ME: Yes.

HARRY: [aloud] I am looking for my power animal. I want to meet my power animal. [silence] Ah, there is the bear again. He is coming towards me. He stops. We look at each other. Not sure if he is my power animal.

ME: Ask.

HARRY: Are you my power animal? [long silence] Wow, the bear said yes. Well, he didn't say it – I just knew. He sat down. He beckoned me towards him. He opened his arms and I just had to – you know – it just felt right – I just had to cuddle up to him. He is holding me. I am smaller now, but I look like I look in real life, not like a child. He is very, very cuddly.

He nudges me with his snout. I...I feel very...well...I feel...that might sound funny...loved. [I observe tears running down Harry's cheeks.]

ME: Just let happen what wants to happen.

HARRY: He is asking me to come along for a walk. I get up and he holds my hand. We walk under the trees, along the river. [silence – Harry smiles] We are in the river. We are throwing fishes at each other. This bear likes to play. We are climbing out of the river. The bear is on his hind legs. He roars. Goodness, this animal can roar. [silence] He just keeps roaring. I think he wants me to roar as well. He keeps pointing at me. [long silence – even bigger smile on Harry's face] I am roaring with him. It's a game. It's fun. My roars are nothing much compared to his, though. Wow, this bear can roar. He is walking backwards, roaring... I am walking forwards, roaring back at him. [long silence – Harry still grins] The bear and I are sitting on the river bank now. He cuddles me again. I am feeling very calm, content...yes, content...peaceful...you know...just peaceful.

This journey was done with a drumming CD that lasted for 20 minutes. When the CD ended Harry thanked the power animal and brought it back with him. The bear had shrunk and fitted into his pocket. I blew the energy of the bear symbolically into the crown of his head. Harry was very moved. We talked for a while about the qualities of the bear and touched for the first time on the subject of anger. This was an emotion that Harry had previously always deflected as he hadn't been ready to look at the anger he held until that moment in the process. It was encouraging to hear that Harry interpreted the game of 'roaring' positively and had enjoyed the display of power. I almost jokingly advised him to practise roaring between sessions and also to imagine that the bear was accompanying him whenever he felt that he needed him around.

Three outcomes of this session are worth mentioning:

1. Harry played 'walking and roaring like a bear' with his son, who was three years of age, and they both enjoyed it. They had drawn a bear together and Harry had promised his son to take him to Canada one day to see a real bear (something they did five years later – I received a postcard).

2. Harry enjoyed journeying with his power animal and we began to use journeying whenever it felt appropriate. The bear provided much advice, nurturing and support during difficult emotional phases in therapy and Harry learned from the dual aspect of the bear, namely that one can be powerful and assertive whilst being gentle and nurturing.

3. The most important outcome was that the bear provided a parental aspect that was completely positive. Harry had been

at times impatient, ignorant and critical towards his 'inner child'. Once the power animal was established, I asked him regularly to turn to it for advice when working with inner child states and the bear's advice was always loving, understanding and nurturing.

CASE EXAMPLE: HEATHER

Heather was a woman in her early thirties. She had married a divorcee ten years her senior, with two daughters aged eight and ten. Heather felt, in her own words, nothing but resentment and anger whenever they had the girls staying with them, which happened every second weekend. Exploring the issue in the first session it transpired that Heather wasn't so much resenting the time her husband devoted to 'his girls', but the fact that she found them 'silly', 'manipulative' and 'stupidly girlish' and couldn't relate to them. She seemed to be genuinely unable to understand why her husband loved them. It was interesting to find out that the time her husband spent with the girls rarely intruded on Heather, who was the manageress of a restaurant, a job that demanded her to be present at the restaurant most Saturdays as well as on Saturday nights and occasionally also on Sundays. In her own estimation, she saw the girls only for a few hours over the allocated weekends.

During the second session I asked Heather to close her eyes and get an image that represented herself, her husband and his children. She saw a circle that represented her husband and his children and another circle, barely touching the first one, which represented her. I asked her to explore the issue further and play around with the circles to find out if they were static or if they could be moved. When she played with them in her mind she felt an incredible urge to rip the bigger circle to shreds. I encouraged her to explore this and find out what would happen. Heather opened her eyes, looked at me, and said, 'I would f…ing kill them' (meaning the children).[4]

Looking at Heather, you couldn't help but get the impression of maleness. Heather had the figure of a slim boy; her hair was cut very short; her communication was direct, with clear-cut, brief sentences; while her tone of voice and her body language struck me as being more aggressive than assertive, holding herself quite straight, legs apart when she sat, hands on hips, leaning forward when she 'made a point'. I asked her to tell me a bit about her own childhood and it turned out that Heather was the 'boy her father wanted'. She was the youngest of three siblings, all girls. After her birth, which was complicated, her mother was advised not to risk any further pregnancies. Heather was her father's favourite. He took her to football matches, taught her to kick-box and how to ride a motorbike when she was 14 years of age.

We began working around the subject of 'being a girl, being a woman', which Heather resented.

I won't go any further into Heather's process, but want to describe her first journey, which was with the intent to connect with her power animal.

Heather's journey to connect with her power animal

HEATHER: I am going down...down...still going down... Nothing happening... [long silence] I am in a strange place. There is a big, big river. I can hardly see the other side. I am standing at the edge of it and I am just watching. I can see fish. Don't tell me that I have a power animal that is a fish.

ME: Ask it.

HEATHER: You must be kidding me. I don't like fish. Ah, there is another animal. Rather sweet. I don't know what it is. Could be an otter. 'Are you an otter?' This is funny. I actually got an answer. It's an otter. [silence] The otter is my power animal. I don't know anything about otters. Doesn't look powerful to me, but it's somehow a sweet animal. I quite like it. It is jumping around in the water...it keeps looking at me...curiously... whilst jumping about. [long silence]

ME: What is happening?

HEATHER: Not much, I am just watching the otter. There was a dragonfly playing above the water, but it flew away. [long silence] The otter asked me to come into the water. I am swimming with her. She is female. I just know that. We are swimming. We dive under and then we come up again. This is actually OK. The water is quite cold. There is water everywhere. I don't know if that's still a river. The otter wants me to dive down. Wow... we are under water now and we circle around each other...playful...She has beautiful eyes. [Heather's facial expression changes. She looks as if she might cry, but doesn't] She is like a little girl, you know...a lovely little girl.

Heather brought the otter back. When she opened her eyes, we just looked at each other, silently. I decided to take a step I usually wouldn't take as I want the client to define the medicine of their power animals themselves. I handed Heather the book I own, which describes power animals and their medicine, and asked her to find the description of 'otter'.

OTTER: Woman medicine; lessons in female energy; teaches about female energy; will care for its young and play for hours. Otter is the true coquette of the animal world. Otter is friendly, trustful and sharing. Otter teaches about 'the freeness of love without jealousy. It is the joy of loving other people's children and their accomplishments as much as you love your own' (Sams and Carsons 1988, p.70).

The book goes on to say that the destruction of jealousy and anger makes space for the female qualities of flowing with the river of life, of sharing and giving as well as receiving.

Both of us sat silently for a while. There was nothing to say. After a while, Heather broke the silence: 'Otter, I didn't even know how a f...ing otter looks.' She laughed. We both knew that she had broken through a layer in one session that could have taken quite a few sessions to break through. Otter hit the spot and Otter was completely understood by Heather. Otter said, 'Come on, sweet woman; it's OK to be a girl; let yourself be a girl, a woman, a playful, giving, loving female and fear not.'

JOURNEYS TO CONNECT WITH A SPIRIT GUIDE

To have a power animal in place is in many cases enough to begin utilizing journeying with your client. Nevertheless, it is beneficial to give the client a chance to connect with an upper world teacher, such as a spirit guide.

The intent for the journey is: 'I am going to journey into the upper world to meet my spirit guide.'

To meet a spirit guide, one needs to journey into the upper world. Again, start in the power place and this time the client needs to find a way in his or her imagination to travel upwards. Many people use tree branches or climb a mountain and start the journey from there. I have never met anybody who didn't get an image that could be used to travel upwards. As I have described in Chapter 6, the upper world journey feels different from a journey into the lower world. One seems to travel through layers and can meet all kinds of spirits and guides. It is essential to give the client time, as upper world journeys can be less clear because the imagery is sometimes hazy and because we are making contact with a world unfamiliar to most of us. If the client meets different 'persons', they are again advised to ask, 'Are you my spirit guide?' If the answer is 'Yes', then instruct the client to have a conversation with the guide, to be with him or her for a while, to ask for advice and to get to know the guide. Some guides are quite stern; others are more loving and gentle. It is my experience that the guide comes exactly in the form the client needs him or her to be. In contrast with power animals, the client should not bring the guide back, but they can bring something that symbolizes the guide.

Discuss the guide with your client, if that feels appropriate, and ask for his or her qualities and wisdom. Let the client express how he or she feels about the guide. Spirit guides, as described in Chapter 6, function as advisors, counsellors and helpers. They generally carry wisdom and knowledge of a higher nature and it is beneficial to call upon them whenever appropriate during therapeutic work, especially work that is emotionally painful or when a certain level of wisdom and guidance is needed.

Homework – power animals and spirit guides

It is beneficial to internalize power animals and guides and to develop a 'feel' for them. Homework between sessions can be given with the aim of doing that. The client may craft something that symbolizes those forces, paint or draw them, write about them, set aside some quiet time every day for communicating with them in the imagination and have them present whenever the situation asks for the energy of the power animal or guide. This will begin to incorporate the energies beneficially into the client's life.

JOURNEYS OF RETRIEVAL, CONNECTION AND LEARNING

All journeys of a psychological nature can start in the lower world. Journeys into the lower world can change into middle world journeys or upper world journeys spontaneously, which is fine. As long as the intent was set up correctly, helpers are called in and the procedure is followed, we need to trust that clients will end up on the level they require to complete the task.

If you want to retrieve a part, or find out about something, or connect with something, the intent is: 'I am going to journey into the lower world to find and connect with [insert whatever the client wants to find]. I ask my power animal and guide to help me.'

If you want to find the source of an issue the intent is: 'I am going to journey into the lower world to find out when [*insert*] was created and what I can do to resolve it. I ask my power animal and spirit guide to help me.'

Journeys to learn about something are interesting journeys and can be profound. We can journey to 'learn about my shadow', to 'learn about One-ness', to 'learn about my connection to spirit', to 'learn about my essence', to 'learn about my tasks in life' and more. When one wants to learn something that is more universal, such as 'One-ness' or 'essence' or 'task', the journey can be set up to lead into the upper world. In my experience though, even if you begin the journey as a lower world journey, the client will travel to the upper world if appropriate. Alternatively, you can leave it open, keeping the intent 'vague' with regards to the world: 'I am going to journey to the upper or lower world to [*insert appropriately*]. I am asking my power animal and spirit guide to help me.'

Another form of journeying to get information and learn is to journey directly to a teacher. This can be the spirit guide or the power animal, or the intent can be kept artfully vague: 'I am going to journey to a teacher who can teach me about [*insert*]. I ask my power animal and guide to help me.' Then start the journey in the usual way and let it unfold.

It is vital to integrate whatever has been retrieved, or the outcome of the exploration, with either the means described in other chapters or with the means you normally use in your therapeutic approach. Keep in mind that if your client journeys to find the root cause of something, he or she might regress or end up in a place that might be emotionally charged. The following example will illustrate this.

CASE EXAMPLE: JOANNA

Joanna was a client who saw me to, in her own words, 'stop me sabotaging myself'. Joanna was 52 years of age. Her husband owned a small but highly successful consultancy business, the offices being part of their estate. Joanna had spent most of her adult life bringing up her children, running a fairly big house, hosting dinner parties for business partners and travelling with her husband to Asia and the Far East, where most of his clients were located. Joanna was a good-looking, groomed, kind of 'classy' woman with a degree in business studies, which, as she put it, came in handy at times, but was never really put to good use, and a lifestyle many would have envied.

Joanna felt that over the years she had cut off parts of herself, which she now missed. She told me that she loved to paint and create installations when she was at school, but that it had been always assumed that she would study either economics or business as her own father had owned a company. She told me about the longing she felt to go to art college, but said she couldn't get a portfolio together. She had tried for three consecutive years and thrown all her paintings, graphics and other projects away again and again, shortly before she had to submit them to get considered for admission. She was now at the same point again. Her portfolio was almost ready, the deadline was looming and her urge to throw everything away had grown stronger.

Those acts of self-sabotage seemed strange. We explored the negative thought processes that had accompanied the destructions of her work, formulated positive beliefs and supportive thoughts. We also did some 'parts-work' around 'the part that wants to destroy the pictures' and 'the part that wants to go to art college' and followed this with some integration work. I advised Joanna to bring her portfolio to me for safekeeping, while we were working, which she 'forgot' to do, in every session.

After the third session and with the deadline being ten days away, I asked her if she would like to try something new, something that might sound strange to her, but might give her some insight. To cut a long story short, we decided to attempt a journey, starting from her sanctuary, with the intent: 'I am going to journey to the lower or upper world to find out what compels me to destroy my pictures.'

Joanna's journey

JOANNA: I am standing in front of a large tree. It's an oak tree. There is a big opening around the tree. I am suddenly quite small. I am falling through the hole… I am still falling…falling…quite fast. I have landed in a strange landscape. It looks like a desert with some big rock formations. It's quite beautiful, very open and wide. Soft, almost golden, yellowish sand, soft sand. There is nobody there, just sand and rocks. Could be quite frightening… [long silence in which I wished that we had established some spirit help beforehand] Something pushes me forward. I am walking towards one of the rock formations. There is an opening in the rock. I am climbing into it.

ME: Repeat your intent, Joanna, and if you need help, just ask for it, aloud or in your mind.

JOANNA: I am in a big chamber. It's quite dark, but I know it's big. I am walking towards a figure that seems to want me to come closer. I am not sure. The figure suddenly seems scary. Massive. It feels threatening. Can I have some help please? Ah, somebody gave me a lamp. I don't know who that is. She, it's a woman, is to my right, but I can't see her. I move towards the figure. This figure is massive. The figure shines in many, many colours when I hold the lamp in a certain way. Oh, now it's all around me, like swirling colourful lights. I am being lifted. I am flying upwards, very rapidly... [long pause] I am remembering something. I remember... It was at nursery. We made a hanger for necklaces out of a wooden cooking spoon. We coloured it in and then we put little hooks on it. This is fun. I use different colours. The spoon hanger looks like a rainbow. [silence] I am in the kitchen. My nanny shouts. She shouts at me. I am crying. I am a thief. I stole a cooking spoon. Mum will hate me when she hears that. Nanny says I am a thief. I am to go to my room and stay there until Mummy comes back. [I now sincerely wish that we would have established a guide or power animal. Joanna looks fragile. Her face seems young, thin, her eyes are moving rapidly]

ME: Can adult Joanna take a look what's happening to little Joanna? [long silence, tears]

JOANNA: I have explained to little Joanna that all is fine. That it was a silly mistake, nothing more. I told her that Nanny is overreacting and that she is not a thief. I am moving upwards, back through the opening. I am back in my special place.

After Joanna opened her eyes, she explained that she had 'forgotten' this incident, but that she remembered it now quite clearly. She had been four years of age when it happened. She had forgotten that the nursery teachers had given them a piece of paper with a message to give to their mothers. The message asked mothers to make sure that the child brought a wooden cooking utensil to colour in. So in the morning she had gone to the kitchen and, as there was nobody there, she had taken the spoon. She said that she remembered that her mum laughed when she was told by the nanny, saying: 'Well, it's hardly the end of the world, Joanna, but in future please ask permission before you take something.'

Joanna was surprised that a minor incident like this might have had such a lasting effect. I wasn't sure either whether remembering and working through this incident would ease the compulsion to destroy her portfolio, but, to our joint surprise, it seemed to have contributed to solving the issue. Joanna handed in her portfolio two days later and enrolled into art college.

Generally speaking, therapists should always take time to integrate the outcome of the journey afterwards if appropriate with the means they would usually use within their therapeutic work and/or use the means described in the later chapters such as embodiment and ceremony. Integrating the outcome doesn't mean to 'intellectualize' the content of the journey. Journeys can be, as I described above, multi-layered, so to analyse the journey or intellectualize it will be counter-productive.

Notes

1   Two informative books on the subject matter are Sandra Ingerman's *Shamanic Journeying: A Beginner's Guide* (2004) and Jeanette M. Gagan's *Journeying: Where Shamanism and Psychology Meet* (1998).

2   The trance-induction leading to the place of power is provided in Chapter 9. Practitioners who are able to use a drumming CD within their space are advised to use it if this is appropriate for the client. You can purchase a drumming CD with journey instructions from my website www.christamackinnon.com or alternatively purchase a shamanic journey drumming CD from Amazon.

3   This is one of the issues we face when untrained practitioners use techniques that can produce powerful altered states, such as journeying, indiscriminately.

4   I remember asking myself if she 'had been killed' in one form or another – and if yes, which part of her – but didn't voice it at the time as this seemed inappropriate and counter-productive at this stage in the therapeutic process.

11 | SOUL LOSS AND SOUL RETRIEVAL

Although soul retrieval will not be described in depth, as it is a journey the shamanic practitioner undertakes on behalf of his or her client, requiring training, knowledge of the different worlds and practice before attempting it, I nevertheless want to outline it, in the form of a brief description and two case examples, because it addresses the mechanism of dissociation, which underlies many issues and conditions we encounter in therapeutic practice, from a shamanic/spiritual point of view. I also want to use soul retrieval as an example to touch on a major difference between shamanic practitioners and the accepted thinking in contemporary psychology and therapy, namely the level to which practitioners get directly involved. On the whole, shamanic practitioners play a much more active role, as they assume that clients cannot resolve certain issues by themselves, such as for example the 'loss of soul'.

THE CONCEPTS OF SOUL LOSS AND DISSOCIATION

In the world of shamanism it is assumed that it is mainly the loss of soul that causes emotional, physical and mental disease and diminishes essential life energy. It is therefore seen as vital to return the soul, or parts of the soul, to the client. The term 'soul loss' usually describes the splitting-off of parts of the soul, as 'soul loss' in its totality would of course cause death. The description of soul loss shows remarkable similarities to what contemporary psychology calls 'dissociation' in that the shamanic concept of soul loss recognizes, like the psychological concept of dissociation, the capacity of human beings to split off parts of their psyche in response to trauma and/ or adverse circumstances.

Dissociation is a device the brain uses to survive potentially destructive traumatic events. It minimizes perception and, later, if the event isn't processed adaptively, it can block access to cognitive, sensory and affective memory or to parts of the memory. Furthermore, the brain uses dissociative devices to disconnect from emotional states and manifesting behaviours of those states, such as anger, rage or sadness, if they cannot be expressed without risking ongoing punishment, be it physical or emotional. This happens mainly during childhood. A simple example is rage, which in most cultures is not accepted and can, when expressed, lead to either direct punishment or to the withdrawal of love and affection by parents. Over time we 'split off' the part of us that is raging or angry, sometimes to a point where we don't feel and accept it any longer as being a part of us.

We all know that dissociation can only take place when the state is altered and that there is a price to pay for adaptive dissociation that turns maladaptive over time. The long-term price to pay for this non-integration of traumatic material or emotionally unacceptable states can be developmental arrest, the manifestation of those defences and parts in distressing, debilitating and incapacitating ways such as anxieties, depression, addictions and compulsions as well as a loss of part of our energies, and our psychological and mental potential. Both contemporary psychology and shamanic concepts understand that dissociation takes place, but whilst contemporary thinking would locate dissociated parts and states within the mind, the shaman assumes that soul loss is a spiritual illness and that the dissociated parts can 'flee the body' and hide somewhere outside, in the case of soul loss mainly in the lower, but sometimes also in the upper, world.

Although it is now widely accepted that we can only dissociate when we alter our state in the way our brain manages, for instance, instantly and automatically when confronted with a potentially traumatic situation, it is not accepted within psychological thinking that such energies could have been split off to an extent that they have become inaccessible, unless somebody who is trained in working in parallel and 'other worlds' accesses them for us. Besides hiding in inaccessible realms, those parts are, in shamanic thinking, also guarded by heavy defences, which are difficult or impossible for the affected person to overcome. During the shamanic journey to retrieve soul parts we indeed encounter quite strong energies, which often show themselves as monsters, reptiles, dragons and other dangerous beasts. They literally guard the soul. The shamanic practitioner will have to overcome those, mainly with the help of spirit helpers, and persuade the soul part to come back. The persuasion of the part is necessary because it is arrested, refusing to come back to a reality that is still perceived as being dangerous.

To retrieve a soul the shaman will journey into the spirit world, accompanied by spirit helpers, with the intent to retrieve a certain part, narrating, at least in contemporary shamanism, the whole journey to the client. Once the shaman has retrieved the part he or she will reintegrate it for the client and together with the client. This is usually done first energetically, by blowing the energy into the body, but also by means of ceremony, and now, in more contemporary practice, cognitively. In psychotherapeutic practice we would attempt a similar form of reintegration of dissociated parts or ego-states, using mainly ego-state therapy, inner child work, parts work, Gestalt approaches and other techniques, but we would not attempt to do it 'for the client' by locating the part and bringing it back. In fact, the generally accepted ethics of psychotherapy might define this level of involvement as borderline unethical or counterproductive.

CASE EXAMPLE: SOUL RETRIEVAL

I am describing a case of soul retrieval here to illustrate this and also the ethical dilemmas one can face.

When running soul retrieval training for professionals I usually demonstrate one or more retrievals, asking for volunteers, before the participants attempt it themselves, working in pairs. During one of the training courses a female counsellor, who struggled physically as well as emotionally with the menopause, asked me to find out if there was a part that needed retrieving so that she could overcome her physical, but especially her emotional, suffering with regards to the menopause. When demonstrating I try to keep the intent for the journey as simple as possible, not necessarily stating anything that would point in the direction of trauma. Thus the intent for this specific journey was formulated: 'I am going to journey into the lower or upper world to retrieve a soul part for Jill that she needs at this moment in time.'

After listening to the drumbeat for a few minutes and calling my power animal and spirit guide to help me, I felt myself descending. I wandered for a while during a barren landscape that I didn't recognize and was suddenly joined by a guide-like figure, also unfamiliar to me. As new guides or the guide of the affected person can show up during soul retrieval I wasn't concerned. The guide called one of my power animals, which is a bird, and I saw myself being carried on his back to the upper world. As I said before, split-off parts often reside in the lower world and it was at this moment that the journey began to feel strange. A moment later I saw a cradle. During soul retrieval the practitioner will narrate the journey to the client, staying away from interpreting, omitting or adding anything. I kept narrating the journey to Jill, but felt increasingly anxious. I knew that the cradle meant something, but as it wasn't for me to guess, I kept looking at it. Suddenly a tiny foetus appeared. It floated through space. As I narrated this to Jill, I was being jolted back into the room by a loud sob. Without opening my eyes I asked the accompanying guide if this was the part Jill would need back. The answer was 'Yes.' Now in the case of an unborn foetus I was convinced that this couldn't be right. So I addressed Jill directly, saying that I wouldn't bring the part back, but that we would talk about it all in a moment. I could still hear sobbing somewhere in the background and it was interesting that the drumbeat changed at that moment in time to the 'calling up' beat. I began to come out of trance and whilst regaining normal waking consciousness I identified the sobs as coming from Jill's partner Ray, a psychologist who also attended the training course.

It turned out that Jill had had a termination six years earlier. Ray was the father of three children in a previous marriage before he met Jill, who had a grown-up daughter. They had agreed not to have any further children and when 'the accident' happened it seemed obvious to both of them that a termination was advised. To Jill's astonishment, years later she struggled with menopausal symptoms, especially emotionally, and during this training course was suddenly confronted with the termination. We opted for a break and Jill and Ray stayed with me to talk about it. It transpired that Jill had contemplated a few times the fact that she now, after the menopause, would never have a chance to have a child with Ray and, although rationally she was in complete agreement with their decision, emotionally she was sad and wondered if the decision had been right for her. She had made a few attempts during the previous year to talk to Ray about her feelings but had accepted Ray's reply, 'There is nothing we can change now,' and hadn't pursued the subject further as it had been, after all, a joint decision and it was, as Ray rightly pointed out, 'too late to change anything'. Ray, who was obviously distressed, seemed to be taken aback by the fact that the termination might have something to do with Jill's menopausal problems and repeatedly said that he wanted to talk it all through. As we didn't have the space within the training group to do that, we agreed to have a session if necessary a week later. When they arrived for that session, they were both smiling and relaxed. They had talked about it, cried some tears and done a small forgiveness ceremony for each other.

GETTING INVOLVED OR NOT?

I have used soul retrieval for quite a few years and taught it to therapists. It is a powerful technique that accesses, more often than not, traumatic, split-off parts and memories. The shamanic view that clients cannot access certain parts and that therapists might have to get more involved is worth considering. Clients might not be able to access certain parts because painful fear barriers are difficult to overcome. If clients work directly with such parts, re-traumatization can be of real concern and there might be states or parts which really cannot be accessed by the client as they are buried deeply or, as shamans would put it, live in realms that are inaccessible. No matter what the reasons, it is a fact that sometimes, in my experience, therapeutic work with dissociated, highly traumatized inner child parts can only take place with the active involvement of the therapist, without disempowering clients and without risking non-integration. The following describes a case which illustrates this.

CASE EXAMPLE: GETTING INVOLVED

Tara had survived multiple abuses from members of a paedophile ring, producing films for an ever-growing international market. Three of the perpetrators, one her own father, were imprisoned. Tara was 24 years old at the time of therapy and very disturbed. She had spent some time in care and had been admitted on several occasions to a psychiatric unit, which she still attended as an outpatient. She was given financial help by a charity to finance her sessions with an osteopath and with me. Tara also attended a therapeutic group for survivors on a weekly basis and received help from social services.

Tara had many 'inner children'. Most of them were severely wounded; unfortunately, some of them seemed dead. This was one of the most tragic cases I had ever worked with, illustrated by Tara's basic belief that it would have been kinder if they (the perpetrators) had killed her. Inner child work, only attempted after about six months into therapy, was difficult for Tara. Her normal state of being was one of dissociation; she really did feel 'dead' most of the time, or, when emotions were felt, she coded them as unbearable rage or as utter despair, which she tried to numb with alcohol. Some of her 'inner children' were accessible and she slowly learned to like them instead of hating them, but some of them lived on an island in a wild river that was occupied by snakes, crocodiles, monsters and other frightening creatures. There was no way she could reach those children. Therapeutic work continued addressing other areas, mainly work to reduce her high level of anxiety (Tara had days of shaking helplessly with fear at home) and her negative beliefs about herself and the world, and to tackle her underdeveloped communication, social and relationship skills; some abreactive work was employed. This was accompanied by Tara's attempt to stop drinking with the help of AA meetings, by treatment through the osteopath and by three-monthly assessments through a psychiatrist.

I remember vividly the session (after about 12 months) when Tara walked into the room announcing to me that she was determined to cross the river during this session to 'bring back those kids'. Miraculously a bridge, which had never showed before, appeared in her imagination and she attempted to walk over the bridge. But the creatures in the river jumped out trying to attack her. She panicked, started to shake and had to open her eyes. Her fear turned into anger, unfortunately at herself for being such a coward, and every suggestion to change the bridge, such as making it higher or safer or wider, was rejected. I had at this point learned to trust the client's resources, so I said: 'Let's just pretend that your unconscious, somewhere deep down, knows how you can cross that bridge safely both ways, now that you have decided to do so. Would you just close your eyes and ask your inner wise self to find a solution?' The answer was very simple. Tara said: 'My wise self told me to ask you whether you would come with me and help me to fight the creatures off.' During that session we crossed the bridge three times. The attacks of the creatures became weaker and less frightening every time we crossed to bring two more children, one in Tara's arms and one in mine, over to the meadow on the other side of the river.

This was an exhausting session. The visualizations we worked with were almost identical. I felt as if I was 'in Tara's world', crossing the bridge. I felt nauseous; my heart was racing and whatever energy it was that showed itself as animals in the water felt threatening. We stayed in verbal contact during the whole session and had to take breaks between crossings. Now, was this projection, was this a tuning into a client on a very deep level or was it an energetic world outside, which we both had to access to retrieve those 'soul parts'? I tend to think that it was a shared accessing of an energetic world, but I cannot know that for certain. Nevertheless, I do know that the island appeared in Tara's future visualizations as being empty. The children were all safely ashore and we began therapeutic work on exploring those parts, healing their wounds, and integrating them during the next few sessions, with more than beneficial results.

I personally think we can learn from shamanic practitioners and become more involved as long as we work ethically, don't interpret for the client, stay away from anything that could re-traumatize and keep our interventions transparent.

12 WIDENING THE CIRCLE

Connecting with Ancestors and Descendants

One of the harmful developments we have undergone in western cultures is our disconnection from our ancestors, a development that now increasingly happens in every region of the world. This loss of connection impacts many levels and areas of our individual and collective life, the most prominent aspects being that we have become, more and more, isolated individuals without roots and have lost sight of the many generations that will come after us and of our duty of care for them.

Apart from a rather intellectual interest in researching ancestral trees, we seem to feel detached from the lines of people without whom we wouldn't be walking on this earth at all, focusing increasingly on youth, which cannot be experienced and wise, whilst disrespecting the elderly, disregarding their life experience and wisdom. I personally believe that the longer we continue this trend the more we will also forget those who will come after us, leaving them a world that will be far from nurturing, if at all habitable. I am not suggesting that we are in the process of forgetting our own children, but if we are honest with ourselves, we rarely think further ahead than a generation or two.

Our current state of affairs is relatively new, compared with the overall history of humanity. Indigenous peoples all over the world lived, as far as we can know, sustainable lives, honouring the ones that came before and considering the ones that would come after. The few who have survived and resisted the pressures of westernization, such as the Hopi Nation and some more aware, or isolated, peoples and tribes, still do so. They had great awareness of the needs of generations to come and honoured that awareness by seeing themselves as 'caretakers' rather than 'exploiters' of the earth. Oren Lyons, chief of the Onondaga Nations, one of the original five constituent nations of the Iroquois, writes: 'We are looking ahead, as it is one of the first mandates given us as chiefs, to make sure and to make every decision that we make relate to the welfare and well-being of the seventh generation to come... What about the seventh generation? Where are you taking them? What will they have?' (Lyons 1980, pp.173–174).

Even now, proclamations from indigenous elders around the world arise from an entirely different level of consciousness than that of our leaders. In 2011 a gathering of elders, ceremony keepers and mandated leaders from the four directions, including Asia, Africa, the Americas, Australia and the South Pacific, saw the need to address four critical issues:

1. Sacred Knowledge – embracing the guidance of our ancestors and elders, to live in balance.

2. Sacred Lands – respecting the rhythms and warnings of Mother Earth to choose wisely.

3. Sacred Children – nurturing the young ones, both near and far.

4. Sacred Generations – providing for future generations, the grandchildren and for all humanity.

(International Indigenous Leadership Gathering 2011)

We have lost this heart-warming focus on providing for future generations and on ensuring that they learn the teachings from the elders and ancestors, who still knew how to live in balance.

I didn't pay much attention to shamanic ancestral work until I participated in an intense, highly ritualized three-day ancestral workshop with Malidoma Somé, an African shaman who has brought some indigenous traditions of West Africa to Europe and America (Somé 1998). He made remarks that struck a chord in me. This man, who was born into a tribe in Africa, basically said that we, in the West, compared to the small, materially poor African tribes, live very one-dimensional, poor lives because we have deadened the mystical within us. Malidoma sees our reconnecting with our ancestors (defined more as a field rather than as concrete ancestors, and therefore not separate from us) as essential if we are to reawaken the spiritual/mystical in us. When we reawaken the mystical in us, as I have stated in different forms in this book, we are expanding, reconnecting the different worlds. He continued to explain that if we don't acknowledge that 'ancestors' are part of us, we stay small and separate. When we look at the question of ancestors from an energetic point of view, we understand much better that they are part of our 'field', that they form a field and are interconnected with our field.

Ancestors, in a traditional sense, are all those people who have lived before us and are now in spirit. They are the ones that share our bloodlines, but also, if one subscribes to certain theories, the ones that form part of our soul groups and, the further we go back in time, the more common ancestors we encounter and the more we understand that we have a connection to all ancestors, to all of humanity. The functions of the ancestors are part of indigenous life. 'In indigenous cultures it is the responsibility of the ancestor to hold the memories and wisdom gained from the past back to the dawn of humankind. It is the responsibility of the living to heal the past, to learn from the ancestors' mistakes and create change' (Pratt 2007a, p.14). It is in this sense that indigenous cultures revere their ancestors, use them as role models, are in contact with them, utilize them as helping spirits, learn from them and live with them on a daily basis.

Ancestors hold the wisdom and memories of humankind, and in that sense, they are role models and advisors. Not surprisingly, taking the breathtakingly fast industrial, military and technological developments of the last few centuries, the devastating wars, the history of slavery, imperialism, fascism and other 'isms' into account, we may not even find many role models in our more recent ancestry and we may feel that they cannot teach us much because their way of life was at times profoundly repulsive. But even without our recent ancestors' devastating behaviours, their way of life, or so it seems on the surface of things, was also profoundly different from our highly technological, consumerist lifestyles.

In shamanism we differentiate between indigenous cultures and our own when it comes to ancestors. Most indigenous traditions distinguish between ancestors that have successfully made the transition to the spirit world, where they belong, and the ones that 'didn't make it'. They are often referred to as ghosts and this term is not positive. Ancestors can only be wise, according to most indigenous beliefs, when they are in spirit form. Ancestors that didn't make it into the spirit world are stuck in the 'world between', where they do not belong and have a negative influence on the living. They need to be helped to reach the other side, a job for the experienced shaman, the so-called psychopomp. This is about the only context in which we hear the word 'ancestral healing' within indigenous shamanism.

In contemporary western shamanism, our focus is also directed onto 'ancestral healing', a practice, as I said, hardly used in traditional cultures. Two reasons are seen as being crucial to this shift of focus. First, there are now many ancestors that don't make it to the other side, as we lack rituals and ceremonies which help to guide the spirits over. Traditionally, at the time of death, the spirit is tended to and energies are cleared via rituals and ceremonies. An example of this can be found in traditional Tibetan Buddhism, where the dead person is helped through Bardo, the world in between, by a Lama, who reads prayers and performs rituals from the Book of the Dead. In most contemporary cultures, especially in western ones, funerals are for the living, rather than the deceased, and not much is done to help the spirit through the stages of transition. Second, over the last two millennia there have been more and more people who 'didn't live well', which over time has resulted in genetic and memory patterns that are detrimental to the descendants. Living well, in a traditional sense, means walking a path with honour, being embedded into a community, being a free human, taking responsibility for actions and rules, keeping one's affairs in order and leaving a world to future generations which is better, rather than worse. If we look at mankind over the last two or three millennia, we realize, as I already said, that we fought big wars, uprooted many people, produced slavery, created starving populations, suppressed whole peoples or wiped them out, destroyed natural communities, habitats and boundaries (just looking at the map of Africa is enough to demonstrate this point), persecuted an enormous number of people and produced many children who were orphaned, not recognized by communities, enslaved and/or treated badly. In theory people who don't live well can't die well, meaning that some of them hang around as ghosts, clinging on to life. Even if they don't linger, they pass on negative patterns to their descendants.

In shamanic terms, both of the above groups create energy fields that are detrimental to mankind and by now we have created vast numbers of such fields that need clearing. There are contemporary modern approaches, one of the latest being Bert Hellinger's Family Constellations approach (e.g. Hellinger 2003), which understand that such intergenerational patterns can reach way back, potentially playing a crucial role in a person's life, and that it is vital to incorporate this knowledge into therapeutic practice, but, in my estimation, we, as a profession, still don't pay enough attention to intergenerational issues. In shamanism we take this issue a step further and widen the field, taking families, communities, regions, nations and so on into account. Clearing such energy fields can be challenging work and needs training.

INCORPORATING ANCESTRAL WORK INTO THERAPY
Clearing ancestral lines

Ancestral healing, which is the domain of experienced practitioners in shamanism, can be incorporated to a certain extent into therapeutic practice, although in more individualized and somehow rather mild forms. The first step is to find the pattern. Clients usually identify patterns relatively easily if they can look back two or three generations and/or develop an awareness for the patterns that repeat themselves in their own lives. These patterns are indicators of unresolved issues in ancestral lines and can be found in addictions and dependencies, in physical ailments, in relationships, in issues of power and control, in how women and children are treated and so on and so forth. We can also identify patterns that might be intergenerational by developing an awareness of what repeats itself in our lives and seems to resist change, no matter how much effort or therapy we throw at it.

Journeying to the source

There are various ways to begin to clear ancestral lines. One of them is to identify the pattern and then do a shamanic journey with the following intent: 'I am going to journey to find the source for this pattern in my ancestral line and ask for ways to clear it. I ask my power animal, spirit helpers and well-meaning ancestors to accompany me on the journey and to help me.'

The journey will unfold in its own way, but it is vital to have spirit guides and power animals present to help. Once the client finds the source, she asks what she has to do to heal it, or to finish the business or break the pattern. Leave it up to the client to ask the guides how to do the clearing and healing. They usually know. She most certainly will come across different ancestors during the journey and it is advised to clear the patterns on each level on the way up. Once the client is back in normal consciousness in your consulting room you can begin to cognitively integrate and to use your usual means to help the client change the pattern in her here-and-now life. In my experience, this will now be easier, after the ancestral lines have been addressed and an understanding has been developed via the shamanic journey.

Timeline

A way I like to work with the past is to combine the idea of a neuro-linguistic programming (NLP) timeline with a shamanic journey. The client identifies the pattern or issue he wants to address. I ask the client to keep the issue or pattern firmly in mind and call in their spirit helpers. After explaining the concept of a timeline, I use a trance-induction or a drumbeat and ask the client to imagine that they float above the timeline, through their lives, back through time.

I then ask them to stop and observe from above every time they see or sense that the pattern we are exploring has been present. I keep the client dissociated on the level above the timeline, asking him to describe to me what he sees or senses (I take notes). We keep going until he reaches the generation when the pattern was formed. I then ask the client to step into the timeline, making sure that his guide and other helpers are with him, and to find out what he needs to do to heal or resolve the issue. When that is done, I instruct the client to float above the timeline again and we repeat the 'healing and resolving' in the same fashion all the way up the line, stepping (re-associating) into the timeline, clearing the pattern, before floating up again, forward in time to the next event and so on.

Ceremony/ritual

I always take time to create a ritual/ceremony with my client after a journey or a timeline-clearing of ancestral patterns. If you work in a time-restricted fashion, you might have to do this in the next session. Most of the time I use a 'letting go' ritual. The pattern that needs to be let go will be embodied (see Chapter 8) by creating a drawing or a piece of craft or sometimes, if time is of the essence, I ask my client to go into the garden and find something that symbolizes the pattern. I then create a fire ceremony with the clients as described in Chapter 14. As well as calling in spirit and guides we will also call in those ancestors that can help. Ancestral spirits are very powerful helpers as they have a direct connection to the client. I find that any ceremony is stronger when the ancestral spirits are called in.

Connecting with spirit ancestors

As well as clearing ancestral lines, it is vital, from the shamanic viewpoint, to be connected with those ancestors that are in spirit and can help us on a daily basis. I have used ancestral connecting beneficially with groups and with individual clients. It might surprise you to learn that this connecting work was felt especially beneficial by people who had survived childhood abuse or neglect, or those who had been adopted or suffered the loss of parents. Some professionals seem to think that things get worse, the further we go back in time. From my experience, I disagree. There is, in every line or network of ancestors, at least one ancestor that clients can not only identify with, but use as a role model and a model of aspiration. I have never met a client who couldn't connect positively with at least one ancestor and the relief is tangible, especially for clients who have had abusive experiences, or experiences of neglect, or both, from their parents. It is a well-documented fact that a relationship with one non-abusive significant adult, such as a grandparent, in an abuse survivor's childhood has a positive impact. Something similar applies to distant ancestral connections.

This reminds me of a TV programme I watched a few weeks ago. The programme was about young, long-term unemployed people who had grown up in households with unemployed parents and who had themselves lost all aspirations and confidence and had stopped looking for work. As well as helping those young people to gain the necessary communication skills, strengthening their motivation and assisting them in applying for work, the programme researchers found for each young person one ancestor who had achieved something in their working life. They then introduced the youngster to the record they had found and offered them a work-experience placement that resembled the line of work of that specific ancestor. The result was astonishing and telling: all the young people were excited that there was somebody they could use as a role model and proud that there was someone in their line who had passed on 'those genes' to them.

I use either a journey or a timeline, as described above, to find and connect with an ancestor who has qualities the client likes, admires and can use as a positive role model. I ask clients to use the following intent: 'I want to meet an ancestor who lived a life worth living, a life that was satisfying, had a worthwhile purpose and left the ancestor feeling content when he or she died.' I tell clients that they can go as far back as it takes. It is my experience that many have to go back quite some time, mostly way beyond the Middle Ages, to find somebody, and that those ancestors are often admired for their 'wholesomeness', 'their honest work', their connectedness to the land and their care for their families and for their courage in standing up for what they believed in. Female ancestors are often admired also for the qualities that made them strong, independent and learned women in the sense that they could plant, heal, write, read and bring up children and were able to take their place as respected, equal members of a community.

Once the client has found this special ancestor I advise them to have a chat, to make a connection and to bring the qualities of that ancestor back into the 'here and now' as – and I stress this – those qualities are theirs by right as they form part of their genetic make up.

The finding of such an ancestor is often an emotional affair, with tears that stem from gratefulness and also relief. With an individual client, I will suggest that they contact this ancestor whenever they feel the need. Usually I also advise them to craft something that symbolizes this ancestor and their qualities and to bring it with them to the next session. I will then work with the piece and also encourage them to put it on the altar so that the ancestors who have positive associations for the client are represented and present.

CASE EXAMPLE: A QUESTION OF IDENTITY AND A HELPFUL ANCESTOR

A fairly drastic example is that of Sarah. Sarah was a homeless young adult with a past of neglect within a violent family. She had spent 11 years of her life in care and foster care and was, when I met her, generally lost, drifting in and out of hostels. Sarah was on the whole uncommunicative, quite violent when triggered and extremely dissociated; in particular, de-realization and de-personalization were the norm, rather than the exception. Sarah was, at that point, heading for an early departure from this life. She self-harmed at times and preferred living rough as she couldn't stand being enclosed within a room or building. She was convinced that nothing, absolutely nothing, about her was positive. We all know that those belief systems can be changed in therapeutic work that is often rather painfully slow, but Sarah was convinced that her 'badness' was inherited and that there was nothing one could do: 'All the people in my family are nasty and so am I.'

She was part of a group run by Mind and also saw a counsellor, her sessions being financed by a charity. I had the chance to observe Sarah in action in the group and I also knew her counsellor, who had participated in some shamanic workshops I facilitated. When asked at one point, I suggested to her counsellor that perhaps, at an appropriate stage in the counselling process, it might be a good idea to lead her back to find some 'sound and positive ancestors' she could connect to. About five months into counselling, the counsellor did just that and the breakthrough was incredible.

Sarah connected with a strong, capable woman, living on the land, bringing up her children. Although struggling to provide, this woman was a loving mother and, above all, she could read and she wrote beautiful poems. Sarah, like so many people who had to learn to dissociate early on, had the ability to access deeply altered, but also very creative, states. And whilst the counsellor rightly tried to re-associate her, keeping her 'in the here and now' as much as possible, during this session, her ability to vividly imagine really came to the fore. She had no doubt that this ancestor existed and, most importantly, she declared that her urge to write was based on more than the need to 'get stuff out of my system'. 'This woman can write beautifully and so can I.' The counsellor said to me that she had never heard such a clear-cut positive statement from Sarah up to that point.

'I can write beautifully' was the beginning of Sarah writing poems for a street magazine. Later she began to work as one of their sellers and stayed in a hostel until she got a room of her own in a shared house. This was not the end of therapy for Sarah nor was it the end of her problems, but it was the beginning of an identity for Sarah that included the word 'writer'. I can only imagine what this means for somebody whose identity had been based on internalized negatives and a past that was, in so many respects, horrendous.

There is much more one can attempt to do to bring ancestral energy beneficially into clients' lives, such as encouraging clients who have an altar at home, to find a piece which represents their ancestors and put it on the altar, to connect with ancestors regularly, to honour them ceremonially and so on. Nevertheless, within the framework of this book I can only give you ideas, hoping that you will find them beneficial.

ANCESTRAL WORK IN GROUPS

Whilst I rarely attempt ancestral healing within a group, as this needs specific attention being given to every participant and therefore demands a certain set-up, I often use the exercise to connect with a positive, admirable ancestor. This exercise lends itself to groups and produces a powerfully positive energy.

Again, either a shamanic journey with the intent of finding an ancestor or a timeline will be sufficient. I always ask group members to have their power animal and/or guide with them when they connect with an ancestor.

If I use a timeline in a group, I get all participants to stand close together in a small circle and then to begin to step back, whilst I drum. I instruct the men to find a male ancestor and the women to find a female one. If done in a circle, stepping literally back, I instruct the members of the group to stop stepping back when they have found what they are searching for. I also 'lead' the stepping back along the lines of 'Now step back into your grandfather's/grandmother's time...then take another step back visiting a great-grandparent...now step back 200 or 300 years...now step back maybe into the Middle Ages...now take another step back in time...' From then onwards I just say 'Step back further in time' until every member of the group is standing still. I might then give some time to writing down the characteristics of the ancestor and exploring how they can bring those qualities more into their own lives.

I will, if appropriate for the group, elaborate on the ancestral work, often creating an ancestral tree, a ceremonial technique I learned from Annie Spencer, one of the shamanic teachers I trained with. All you need for this exercise is a bunch of branches and some coloured wool or ribbons. We put the branches, which have been cut ceremonially beforehand, in the middle, form a sitting circle, and then take it in turns to 'tell the story of the ancestor' whilst weaving/binding a ribbon or piece of coloured wool around the branches. The telling of those ancestral stories is usually quite moving, connects the participants with each other and brings the positive ancestral spirits into the room, where they stay until the end of the group. We then burn the tree ceremonially at the end of the session, sending our gratitude and thanks to the ancestors and asking them to be with us, supporting us in our lives.

CARING FOR OUR DESCENDANTS

Another aspect of shamanic thinking, closely linked to the idea that we are embedded into a network of ancestors and descendants, is the duty we have to be caretakers of the earth and with it a duty to care for future generations. One of the ways to attempt incorporating this into therapeutic work is to journey to, or for, descendants. I only want to touch on this subject briefly, as it doesn't lend itself too well for integration into contemporary therapy.[1] In shamanically orientated groups, however, we sometimes include a journey to the descendants, with the intent: 'I am going to journey forward in time to meet one of my descendants and find out what I can do now to make their lives better.' It is not surprising that the majority of participants journey to a rather frightening place. Usually those places are sterile, barren and quite desperate. It seems to me that we all have developed an understanding that, if we continue our development in the current way, the generations that come after us will have little of the natural world left. It is also interesting to experience that most participants do not quite know what to do about this until they journey with the intent: 'What can I do now to make their lives better?' Every single participant I have ever come across found at least one concrete way in which they could contribute to a better life for their great-great-grandchildren or beyond: switching off the lights, cleansing energies around the house, getting involved in environmental work, writing about it to raise awareness, praying, doing regular ceremonies, representing the descendants on the altar and so on.

I usually instruct people to discuss what they want to do in pairs and to make a plan. If it's within the scope of the group, we often create either a group drawing or an object for our descendants, weaving good wishes into the drawing or object and keeping it positive throughout. Again, the crafted piece will stay in the room until the group finishes, when it is then burned ceremonially. Alternatively, if we have crafted individual pieces, the participants take them home.

The embedding of people within a network of past and future relations reminds us that we are not the beginning and the end, but part of lines and networks, which bring with them support and help from the past, but also a duty of care for the future. This expands our consciousness and reconnects us to something bigger and wider than ourselves, giving us more roots in the process, all badly needed in our disconnected, individualistic twenty-first century.

Note

1   It is appropriate when decisions have to be made that involve descendants, as in the case example 'Teresa's story of visiting her descendants' in Chapter 13.

13 MYTHS, STORIES AND TEACHING TALES

A concept closely connected to any spiritual/shamanic way of thinking and working is that of myths, stories and teaching tales. The need to create myths and tell stories is certainly as old as humankind, and has been used by all peoples of the world since ancient times to pass on knowledge and traditions, to instil morals, ethics and values, to make sense of individual and collective experiences and the functioning of the world as well as to teach about creation and life, love and relationships, the mystical and the sacred and the forces of the universe. There are countless indigenous stories that serve a therapeutic purpose, or could be adapted to serve it.[1]

Stories work their magic on different levels. They encourage us to reflect, they aid creativity, they train the imagination, they provide teaching and meaning without being directive and they connect with, and activate, parts of our brain that can work with archetypal material, which already exists within the individual and collective unconscious. Some of the most profound stories that influence us all, whether we are aware of it or not, or whether or not we pretend that we are immune to their influences, are creation stories and other stories that are based on our religious/spiritual cultures. The creation stories of a culture will influence the way the people within that culture define themselves, the way they see the world and behave within it. They are closely connected with the basic beliefs of a culture, forming the basis of a world-view that reaffirms and guides how people relate to both the spiritual and natural world, as well as to each other. For millennia Christian creation stories have shaped Christian views of humans, their place within creation and, this is vital, the worth of other species and the worth and self-worth of men and women.

For example, in Christian creation stories I am the 'crown of creation', made in the image of God. This implies that all other creatures are beneath me and it is therefore not surprising that I feel inclined to treat them as such. As a woman I am created out of a rib of another human being. This implies that I am not only second in the hierarchy but also worth less, because I have been created out of a part. If I am then later on described as a 'temptress', responsible for humanity's 'fall from grace and banning from paradise', it will be difficult to see myself as an equal. If our creator is furthermore 'male' and if our most divine figures are all male, God, the father and Jesus the son, and if the only widely accepted divine female is a virginal mother, it will take a long time to eradicate subconsciously held beliefs and attitudes towards the feminine. In contrast, if I emerge, as in some North American indigenous creation stories, from a previous world that is interpreted as the 'womb of mother earth' and helped into creation by a female midwife, such as the spider woman in Native American stories, then the feminine is inherently worth more.

What strikes most people when reading creation myths of a more indigenous, earthy kind, like the ones we find in Aboriginal or Native American cultures, is not that they are 'lovely'. Many of the stories are quite wild, with the birth of the world and of humanity being described as tough, complex and sometimes even brutal processes. What strikes us is the understanding that the earth and everything within it is 'alive', the equality and interconnection between the male and female forces at work in creation and the inclusion of animal spirits. Spiritual systems, practices and concepts that are based on nature by their very definition cannot give weight mainly to the masculine principle and define one living species as being superior to another. By being closely connected to the natural world, by understanding that human beings are not separate but an integral part of nature and by observing natural laws, it becomes obvious that every piece of creation needs the male and the female, the yin and the yang, the active and the passive, the seed and the womb, and many indigenous creation myths do reflect this.

Stories that are read to us in childhood, mainly the many fairy tales, will also profoundly influence us. They introduce us to archetypes, to the fair princess and the heroic prince, the good and the bad mother figure, the evil and the shadow in the form of dragons, monsters and 'bad people', which have to be overcome, and also to emotions such as envy, greed, fear, sadness, compassion and love. They help us to understand cycles of fear, and overcoming fear, and cycles of tension and release. Most importantly they present us with worlds beyond our ordinary reality, allow us to immerse ourselves into them and identify with the characters of the heroes. Immersing ourselves in such archetypal worlds, we can utilize those parts of the brain that understand the timeless concepts of the conflicting forces at work within humanity's soul and spirit. It is this understanding on levels beyond our conscious awareness that shapes our walk upon this earth. Contemporary children's fiction and films run on the same themes. The phenomenal success of the Harry Potter books and films, and before that the success of Philip Pullman's stories as well as the earlier success of J.R.R. Tolkien's *Lord of the Rings* series, shows us the great impact of stories that take the magical, archetypal realm into account.

Clarissa Pinkola Estes, the Jungian analyst and author of the successful and profound book *Women Who Run with the Wolves* (1992), talks about this process of identification every good story allows to happen. She stresses that to hear the story allows the listener to step out of themselves and slip into the hero's or heroine's personality, allowing them to have the adventures, slay the dragon and either win or lose. Estes calls this 'sympathetic magic'. It allows the mind to step away from the 'I' and to merge with another reality, dive into another level of consciousness, where the 'I' can learn and bring the learning back to a consensual reality.

A good example of this is the ancient story 'Sealskin, Soulskin' (Estes 1992, p.258). It is one of my favourites and I have never met a woman who could not, and did not, identify with the seal woman of this story on one level or another. The story is a tale consisting of many layers, but it is mainly about 'homecoming' to the self, about steps of initiation, about losing the soul and regaining it, and the price that has to be paid.

SEALSKIN, SOULSKIN

The story unfolds as a lonely man observes a group of very beautiful, naked young women on a rock. Their enchanting laughter and movements lift the loneliness of the man and, as though he was meant to, he steals one of the sealskins that lie on the rock. Later, when the women try to put on their sealskins, to dive back deep into the sea, where they lived as seals, one of the women misses her skin. The man steps forward and asks the woman to marry him. 'Oh, I cannot be your wife, for I am of the other, the ones who live temeqvanek, beneath' (Estes 1992, p.259). The man persuades her by promising her to return her skin after seven years of marriage, and that she would be free to go as she wishes. She becomes his wife and bears a son, a son she loves beyond all comprehension. She teaches the son about the world she comes from in the form of stories of whale and walrus, seal and salmon.

As time goes by her flesh begins to dry out and cracks, her hair falls out, she limps and grows thin and her eyes, once so very beautiful, become ever more dull. One day, after more than seven years, she demands her skin back. Her husband refuses, accusing her of planning to run away, which would make her a bad wife, and, even more despicable, a bad mother, and with that, he leaves the house.

The boy, who has been crying himself to sleep hearing the row, is woken up by a loud call of his name. He runs to the sea, just to see a big old seal's head disappearing into the sea, whilst he stumbles over a bundle. He lifts the bundle and his mother's 'soul passes through his skin' (Estes 1992, p.260). He takes the skin to his mother who puts it on. The child, who knows instinctively, cries and begs her not to leave him. The seal woman is torn: 'She wanted to, but something called her, something older than she, older than time' (Estes 1992, p.262).

So, in the end, she takes her child and she runs to the water and they both swim out, being greeted by the old seal, the boy's grandfather. They stay for seven days, during which the seal woman regains her power and beauty and then, as the child's time has not yet come and he needs to go back to the topside world, she and the old seal take him back ashore, and they both weep.

When placing the boy onto the stone she says 'I will always be with you. Only touch what I have touched...and I will breathe into your lungs a wind for singing of your songs' (Estes 1992, p.261) and, at last, the old seal and seal woman tear themselves away from the child.

And, so the story goes, he grows into a mighty drummer and singer and to this day he can be seen often kneeling on the rocks, talking to a female seal that comes to the shore. 'Though many have tried to hunt her, time after time, they have failed. She is known as Tanqigcaq, the bright one, the holy one, and it is said that though she be a seal, her eyes are capable of portraying those human looks, those wise and wild and loving looks' (Estes 1992, p.262).

This is a profoundly touching story of the dangers every woman faces, losing her true nature, her soul. This is also a story of the price one has to pay for losing the soul, and a story of the price one might have to pay to regain it. It teaches us about the steps we must take and it, in a way, laments the loss of guidance women face now. I can not agree more wholeheartedly with the words of Dr Estes, who observes: 'Because matrilineal lines of initiation – older women teaching younger women certain psychic facts and procedures of the wild feminine – have been fragmented and broken for so many women and over so many years, it is a blessing to have the archaeology of the fairy tale to learn from' (Estes 1992, p.264).

Besides teaching, passing on knowledge and being used for entertainment, ancient stories told and retold and enacted also help to process adverse events, especially those that threatened survival. We have lost this natural way of processing. The processing of frightening events is vital, for the individual well-being as well as the collective. Our ancestors were certainly confronted with situations that were very frightening, many of them life-threatening. We can get an idea of how these situations were processed when we look at ritualized story enactment in indigenous tribes, and it seems obvious that besides using them as teaching tales, the telling and re-enacting of such stories within the family, tribe and clan enabled the brain to process those materials cognitively and emotionally.

Let's assume that somebody was attacked by a wild animal, or that a tribe was subjected to an attack or a natural disaster. Their brains, just like ours, would have activated the fight or flight response – via activation of the hypothalamic–pituitary-adrenal (HPA) axis – through a string of complex neurological, chemical and physiological mechanisms. This autonomic response gets us physically ready to either run or fight. Mentally it shuts down to a greater or lesser degree responses that might disadvantage us, namely feelings like fear and anxiety and perception of physical pain, and it focuses our attention away from 'everything unnecessary for survival'. Or, in contemporary terms, it dissociates us as much as possible, creating a state of mind that gives us the best chance of survival. To survive as a species in the early times of mankind, we had to develop a brain capable of producing this appropriate physical and mental state within split seconds of perceiving a threat.

Once a particular threatening incident has been survived, the brain returns to 'normal' and we enter a state that psychologists call the 'acute stress reaction'. During this time the full impact of the event is being experienced: we feel the feelings, the memory of the incidence seems to haunt us, we might have nightmares about it, we might have physical anxiety responses in the form of shaking, heart racing, nausea, we might feel dazed or very tired or have all of the above symptoms. Whatever happens, our brains obviously want us to work through the incident, to process it. When we are given the time and means to process we are enabled to look at the event, reflect, let go of the distressing emotions, learn what we need to learn, put the event into context and come to terms with it and, with that, we move on. In other words, the processing of such frightening events takes place cognitively through thinking about them, talking about them to other people, and by letting our feelings, in the form of sadness, anxiety, anger or grief, surface and express themselves. If we are allowed to do that and are supported in that process, we will arrive at a point of acceptance, with a memory that is contextualized, stored away within a context, whilst we have learned what we needed to learn, a learning that is accessible for future reference. This form of acceptance still gives the event the weight it deserves, but doesn't force us any longer to act and react out of a conditioned fight or flight, or out of a feeling that relates to a past event rather than to what is happening at present.

Unfortunately, today, when left to our own devices, we often avoid processing, as this can be painful, using mechanisms that prevent processing, and instead numb us down or distract us, such as using alcohol or drugs or a focus on other things, such as work.

In indigenous traditions, even if expression of direct emotions might not be obvious, the telling and re-enacting of such stories is encouraged. The practice is taken seriously and given the weight it deserves. Whole groups enact stories of hunting, of danger, of attacks and of frightening experiences. They are always resolved, as they should be. But it is not only the telling, it is also the re-enactment that processes the bodily memories and brings them to a positive conclusion.

STORIES IN THE CONSULTING ROOM

Besides using traditional myths and stories, spontaneously crafted stories are also used as a shamanic tool. Shamanic practitioners tell stories with the intent to aid healing and to restore balance and harmony by calling in essences and energies such as animal spirits, plant spirits, ancestors and guides via the story. Another way to work with stories, which some contemporary shamanic practitioners use, is to enable clients and group participants to create their own stories and myths. This way of working with stories can be transferred into the consulting room and interspersed in the therapeutic process and will therefore be the focus here.

I was introduced to working with stories during training with Sandra Ingerman, but have observed other practitioners and teachers, such as Victor Sanchez, a Huichol shamanic practitioner from Mexico, and Annie Spencer, a British ceremonialist, working in various ways with stories. Especially when talking about creation myths and stories of a more mystical kind we realize how unimaginatively narrow the stories we tell ourselves are, how much they narrow and restrict our sense of self, our sense of where we come from and what we are here for. My first experience of exploring the story of my own creation certainly made me realize not only that the negative stories we keep telling ourselves keep us stuck, make us repeat patterns and influence our very way of being and reacting in the world in a non-beneficial way, but also how narrow and limiting the stories we tell ourselves are. Our stories, which have either been told to us or, alternatively, have been told to us by ourselves, are based on our experiences and memories. No matter which way we acquired them, they are stories, based on aspects of a narrow reality, which we believe to be 'absolutely true'. Once we are enabled to enlarge the context of our stories, our world widens and becomes enriched.

CREATION STORIES

Creation stories within much western culture are either based on Christian teachings or, if we talk about ourselves, they are kept within the boundaries of our family, our conception within the relational structure of our parents and our own upbringing. Once we widen the field in which we are embedded, our perspective and our idea of who we are and what we are here for can change profoundly and usually beneficially.

CASE EXAMPLE: PETER'S CREATION STORY

I want to give you an example. We know that, for instance, early abandonment will almost certainly lead to a degree of attachment problems, low self-esteem and issues around trust and belonging, which later on will have, for instance, effects on their way of relating as adults. I worked with a client whose mother left the family when he was six months old. Several reasons led to his father being granted custody and his mother to leave the UK, breaking all contact. Besides this early abandonment, my client's childhood experiences seemed positive. The father remarried soon afterwards and the new mother, the only one my client consciously remembered, seemed to have replaced his birth mother in a very positive way. My client felt much loved and cared for and he had a strong bond to the woman he called 'Mom'. His father and stepmother had no further children and he was adored by both of them, with his father, a medical practitioner, spending a considerable amount of his spare time with him, doing 'boy's things' like riding bicycles, teaching him tennis, taking him camping and so on. He always saw his stepmother as his mother until they told him at the age of seven, when his father thought that he was old enough to be told.

Peter, who was 26 when he consulted me, had studied chemistry and worked as a researcher, but in his heart he was an artist; his passion and love was to paint. His presenting problem was a curious inability to come to a decision that, according to his own words, would determine the life path he would follow. He felt that he would like to quit chemistry and work as an artist, but had put the decision off for years. He felt an increasing pressure to make a decision because he was keeping himself in limbo, not taking his career in chemistry seriously. He still hadn't started work on his PhD, which was a necessary step to further his career. Nor had he enough time to paint. He also felt more and more unhappy in his research job. He wanted to come to a decision without discussing this with his girlfriend or his parents, as he always ended up more confused after such talks because each of them had their own agendas. It seemed that his mother supported him in his longing to paint and that his father and his girlfriend, in rather indirect ways, conveyed the message that they would prefer him to work on his career in chemistry. He made it quite clear that neither financial nor security considerations held him in his current job. He was, first, convinced that he could make a living as an artist and, second, he told me that he had savings as his grandparents had left him a considerable sum of money.

I didn't want to touch on any early abandonment issues, but had a strong inkling that somehow, somewhere, this paralysing tension he had created in his life by not following his love for art had to do with his birth mother and his father. I asked him therefore to tell me a bit about his mother and, to my surprise, he immediately said: 'Well, she was an artist, a photographer, didn't I mention this? My father said that she was emotionally very fragile, diagnosed with bipolar disorder and later on she had a "break-down". That's why he had custody of me and that's why we never saw her again.'

We looked at the fears surrounding 'art' and it turned out that there was a part of Peter that wanted to protect the father from having to 'deal with yet another artist' and a part that wanted to 'please the father' and a part that was afraid of 'triggering emotional turmoil inside myself when I focus solely on painting'. Another part, that wasn't clear cut at all, pointed in the direction that Peter might be afraid of being confronted with his emotions surrounding the subject 'birth mother' if he followed professionally in her footsteps.

Before addressing such issues on a deeper level, which I had the impression Peter wasn't ready to do, I asked him if he would be willing to try something 'a bit unusual' and suggested a 'learn about my creation and my task journey' process. Peter agreed without hesitation. Most clients expect to stay within the earthly realm and most of them will be surprised by the fact that the earthly realm plays a minor role in their story. Peter proved to be no exception.

Peter's journey

Peter went straight into the upper world. He journeyed past clouds and went through layers upon layers until he arrived way out in a galaxy that was still creating itself. He observed stars and stardust clouds; he described wondrous creatures of a sublime, energy-like quality and shining of intense lights in different colours. Suddenly he stopped narrating. After a few minutes' silence I ask him gently if he would like to let me know where he is and what is happening. His facial expression changed to one of sheer joy. 'It's very beautiful here. I am waiting to be born. It's not my time yet, but I am sure, I will know when it's the right time.' A few more minutes passed and, as suddenly as he had stopped, Peter began to narrate the events to me again: 'I am being in a void. I am not solid. I am like a whirling mist. I am made of different colours. I am flying with immense speed in a void. I am almost non-existent, but I know I am going to get bigger and more solid. I am one of those light-creatures. I am colourful, made of colourful light,' and I can see the earth approaching. I feel more solid now. I am about to land. I am choosing the town of my birth. I am choosing where I want to land. I am being drawn to the home of my childhood. The house looks dark, like a shadow. I want to dance around in that house, making everything sparkle.'

At this point Peter opened his eyes. He looked disorientated. 'I am to create from the dark and the light. I am to fuse the dark and the light. That's my task.' He closed his eyes again.

I always ask clients to write the journey up in the form of a story and, if they are willing to do that, also to draw or paint it. Here is Peter's:

Peter's written story

> I come from far, far away. For a long time I lived between the stars in a vast space. I was quite tiny. I didn't consist of something solid, but was made of colourfully flowing, whirling rays that were held together by something invisible. I danced and whirled a lot, together with others, who were just like me. The place I lived in was a place of great freedom. One day I just knew that it was time to leave this place. The moment I knew, I felt as if I were surging downwards at great speed. I fell and flew and fell. At one point the earth approached. I still fell at great speed. Then I saw the house I would enter and the images stopped. I just saw the house, like taken as a still picture from above. Then I heard a voice, very clear, that said, 'Create from the light and the dark. Fuse it. This is your task.' I experienced great joy because I knew that the voice was not talking about chemistry. It was talking about art. I had confirmation that I am meant to be an artist. I am here to paint the light and the dark. I am here to create from opposites – to fuse them.

Peter's creation story is, so he told me when he saw my practice partner for a session of smoking cessation, about two years later, his most cherished painting. It hangs on a wall in the house that, with a large studio attached, is now his home. He has become quite successful over the years. I am still following his progress as a painter and sometimes I see one of his exhibitions. We saw each other another four times in all. I can't judge if this second session provided the complete 'breakthrough' or if the therapeutic process helped Peter to finally make one of his most important decisions, namely to quit his job and to be the artist he was meant to be. I do know though that the creation journey put his early life into a much wider perspective and that the process of 'fusing the light and the dark' is ongoing in his painting.

ARCHETYPAL STORIES

Using an archetype as the main character of a story provides us with rich material that is already present in the client's memory on a deeper level. I generally use an archetype in the title if I give the writing of a story as homework, which I personally like to do because it helps the client to safely address certain issues without having to be direct. Tanya's story provides a good example of how fruitful this approach can be, especially with younger clients or with clients that like writing.

CASE EXAMPLE: TANYA'S 'PRINCESS' STORY

Tanya was referred to me by her GP. A previously lively, intelligent and creative A-level student in her final year, Tanya had turned over the period of a few months into a person who was diagnosed with depression and insisted on leaving school. The change in Tanya seemed to have developed after meeting her father, whom she only saw sporadically, on occasions such as birthdays or at Christmas. Tanya's parents had divorced when she was 11 years of age. The divorce was fairly traumatic as it was partly based on the father's criminal activities, which had caused massive strain in the family over a period of time. Tanya carried much. She carried the anger and frustrations of her mother, the betrayal she had felt when it turned out that the father, who was her playmate during childhood, was 'a bad man', as well as her own anger and grief. Above all she carried lots of confusion, her 'love/hate' relationship with both parents as well as her outward appearance being just some of the indicators. When I saw Tanya I was taken aback at how dissociated she seemed. Her face was a mask; her voice was monotone and her answers monosyllables of emotion-free content.

When I asked her in the second session to close her eyes and to find an image that would represent the way she felt, she produced one that could have come out of a psychology 'textbook'. She saw herself in a bubble, with a storm raging outside it. The bubble couldn't be entered. When I asked if she had the power to come out, she was adamant that she could, but that she chose not to as she certainly didn't want to step into the storm. In my mind it was clear that Tanya needed to be re-associated with her feelings and that this might be painful for her. The symbolic storm, as well as the safe, non-penetrable bubble and her certainly traumatic experiences during her parents' final years of marriage, left little doubt that she could be flooded, which I didn't want to risk.

Taking Tanya's young age and other indicators into account I felt that I had to 'catch her imagination', give her some insight and begin to re-associate her.

I suggested that she write a story entitled 'The princess in the bubble' as homework. Tanya returned the next week, handing me a notebook. She seemed relatively pleased with herself and I asked her if she wanted to read it to me or if she would like me to read it. To my surprise, Tanya answered: 'I can read it to you.'

Tanya's written story of the little princess

Once upon a time there was a little princess. She thought that she was a pretty and lucky princess. She lived in a pretty house with many toys and dolls and a garden and a dog. The Queen and the King were very old, but they went for walks with the princess and they played often with her. One day the little princess woke up and she heard loud voices. It was the Queen and the King arguing. The little princess was afraid and was hiding under her blanket. From then onwards the little princess woke up repeatedly, hearing them shout, but she always hid under the blanket and in the morning everything was over, as if it hadn't happened at all. One day the King said to the little princess that he would move out for a while. The little princess didn't understand this, but after a few months the King came back, and everything was OK, except that now the King and Queen also argued during the day. One day the shouting got so bad that the princess couldn't pretend any longer that she hadn't heard them. After all she was now a big girl. When she heard loud voices again, she went down the stairs, found her mother crying and her father disappearing into the garden.

She tried to hug the Queen but the Queen just pushed her away: 'if it weren't for you, I would have left him long ago,' the Queen shouted at her. The little princess didn't know what to say, so she quickly created a bubble and disappeared. She turned very ugly in the bubble and she felt very lonely, but also very safe. From then onwards, whenever the King and the Queen rowed she disappeared into the bubble. Then, later, she also took the bubble to school, just in case.

After a while the King moved out. The little princess came out of the bubble sometimes, but the Queen talked all the time about how bad the King was and how angry she was that she had wasted many years with him and that all that had gone wrong with the princess was the King's fault. So the little princess was very sad and very angry herself, because it was her fault that the Queen had spent many wasted years. So whenever the little princess came out of the bubble, she tried to be very nice to the Queen. She didn't want to see the King, because he was bad, so she only saw him when it was really important, like on his birthday. But then, whenever she needed to she could run back into the bubble, which she did often, especially when the mother talked about the bad King.

As time went on the princess grew up and the Queen found another King and everything seemed OK, except that the princess had no explanation why she felt so angry with herself and why she didn't like herself. Sometimes she wanted to cut herself into little pieces, but she never did because she learned how to carve and she learned that boys liked her, no matter if she was angry or not, which felt nice.

Now the little princess is back in the bubble. She went back into the bubble because the Queen wouldn't stop talking about the bad King after the princess saw him for his birthday. It's better in the bubble because the princess can't hear anything when she is in the bubble.

By then Tanya had tears in her eyes and so had I, understanding that she had just told me in a nutshell about the hurt and anger she felt, and the unjust responsibility that had been placed upon her. We spent four sessions after that, working mainly around her issues with her mother. Tanya cried a lot during that time and got suitably angry, always feeling guilty when she did so. We introduced an old wise person during a visualization, who could help Tanya along with advice, and after six sessions in which a lot of anger towards both parents and despair had been addressed, Tanya returned to her studies. The rest was a matter of time and patience.

Stories, especially those that include an archetype, work on many levels. The dissociation helps clients to express without immediately judging themselves, and without trying to write 'perfectly'. It puts things into a bigger perspective and lets them access material that would otherwise not easily come to the surface. In Tanya's case the 'bad father' was only one of the issues and that the 'emotionally vulnerable, but also angry, transferring mother' was what overwhelmed her in the end, prompting the creation of the bubble. It was this insight which moved our work fairly quickly in the right direction. Tanya had always blamed her father for everything, protecting her mother and herself.

FUTURE STORIES

Another way of creating stories, inspired by my shamanic experiences, is to encourage clients to travel into the future. As discussed, in shamanism attention is paid to how our actions will influence future generations, and I find it therapeutically beneficial to utilize this way of thinking with clients. I will install a light trance, or start from the power place, knowing that the visualization will deepen the state as the process moves along. Before we go into the future I will do either a journey or a simple visualization to establish a spirit guide, as such a figure can be very helpful when journeying into the future. The intent for the future story can be along the lines: 'I am journeying to find out about what happened to [*insert appropriately*] in the future and I am asking my guide to help me with that.' I then instruct the client to journey 'up' and to let the journey unfold. Here is Teresa's journey and story.

CASE EXAMPLE: TERESA'S STORY OF VISITING HER DESCENDANTS

Teresa was a very attractive lady in her late thirties. She held a title by marriage, lived on a large country estate, had two children and employed more staff than she could remember. She worked for two days in London in a gallery as a fine art dealer. She made it quite clear that she didn't need to work as the estate of her husband provided more than enough for her lifestyle, but that she chose to work because she 'got bored at home'. Her presenting problem was her sleep disorder and I had planned to just use hypnosis without going anywhere near any deeper issues. It transpired, whilst taking a case history, that Teresa was originally from South America, coming herself from a rather wealthy background. She had been to boarding school in the USA and then studied in the UK, where she met her future husband. When Teresa began to talk about her husband she began to sob, telling me that her problems had nothing to do with sleeping but that it was her marriage that was failing and that she wanted to go back home, or at least back to the USA. She seemed to hate everything about her life and about Britain, from the weather to the British way of being conservative and controlled, to her husband's circle of friends and especially her husband, whom she described as cold, arrogant and only interested in having more children.

All that occupied Teresa's mind centred around one question: 'Should I divorce my husband and return to the USA or home to my parents?' The magnitude of that decision was apparent to her, especially as she was worried that she might rarely see or even lose her children, who were both boarding in the UK, loved the estate and their father, and, in her words, would be fought for in court by her husband. Teresa cried many tears and we looked at the issue from many angles; she tried, encouraged by the sessions, to speak to her husband, but they ended up rowing without resolving anything. I suggested that they see a relationship counsellor but, unfortunately, her husband refused. It was during our fifth session that I introduced her to journeying. She absolutely loved it. Her South American soul seemed to resonate with guides and animal spirits and the magical world of archetypes. I decided to work with a future story, to see if there was something that could help Teresa to come to a decision. By now she was sleeping fairly well as she had our sessions to address her worries, but she was nowhere nearer to deciding and nothing was changing in her marriage. The opposite seemed to be the case; the more Teresa tried to address the issues with her husband, the more he was absent, spending time in London and, whenever she was in London, he spent time on the estate.

Future journeys have to be far enough in the future and also wide enough to have an effect. I asked Teresa to journey into the future landing somewhere in about one or two hundred years from now, where she could meet one of her descendants.

Teresa's journey into the future

Teresa flew a few times around the world, landing to her astonishment in Chile. She landed somewhere in the countryside on a big estate. The house looked very futuristic, like a massive glass dome, and so did the greenhouses that spanned many square miles. Teresa described the walk she took between the greenhouses, meeting an elderly man, whom she identified as her great-grandson. She had a rather emotional chat with him in which it transpired that he was one of the last farmers who grew 'normal' food. Most of the food, he told her, was now created artificially, as most of the land was not suitable for farming any longer. She also met two younger people, who were her great-great-grandchildren, whom she described as delightful. She went riding with them, seeing some rather devastated landscapes. The young people told her that their father had learned the secrets of this kind of farming from his forefathers who lived in England and moved to Chile only a generation ago.

The journey suddenly changed and Teresa was catapulted into the upper world where an old female guide was waiting. The guide pointed to an empty space and said to her: 'No matter how you decide, there are forces between heaven and earth that you cannot control. You have to base your decision on what is best for you and your children and you have to trust that all will be well.'

Teresa's written story of her journey

Once upon a time there were some big fruitful lands, where people sowed and reaped and there was plenty for everybody. But people were greedy and, for reasons that I cannot know, the lands were devastated and lay barren. Nevertheless there were some people who still knew how to grow vegetables and corn and they built giant greenhouses to do that. One of the people who knew how to do that was a farmer whose forefathers had lived on a vast estate in England. That farmer and his family, who are my descendants, still lived a life worth living, contributing to the keeping of an ancient knowledge, that of farming in greenhouses. I am very proud of my descendants. They touched my heart. I know that I have made the right decision.

One week later Teresa spoke to her husband. This time she told him how very unhappy she was in the marriage and that she wanted a separation and time to be alone. They decided to separate. Two weeks later Teresa moved into the couple's flat in London and began to train as the gallery's buyer with the prospect of being made responsible for the US market. Teresa still lives in London, whilst the children, when back from boarding school, divide their time between the estate and London. I saw Teresa four more times. We discussed questions along the lines of 'how to talk to the children' and other, more practical issues. It was by no means an easy time for all the people involved, but Teresa had made a decision that was right for her and her children.

THE SET-UP FOR WRITING STORIES

Generally, my preferred way to work with stories is via journeying, translating the journey into a story, or giving the construction of a story as homework. I am very precise about what the story will be about. If the story is to be based on a journey, the client and I formulate the intent for the journey together. I will ask the client to transform the journey into a story, in writing, and preferably also draw or paint or craft something that symbolizes the story.

If the story is not based on a journey but written at home between sessions, we agree on a title beforehand. If possible I make sure that the title includes an archetype or at least a strong value and I always instruct the client to take a few deep breaths, put him or herself into a light trance state and to state his or her intent – for example, 'I am going to write the story of the little princess in the bubble' – a few times before beginning to write. I advise writing the story in the third person and letting the story flow, rather than trying to create something 'perfect'. I leave it up to the client how much of the story they want to read to me in the next session, but I do tell them that it would be beneficial if they could share the story with me. I also advise clients to use their imagination in the form of visualizing, rather than just focusing on words, thoughts and sentences.

Another way of creating a story is to use the power animal, if the client has already connected with it. Titles such as 'Wolves hunt in packs' or 'When the mouse had enough' or 'Of bears and birds in cages' or 'The wisdom of owl' seem to work very well. I assume that such titles remind the brain of fairy stories, activating the creative forces we all had available to us during our childhood years, and lend themselves for a more 'instinctual' kind of writing.

Here are a few titles that come to mind, which I have used over time: 'When the prince decided to fight the dragon'; 'The little prince and the step-mother'; 'Sky dreams and earth realities'; 'The day Red Riding Hood met the wolf'; 'Of flowing water and breaking dams'; 'Of fire and water'; 'Angels and broom sticks'; 'Sisyphus is tired'; 'The freedom wheels'; 'The hero goes on a journey'; 'Eve in her element'; 'When princes turn into frogs'; 'The fire in my soul'; 'The little tree that touched the heavens'; 'Stirring the cauldron'.

The title of the story is important as it has to reflect in an artfully vague, but meaningful, way the issue you want the client to explore. The vagueness gives the client's creativity a wider field to express itself whilst the reference to the issue has to be meaningful. The title 'Sisyphus is tired', for instance, leaves the field of exploration wide open. The client can describe how Sisyphus feels when he is tired, why he is tired, what he does when he is tired, who he blames for being tired, whether he is fed up being tired or if there is help for Sisyphus and so on and so forth.

It is vital never to react negatively or be critical about the story that is written. In fact, this is not difficult. All the stories I have heard over the years are amazing, even those of only a few lines long. I will end this chapter with such a brief story, written by a student who had overcome his addiction:

THE LITTLE LAMB AND THE HIGH WALL

One day the lamb decided that taking the risk to jump over the wall was better than walking to the slaughterhouse. He wondered why it had taken him so long to understand that. He explained this to all his friends and asked each of them to come with him. His heart grew very heavy because they all said 'No, we don't know what's behind the wall and anyway, it's too high. You will never jump over that.' With much doubt in his mind and fear in his heart he tried to jump over the wall, alone. He failed miserably. The other lambs said 'You see, we told you so,' in a rather self-righteous way. The lamb tried and tried all day at different spots on the wall. At one point he arrived near the wooden gate and just as he wanted to jump again, he saw that the gate was open, just an inch, but nevertheless open. He gave it a push, walked through and never looked back. *The gate is open. You just have to find it.*

Note

1   Myths and stories are also part of numerous western therapeutic approaches such as Jungian analysis, psychosynthesis, psychodrama and drama therapy as well as NLP and Ericksonian hypnosis, to name but a few.

14 | THERAPEUTIC WORK WITH RITUAL AND CEREMONY

Ceremonial work is one of the most beautiful, profound and enchanting ways of connecting with the powers of the universe and with deeper levels of ourselves. Ceremony and rituals are used in all spiritual systems and form one of the cornerstones of shamanic work. Ceremonial and ritualistic work is traditionally used for healing, for rites of passage, for blessings, initiations, dedications and cleansing, for the shaman's flight, for giving something back to the earth, for expressing gratitude, for divination and for quests about meaning and purpose.

The words ritual and ceremony are often used interchangeably, although, strictly speaking, rituals follow a set pattern and are repeated over time, while ceremony, being less formal, allows us to be creative and spontaneous. The ceremonial work I will be focusing on here is based on a creative act, in the sense that we decide for what purpose we want to create a ceremony, and when and how the ceremony is performed. This way, ceremonies can be created with individual clients or with groups to suit therapeutic purposes.

Much has been written about rituals and ceremony and their wide-ranging effects. The symbolic elements used in rituals and ceremonies are charged with meaning, eliciting powerful psychological responses. As I have stated before, ceremonies can create whole brain responses, and these profound responses can, according to Ernest Rossi, who taught me much I know about Ericksonian hypnosis, reach as far as to modulate alternative gene expressions facilitating health, rehabilitation and healing, meaning that they can switch genes on or off (Rossi 2004).

Ceremony is a vehicle to make us aware of – and to integrate – aspects of our multi-dimensional selves, our conscious self and our unconscious patterns, with something deeper, which we can call our soul, as well as with something greater than ourselves, in shamanic terms, with 'spirit'. Ceremonial work helps us to create a bridge between our mind and soul, between the sacred and the mundane. In fact, it helps us to turn some of the ordinary into something sacred. Once we enter a ceremonial space, we are reminded that the line between our everyday world and the world of our soul, or even the divine, is fine and easily crossed. Malidoma Somé, one of the African shamans I have worked with, echoes this by defining the purpose of ritual as a way 'to create harmony between the human world and the world of the gods, ancestors and nature' (Somé 1994, p.32). He also reminded me, in a workshop I attended, that 'beauty brings us closer to the sacred', and it is worth emphasizing that ceremonies should always be created in the most beautiful way possible.

Ceremony and ritual also function to contribute to harmony in the intrapsychic and interpersonal human worlds through creating a whole-brain experience. In therapeutic terms, we could say that ceremony not only provides us with the means to enter an altered state and experience deeper levels of ourselves, but with an experience that our brain interprets and stores as being meaningful. Creating a ceremony or participating in one can therefore be transformational. It is our myths, stories, experiences and memories that shape how we see ourselves and the world around us and, especially, how we dream and build our future. In contemporary shamanic terms, every time we participate in a powerful ceremony, we create a drama that expresses ritually and symbolically our gratitude, or how things might change, or how we want things to be at their most healthy, harmonious and beautiful. Through it we create a memory of that experience; a memory that will not only affect our future, but can change our view of the world and ourselves. If, furthermore, we take the concept of collective consciousness seriously – namely that, as humans, we create and tune into a pool of all human ideas, dreams and activity – then we will understand the shamanic idea that, when we conduct a powerful and beautiful ceremony, we are feeding the dreams and experiences of beauty and harmony into the general pool for all to be touched by them.

Ceremonial work is moving. I have never encountered a client or a group participant who couldn't relate to it. Created and executed well, ceremony touches even the hardest sceptics, as it seems to reawaken something deep within us, almost as if we all carry positive ceremonial memories. I fell in love with ceremonial work when I started to get interested in shamanism, and to create a ceremony always gives me pleasure.

Generally speaking, in ceremony we enter into a symbolic enactment, and what we enact in a ceremonial way, as I have already said, has meaning for our inner world, our inner being. Sobonfu Somé (1999), a female African shaman from the Dagara tribe of Burkina Faso, whose name means 'keeper of the ritual', observes that when we create a ceremony we suspend the normal time and space continuum and enter into the present. Ceremonial work brings us into the present, as all that seems to matter is happening within the ceremony, as it brings all participants into a higher place of consciousness within themselves.

TRADITIONAL CEREMONIES AND RITUALS

There are many well-known indigenous ceremonies: the sweat lodge ceremony, the pow-wow, the fire ceremony, Navajo healing sand-painting ceremonies, Celtic ceremonies to honour the cycles of nature (such as solstice or full moon ceremonies), ancestral ceremonies, especially in Africa, and many more. Some of those traditional ceremonies are ritualized, in the sense that they are formal rites, representing traditions that have been practised repeatedly and over time in the same form, following a set pattern.

Before we look into how to create and structure a ceremony in a therapeutic setting, let's look at a few well-known shamanic ceremonies, to develop a feel for ceremonial work. Many traditional ceremonies are substantial, long-drawn-out affairs, such as the Gabonese healing and initiation ceremony, which I have described in Chapter 5, or the sweat lodge ceremony, which takes at least

12 hours, and the Vision Quest ceremonies, which can take a few days and nights. The ones described in this chapter are shorter and therefore elements of them can be adjusted to work in a consulting room.

The ritualized *ceremony for couples*, described by Somé (1999), is quite simple, but profound in its underlying wisdom. Somé relates how, in contrast to western understanding, two people who come together as a couple are defined within her culture as two spirits in a body. A union of two spirits should not be undertaken if there are any residues of resentment. Before they make love, couples are therefore required to 'speak their truth', clear resentments and finish unfinished business. A ritual is used to achieve this, the space is prepared and certain rites are performed. The couple sit back to back, and each of them takes it in turns to speak. They express what has annoyed them, what they disliked, what they resent in the other. Normally, the couple will do that 'in private', but if the resentments and misgivings are strong, the whole community will bear witness. Afterwards, the couple cleanse, leave the village and find a place in nature to make love.

The *fire ceremony* is probably the best-known ceremony of all and can be found in many indigenous cultures. I have participated in a traditional fire ceremony with Quechua shamans in the Andes in Ecuador, where I spent some time learning. This family of Yachaks, the Quechua word for Bird Shaman, is one of the powerful circles of indigenous shamans who live in South America, including in the Ecuadorian Andes and the Amazon. Their ceremony is created with three fires, representing and honouring the three mountains I have described earlier. Its purpose is to offer healing to the land, the community and Pachamama (the earth) as a whole. I have also participated in various fire ceremonies in North America and in Europe and, although each was slightly different, the ceremonies had some ingredients in common.

The first step is to create an offering. Each participant crafts an object, which can be as simple as a stick, decorated with yarn, or a letter, a drawing or a bundle. It is vital that the offering is constructed with focus and intent and in the right spirit. Then the wood is collected in a 'sacred manner'. This means that we understand that we take something from nature and use it for a sacred task, so we collect it with attention, focus and intent. In most traditions, thanks are given for whatever is taken from nature and we therefore give thanks for the wood. When the fire is lit, often in a specific way, spirits are called in, either by the ceremonial leader or by each participant, to create a sacred space. Often, sacred herbs or oils are put into the fire as offerings to the spirits of the four directions, or the elements, and to Great Spirit or Pachamama, or to all of them. Either chants or rattles or drums are used to connect with spirit.

After this, each participant puts into the fire an offering crafted to hold his or her intent, such as gratitude, giving something back to the earth or calling something in. Often the intent is spoken aloud whilst the offering burns. After giving the offering, the participant puts their hands through the fire, bringing the smoke first to the belly, then to the heart and then to the third eye. After each participant has completed the offering, the ceremony finishes by thanking the spirits, by more rattling and chanting or drumming.

The *Navajo healing ceremony* has been used and adapted to different needs over time. The basis is formed by a sand painting, similar to the mandalas created by Asian monks, which is created with the intent of achieving balance. The Navajo sand painting expresses perfect balance and therefore the healing ceremony is usually about balancing. Indigenous people have special chants and songs that call in spirits to help restore balance. I have experienced sand-painting ceremonies in different forms and they are also used to release. If created for release, a mandala is created. One can place items around the outer edge to 'catch spirits'. Then something, which can be a simple stick or an elaborate created object, is used to represent what needs to be 'let go'. One can 'blow the intent of letting go' into the object. The object is then, with intent, placed into the centre of the mandala to allow whatever needs letting go to be released into the earth. The release takes place by scattering everything back into the earth. Additionally, the object can be burned, which is again done ceremonially. It is important to hold the intent of 'releasing with love' in mind during the ceremony.

The *pow-wow* is another well-known ceremony. A circle is formed, spirit is called in and a talking stick is passed round. The person who holds the talking stick speaks, whilst everybody else listens, respectfully, with the heart. The talking stick is passed round for as long as it takes, until every person in the circle has spoken all the words he or she needed to speak.

The basic aspects of all *seasonal ceremonies* that mark the beginnings and endings of nature's seasons are rooted in shamanic traditions. For instance, the various winter solstice celebrations amongst the Siberians, the Saami in Lapland, the Altaic and others all focus on the shaman leaving his body and being guided to the Northern Star, via the Sacred Tree or the Pole of Ascension. The winter solstice ceremonies centre around moving from the dark night of the soul into the lighter days of spring, into revealing, growing and receiving the gift of blessing. The shaman flies to the Northern Star, carrying the burdens of the souls – the soul essence of each participant – with him and returns with a blessing for each of them. In more modern terms, the winter solstice is a time to let go of old grudges and negative feelings, unburden, forgive, give thanks to the blessings of the year left behind and call in the new, opening to the light of spring (Grigori 2010).

ADAPTING CEREMONIAL WORK WITHIN A THERAPEUTIC SETTING

In a contemporary therapeutic setting ceremony can be used to mark transitions, to resolve, celebrate, embody or let go of something or to call something in. You can use it to resolve an issue, celebrate an achievement, let go of something that doesn't serve you any longer in your life, or call something that you would like to manifest. Ceremony lends itself to speak or to hear the truth, to finish unfinished business, to give thanks, to send out wishes and prayers, to release or give away fear, anger or grief, or to call in something that we want to attract. No matter what the purpose of your ceremony may be, ceremonial work is transformational.

Ceremonies are fun to create, but unfortunately they lend themselves more to working with groups than with individuals and to a less time-restricted setting. Nevertheless, one can use them in one-to-one sessions, as they don't have to be elaborate and can involve any number of people. You can also advise clients to do ceremonial work at home, between sessions, to consolidate change, turning over time a ceremony created in the consulting room into a ritual for the client. There are three vital components to every ceremony: there must be a clearly defined and stated intent, spirit must be invited and a symbolic representation and/or enactment must take place.

I have created many ceremonies over the years and have used them with individual clients and with groups. With individual clients, I usually keep them brief and to the point. The one I use most with individual clients is an adaptation of the fire ceremony, usually in the last 20 to 30 minutes of the session. I also sometimes give ceremonial work as homework. The intent is usually determined by the outcome of the session, such as to let go of something or to call something in or integrate something.

Fire ceremony with individual clients

To create this, I use simple things, such as pieces of paper and colouring pens or small twigs and wool, which I keep in a box in my consulting room. I ask my client to use whatever she fancies to create something that symbolizes what she wants to let go or call in or integrate. This can be a small drawing, a twig decorated with some wool, or some writing on a piece of paper. I set a time limit for the task, as this focuses the mind, and the client is instructed to hold the intent during the whole process of crafting. We then build a circle, using stones (in my room, there's a bowl filled with hand-sized stones). The stones are chosen by the client and laid down by me. I might burn some incense, dim the lights and light some candles whilst my client crafts the item. Then my client is asked to sit with me inside the circle and to close her eyes whilst I call in spirit with the help of a rattle or a drum or, if the energy feels heavy, with the help of a singing bowl or Tibetan bell. If you don't like to use any of these, play some soft music in the background. I tell my client that she can call in spirit or spirit helpers silently, in whatever form she would like, according to her own belief system. After we have invited spirit, I ask my client to hold the object, to state her intent, to really feel what she wants to let go or call in or integrate, and then I instruct her to burn the object in a bowl with a candle, which has been placed in the circle beforehand. In winter, I often use the fireplace in my consulting room, having lit the fire beforehand. The client is encouraged to state the intent – for instance, 'I am letting go of [*insert appropriately*] with thanks, asking [*insert appropriately*] to help me' – a few times whilst she watches the object burn. If there is more than one issue to address within a ceremony, make sure you allow more time, asking the client to create something for each issue. When the object has burned – fast if it's a drawing or a letter and a bit more slowly if it has been made of another material – I ask my client to close her eyes again and to imagine that whatever she has just worked on is already happening. I give thanks to spirit again, encouraging the client to do the same, silently or aloud, if that feels right. We then put the stones back into the bowl and finish the session by thanking spirit.

Affirming and honouring aspects of ourselves

This ceremony will take a whole session and needs some preparation. You might be familiar with the 'wise woman or wise man' visualization, where clients are asked to imagine meeting a wise person and asking for their advice. In more shamanic-orientated work, we would set it up in a more ceremonial way, rather than involving only the visual.

This ceremony around the wheel is to meet and to honour four aspects of yourself: the magical spirit child in the East, the inner man or woman in the West, the wise adult in the North and the trusting, creative playful child in the South. The client is 'the witness' in the centre of the circle. I have used it when we were at a stage where a client needed to get to know and honour inner aspects of herself.

First, build up a circle, using bigger stones for the four directions, South, West, North and East. The space has to be large enough for the client to be able to sit in each direction, facing the centre. Call in spirit.

The first round: your client sits in the middle, facing each direction in turn, beginning with the East. Ask your client to imagine her 'inner spirit child' in the East, stressing that the spirit child can come in all shapes and forms, but that it is magical, spirited. Ask your client to describe whatever image comes to her. Take notes. Do the same for the other three directions, stressing that these are positive aspects, not influenced by life events.

The second round is the more powerful one. This time the client will sit in each specific direction, facing the centre. You can sit in the centre, being the witness. Ask your client to begin in the East, closing her eyes, taking a few deep breaths and then remembering the image. Now ask your client to begin to embody the magical child, feeling as if she were this magical, spirit child. Ask your client to nod her head when she has a sense of being the spirit child. Now ask your client to speak, starting 'I am [*insert appropriately*]'s spirit child… I am [*whatever comes out*]'. Encourage your client to speak freely, letting come what wants to come. Sometimes it is one sentence; sometimes clients speak for much longer. It is important not to ask for more, not to comment and especially not to judge, neither positively, nor negatively. When there is silence, ask the client to let the magical spirit child go and, in her own time, open her eyes, coming back to the circle.

Then proceed to the South, repeating the exercise until your client has completed the circle. When the client has completed the circle, and has embodied all four aspects, ask her to come back into the middle, close her eyes and silently reflect, honouring and giving thanks to her beautiful inner aspects.

It is important to give thanks to the spirits you have called in and also to clear the space together with your client after the ceremony. It is advisable not to discuss the ceremony and what happened afterwards so as not to intellectualize what should be left to work its way through the system, unless you feel that there is some integration work to be done. After a ceremony such as 'honouring the four aspects', it might be beneficial to give homework that refers back to the aspects and then, should this be the client's need, to discuss whatever needs talking about in the next session.

CEREMONIAL WORK WITH GROUPS

All traditional ceremonies described, including the ones I have outlined for use with individual clients, can be used with groups. The possibilities with groups are endless and, of course, the energy of the group will make the ceremony more powerful.

Tree ceremony

Another ceremony I have used in an adapted form, mainly with groups, is 'the tree'. This ceremony works beautifully inside or outside, if the group is larger than six people. I either collect big branches beforehand or send some group members out to collect them. I use a big container that is filled with sand. The branches (about 1 metre in length) should ideally be from trees. They need to be cut ceremonially – asking permission and giving thanks – or collected from the ground. The 'branch tree' is put in the middle of the room and I put a tray with different coloured wool and scissors, ready prepared for the ceremony, next to the 'branch tree'. The group forms a wide circle around the tree, sitting down if it's a big group or standing up if that feels better. I call in spirit, encouraging the group participants to do the same silently, with their eyes closed. We then chant or rattle or drum for a while, if that feels appropriate. Then each participant takes it in turns to walk around the inside of the circle – clockwise or anti-clockwise (it doesn't matter which, as long as every person walks in the same direction) – to build up an energy field. When they reach the tree, they cut a piece of wool and wind it around the branches, stating their intent out loud.

Let's say we create the ceremony to give thanks. In this case, each participant would take a piece of wool, wind it around and state 'I give thanks for my health, I give thanks for having a loving family, I give thanks for having a job I like and that sustains me, I give thanks for my children, I give thanks for having the means to participate in this workshop' and so on. People will give thanks until the piece of wool they have cut has been wound around the branches. Some of them will cut a long piece; others will cut a short piece. It is always right. In a big group, you will end up with a bunch of beautifully decorated branches, usually astonishingly harmonious in shape and colour. When all participants have finished, we thank spirit, and drum or rattle again. This time I take the level up, rattling faster and louder, until it subsides by itself. We thank spirit, put the tree onto a table in the room outside the circle and usually have a break, to break state. The branches will be either ceremonially burned or buried at the end of the workshop.

This ceremony can be used with any intent. I have used it to 'call in blessings', 'let something go', 'call something in', 'remember something with love', 'forgive someone', 'honour ancestors', 'tell my story' and many more. If conducted in a group, it is always moving. It opens participants' hearts, they get to know each other on a deeper level, it builds community and connects them on a level of soul.

CASE EXAMPLE: DEEP IMPACT OF A SIMPLE CEREMONY

I used the tree ceremony with a group of philosophy students from a university who had booked a weekend with me to experience shamanism. We used the ceremony to give thanks for all the good things in our lives. After a brief meditation to 'remember all the good things', we began the ceremony. One of the students, who seemed to be an outsider in this quite lively group of young people, cut a very short piece of wool, made a bow on one of the branches and said: 'I give thanks to my mother for smiling at me before she died.' Tears streamed down his face. You could literally feel the group holding their breath. I said, very quietly: 'Do you want to tell us more about this?' And he replied: 'All I remember about my mother is this smile. She died when I was four years old.' Needless to say, the whole group was visibly moved. I stepped into the circle and asked him quietly if there was anything we as a group could provide for him at this moment in time. He held out his arms to me. We hugged and the young people all started to move closer towards their fellow student, putting their arms around him and each other. As you might imagine, tears and joy mixed as I stepped back, leaving them to it.

I saw him for an individual session after the weekend and he followed my advice and worked with the student counsellor at his university for a few sessions. His life changed after this simple ceremony. He became more outgoing, more integrated in the company of his fellow students and, most amazingly, when I spoke to him a year or so later he was still in a relationship, which had started a few months after the workshop, with one of the girls from that particular group.

HOW TO STRUCTURE A BASIC CEREMONY

1. Find the intent with your client or with a group of people.

2. Decide how you want to create the ritual.

3. Define the space: I usually use stones to create a circle. The ceremony takes place inside the circle. Anything that is available can be used as long as it clearly defines/marks the space.

4. Call in spirit in a way that is comfortable for you and the people you are with. Do this aloud: for example, 'I am calling in spirit to bless the ceremony we are about to do and to help us with it.' (This is the simplest form, but of course you can elaborate – calling in ancestral spirits, the spirits of the four directions and also specific guides in the form of spirit guides and power animals.)

5. Transform the space into 'sacred space'. Cleanse it by walking around it with smudge or use sound in the form of a Tibetan bell, a singing bowl, a drum or rattle. Build a little altar. A simple cloth on the floor will do. Then put on the cloth a centrepiece that represents the intent of the ceremony…a candle, some flowers, a stone or whatever else feels appropriate. When you put it on the altar, speak the intent aloud. Then have every person place an object on the altar. They can say whatever they want to say while doing that. Last but not least, put something there to represent the spirits you want to be present. I generally use fire, water, earth and air as well as something that represents 'spirit in general'. What you use must relate to the intent, the people involved and the spirits you want present, and it is important to make it as 'beautiful' as you possibly can with the means you have available as beauty brings us closer to the sacred and the shrine is to become a seating place of the spirit (Somé 1994).

6. Call in spirit again. State your specific intent and ask for help to achieve the intent.

7. Do the ritual, involving everybody as much as possible. There are many, many ways besides the ones I have described above. Use your imagination.

8. When your ceremony is finished, do something to mark the end, for example drum, rattle, chant or meditate for a few minutes. Do whatever feels right and supports the people and the intent. Give thanks to the spirits you have called and to other helping energies.

9. Clear the space.

10. Walk away! It's done. Go back to normal reality.

15 | THE MEDICINE WHEEL AS A PSYCHO-SPIRITUAL AND THERAPEUTIC TOOL

Having already introduced the Medicine Wheel as a map in Chapter 6, I will focus here on the human wheel and how we can adapt it to working therapeutically with clients. The basic human wheel places the human psyche in the centre. It tells us about the cycle of life, how the stages are connected and evolve and how the different aspects of it are linked. It can be utilized as a vital tool to work towards personal growth, towards the development of every human aspect, and it is a tool for transformation. I will therefore describe the directions further and remind you briefly about the functions of the circle and the diagonals before outlining some of the applications in therapeutic practice.[1]

The primary lesson that the wheel teaches is about balance and that all aspects are connected. The centre of the wheel represents metaphorically many things, including the centre of the self, spiritual illumination and the gateway to ascension. When we start to bring ourselves into balance in all the aspects represented in the wheel, we will naturally move toward that centre. Rumi, the famous thirteenth-century Persian Sufi mystic, expresses this so very beautifully when he says: 'We come spinning out of nothingness, scattering stars…the stars form a circle, and in the center we dance.'

The human wheel connects the eight directions in a circle, which represents the feminine way, the holding and all encompassing. It also connects the directions via their diagonals, which represents the masculine way in the form of straight-line energies. Both, together with the centre, create 'the whole'. The human wheel also includes the light and shadow aspects of each direction, as we can only experience and name everything in the manifested realm through their opposites. Shamanism acknowledges the dark and embraces it because, without the polarity of both light and dark, there can be no life and no challenges, no illumination, no development, no change and no unfolding story. Evolution, theoretically at least, happens when we keep the dark at bay, reducing, transforming or transcending it, whilst increasing the light.

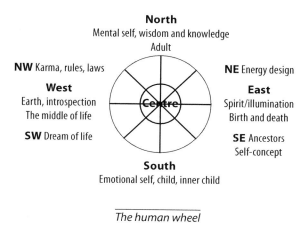

The human wheel

THE EAST

The East is where it all begins and ends and begins again. It is associated with illumination, with light, ascent, enlightenment, with the upper world and with spirit. It is where we seek higher vision, creativity and illumination. The East is also the place where we will reap the fruit of all we have worked on as we travel round the wheel of life. We will either reap illumination, or delusion and grief. We will be either 'in spirit' or be realizing that we have not lived the life we could have lived, that we have missed out, that we didn't make good choices.

Light: The power aspects of the East are prayer, stillness, meditation, creative acts and ecstatic and other spiritual practices that bring illumination. The East is also the place of the 'spirit child', an inner light aspect.

Dark: The negative aspects of the East are abuse and misuse of spiritual power and spiritual power and development that is not grounded. This especially applies to the 'energy' aspects of spiritual practice as energy is, in the final analysis, just energy and can lead to self-inflation as well as burn-out. To give it positive direction in the world, we need the compassion of the South, the grounding of the West and the wisdom of the North.

THE SOUTHEAST

The Southeast is the place of the ancestors and of our self-concept. It is the place that symbolizes our talents and gifts, the legacies we bring with us through our ancestors, our DNA, our cosmologies, our beliefs, mythologies and our early imprints. It encompasses all aspects of us at a given time.

Light: The power aspects of the Southeast are the questions we can ask to establish our authenticity: Who am I? Where did I come from? Why am I here? The light aspect is that we have the power of self-awareness, self-appreciation, self-acceptance and self-love.

Dark: The negative aspects of the Southeast come to the forefront when we resign to our negative self-concepts and keep seeking validation outside ourselves.

THE SOUTH

The South is the place of warmth as the sun reaches its highest point. It is the time of growth and is therefore the place where the growing child resides, with its beauty, innocence, playfulness and wonder, but also its wounding. The South is, in psychological terms, associated with the 'inner child'. It is the place where we encounter our emotional self; our emotional patterns in the form of fear, anger, hurt, pain, shame and some deeply held core-beliefs that stem from childhood.

Light: The positive aspect of the South is our capacity for trust and innocence, of childlike magical play. The authentic self-aspect of the South is our self-awareness and self-confidence, the belief in our own inner worth, the belief that we are unique, that we are worth being loved and that what we create has worth also. This aspect is supported by the positive affirming experiences of our past.

Dark: The negative aspects, the shadows of the South, are the debilitating childhood beliefs that we are not loveable and that we are worthless and powerless. We can find those in the stories we tell ourselves that support them. Here we place our addictions, our self-sabotaging behaviours and the debilitating emotions stemming mainly from the wounding of our childhood and early adolescence.

THE SOUTHWEST

The Southwest is the place of the dream. It is the place that symbolizes the underlying dream of the manifested life we create. The dream is usually based on our learning, our beliefs and on how we process our experiences.

Light: The power of the Southwest is our ability to create the life we want to create. This is supported positively by our empowering beliefs, by our ability to envisage a 'positive, contributing and fulfilling life path' and by our conscious effort to create that dream.

Dark: The negative aspect is created by our, mostly unconsciously, drifting through life, by walking on a path that we haven't consciously chosen and created, by living other people's dreams. Supporting the negative aspect of the Southwest are our disempowering beliefs, our self-doubts, our negative self-talk.

THE WEST

The West is the place of sunset, of dusk, of the transition from light to dark. The West is the end of the growing season. In human terms it is the end of growth if we avoid introspection. The transition place in the West is about shadow. It is not quite dark, but also not light. The West is the place of earth, of the physical, of manifestation. It is the underworld, the lower world, the world of caves and holes.[2] The West is where we introspect, where we look at the hidden, the dissociated and the repressed; that which the ego doesn't want to see as part of our self. It is the place of the wild soul, where the introspecting hero has to travel to self-discover and confront the demons so that she can connect with all of herself, diminish the powers of the dark forces and take responsibility. It is also the place of vision, of the dreaming.

Light: The powers of the West are introspective, facing our shadow and our own death, and being able to take responsibility. In the West we are called to shine the light of awareness on the world within, to introspect deeply, and thus get to see how we have manifested our outer world. The West is also the place of the 'inner spirit adult', a light aspect of the opposite sex.

Dark: The negative aspect of the West is giving into the fight of the 'ego' to avoid introspection, to avoid the shadow and to keep everything as it is. It is the rejection of taking full responsibility for our own growth and development and for the manifestation of our lives.

THE NORTHWEST

The Northwest is the place of rules, laws, Karma and justifications.

Light: The power of the Northwest is the acceptance of 'Karma' and learning from our life's lessons. When we take the power of the Northwest we begin to consciously create and design our own rules and laws, choosing those that empower us and help us to lead positive, creative lives.

Dark: The negative aspects of the Northwest are the laws and self-limiting rules we follow that are based on our unquestioned socio-cultural beliefs.

THE NORTH

The North is cold, dark, the place of night and of winter, where growing has stopped. It takes skill and endurance and knowledge to thrive in the North, and the North is therefore linked with competence, skill, knowledge and wisdom. In human terms the North is the place of the mental, the adult thinking self. Our thought processes, our beliefs and our philosophies are represented in the North. It is the place of the wise adult, the one that has healed the emotional issues in the South, learned through introspection in the West and has gained wisdom and intuitive knowing.

Light: The power of the North is our ability to 'stop the world', so that we can look at our thought processes as well as our philosophies and beliefs. Our ally in the North is this rather elusive quality of instinctual knowing, a knowing that is based on deep inner wisdom available to us when we are 'in the present', in alignment with spirit, when we have developed a knowing of how things are meant to be.

Dark: The negative aspect of the North is what we call 'knowledge' that is based on our unquestioned belief systems, theoretical constructs and ideas adopted via our culture and upbringing and the thought processes that reinforce them. It is 'knowledge' that is not grounded in wisdom and not based on deep inner knowing that comes from experience, work on growth and deeper intuition.

THE NORTHEAST

The Northeast is the place of the design and choreography of energy, our life's energy. It is what we focus on and how we use the energy we have available to us.

Light: The power of the Northeast is our capacity for choosing how to choreograph and design our lives from an energy point of view. Ideally, we choose from the highest place within us, which will lead to a life lived in harmony with our own and the world's highest good.

Dark: The negative aspects of the Northeast are our unconscious choices, which are based on our psycho-cultural conditioning and not on self-knowing through introspection, and are therefore not aligned with our soul's longing and our spirit.

The circle as a developmental map

I have described this map in detail in Chapter 6. Please refer back to it. Here is just a brief reminder: We start in the East, the immaterial, being born, a spirit in a body. Then we travel through the Southeast and South, and the beliefs we adopt, the abilities we develop and the thought and processing patterns we hold stem from that time, forming the 'mostly unconscious' basis of the Southwest, namely the dream we hold. We manifest and live the dream, our whole way of life, in the West we are asked to question and introspect. When we have done this, we begin to move towards the Northwest, changing the patterns we have held so far unconsciously into rules that support the life we want to lead. Only if we do that will we be able to become the 'wise adult' in the North, changing our design of energy in the Northeast to focusing on what really matters to us and, arriving in the East, reaping an inner state and an outer life that is in alignment with our soul's direction and spirit's desire to manifest itself to the highest potential through us. The work in each direction influences the other directions.

This developmental map can be applied to all things 'human'. Let us look, for instance, at a creative process. We start in the East with an idea. Then we travel through the South, where our emotional self begins to get involved. More often than not we begin to doubt that we can do what needs to be done. Many ideas stop right there. The dream (idea) is killed in the Southwest, never being developed, let alone manifested. We can overcome this by moving further, introspecting in the West, tackling our doubts by giving our insecurity and fears from the South a 'reality check', calming them down, and then we can change our unconsciously held rule in the Northwest from 'I can't do this' into a conscious 'I can and will do that'. Once the creative process has reached the North we have a realistic, but not 'cut-down', act of creativity. As we travel through the Northeast our energy design will be one of focus on the task; we plan, work and produce. With this we reach the East, where we reap the fruit – and then? Well, then there is a new idea being born and we repeat the journey. Over time our journey gets faster, less painful, more productive.

The diagonals as determining and balancing opposites

The following is just a brief reminder. Please refer to Chapter 6 for a more in-depth description of the diagonal forces. North and South is the personal axis of the wheel. The intelligent, thinking, skilful, leading adult needs the emotional, playful, delighted and wondrous child, and vice versa, to achieve balance. East and West is the spiritual axis of the wheel. Spiritual energy is aimless without grounding in the West. The laws and rules, the Karma, of the Northwest are determined by what we bring into the world via our genes, our culture and our early childhood experiences in the Southeast. Changes in each direction influence the other. In the Southwest and Northeast, our dream of life directly influences the design of energy and vice versa. If our 'dream' is disjointed and fragmented our energy design cannot be directed; if our energy is 'all over the place' we cannot manifest a 'proper dream'.

THE MEDICINE WHEEL IN A THERAPEUTIC SETTING

There are as many ways to work with the wheel as you can imagine. I have brought the wheel to your attention to introduce it as a map. It is a reminder that if we want to live a positive, authentic and contributing life, we need to address all aspects. The light and shadow aspects of each direction I have listed will, besides the examples below, hopefully give you ideas and insights into the kind of questions one can formulate in each direction whilst addressing specific issues. In shamanism we believe that we all carry the 'sacred hoop of life' within us. Therefore, if you call in spirit, have a clear and honourable intent, open your heart and ask your highest self for guidance you can trust your intuition when working with the wheel.

It is advisable to work with all the aspects of the wheel – here with four or eight directions as well as the centre aspects – when addressing any issue. Let me give a few examples: We can of course change one or two debilitating beliefs in the North, or thought processes that reinforce a certain problem, but the deep wounds of the South can still, when triggered, throw us into emotional turmoil.

The decision that we will strive to dream a 'proper dream', one that gives us pleasure and contributes positively to the world, will not lead to the manifestation of such a dream if we don't know how to create an energy design that supports it in the Northeast, or if we have internalized belief systems and self-concepts, unconscious and deeply buried, that will throw us into self-doubts, self-sabotage or make us stumble at the earliest hurdle. It is certainly of little value to have many ideas in the East without being able to manifest them in the West because our bodies are too weak to produce the energy to take the necessary steps in reality, mostly through hard work, to turn the idea into something concrete. To engage in spiritual practice in the East, hoping that this will automatically heal our emotional self in the South, is an illusion. Spiritual practice will help to put it all into a wider perspective and also help us to centre, to stay calm and to focus, but it will not automatically heal the emotional body. If we cannot focus in the Northwest we will not be able to manifest our dreams in the West. If we cannot temper our emotional selves with the wise thinking mind in the North, we will be at the mercy of our feelings. If we do not confront our shadow at a point in our lives, we will not only deprive ourselves of vital energy and of many facets of ourselves, but we will be surprised one day when it raises its destructive head in one of its many forms. Last but not least, without introspection in the West and without questioning the rules we follow, we are bound to succumb to society's pressures and 'easy ways' to lead lives we do not necessarily want to lead.

The list could be endless. The wheel gives us a practical tool to explore all the areas, no matter what kind of issue or question we address. It offers us a tool to get a snapshot of 'all of ourselves' at a given moment in time. It can show us where we need to pay attention, in which directions we hold contradictory forces, which directions need to work together and so on. The wheel gives us diagonals we can address, it provides us with helping attitudes and spirits in each direction, shows us the light aspects of the directions, which can help with the darker aspects, and much more.

The wheel addresses all aspects of the self, the conscious aspects of our ego, the hidden, more unconscious aspects and that which is based on 'soul and spirit', with the aim of integration to the highest possible extent at any given moment. Shamanic work, in contrast to widely practised psychotherapy, is about assisting people to create a life that is in tune with spirit and soul, without denying the 'I' and without denying the dark side of things. In that sense it has to be about the relationship between the ego and the spiritual also. Only a well-developed person, one who is stable and can be in the world, will be able to manifest in the world, without being, for example, influenced by the shadow or becoming emotionally fragile when encountering the first challenge. We all know countless examples of religious people who seem to have ignored their own dark side by projecting it on to some kind of 'evil or devil' outside themselves. The resulting atrocities, which have been committed by representatives of all churches, show how little the emotional and mental was influenced by their spiritual practices. We also know contemporary spiritual leaders of the New Age and other varieties who have, and still do, abuse their powers by using their status with their followers to gain sexual gratification, feed their self-esteem with the submission of their followers and enrich their wallet rather than their disciples. A spiritual person with a well-developed 'I' has a sense of self-worth, is aware of his or her own shortcomings, doesn't need to project dark desires, forces and prejudices on to others, introspects whenever necessary, knows that we are all equally on a journey, has passion and compassion and can function well in the world, without being of the world, without being attached to that which is of the surface. A spiritual person with a well-developed sense of 'I' has the ability to cultivate discernment, is humble because she knows that whatever she is given is not solely of her making, asks for advice from 'spirit', wrestles with her conscience, knows that power is seductive and that seekers can be vulnerable and strives to be generally aware and conscious, especially of the higher and sacred.

If we look at the wheel from this perspective in a developmental way we find that, from the Southeast to the West, the wheel is more about ego-development, especially within our contemporary societies. In more ancient systems we would have more spiritual input, especially through ancestral connections and general spiritual activities, at the latest through an initiation rite between puberty and adulthood, which would bring spirit to the forefront.

THERAPEUTIC WORK WITH FOUR DIRECTIONS

If you want to use the wheel it is beneficial to build one in a sacred/ceremonial way, together with the client, as described earlier, calling in the spirits of the four directions as well as 'spirits of above and below', 'Great Spirit' and spirit helpers before beginning the concrete work, with the client being in the centre of the wheel, preferably centred and in a light trance state. Make sure the client has called in his or her spirit helpers as well. If you do not want to attempt this, or if such a way of working is not possible in your practice, you can utilize the wheel in a way you would use a guided visualization, but make sure that you have 'spirit' present.

No matter which method you use, guide your client through the directions, stating the questions in each direction, and write down the answers your client receives. Let the client explore every direction on the wheel and note everything the client describes. Do not interrupt, interpret or get into discussions during the exercise.

Getting a snapshot

The following is a simple, but very effective, exercise with the aim of tuning into the four major aspects of the person, namely the emotional, child self (South), the mental, adult self (North), the physical/manifesting self (West) and the spiritual self (East).

Turn South: Which image represents the South? How do I feel in the South? What is my task right now in the South? Is there anything that needs healing/changing in the South?

Turn West: Which image represents the West? How do I feel in the West? What is my task right now in the West? Is there anything I need to change in the West?

Turn North: Which image represents the North for me? How do I feel in the North? What is my task right now in the North? Is there anything that needs changing in the North?

Turn East: Which image represents the East? How do I feel in the East? What is my task right now in the East? Is there anything that needs changing in the East?

Centre: Let it all go and centre. Experience the calmness of the centre. Whilst the wheel of life is turning, you can stay calmly in the centre.

Second round: how to work towards change

Depending on the answers the seeker received to the above question 'What needs to change?' it is a good idea to travel around the wheel a second time, to receive more concrete guidance. The question to ask in each direction is: 'How can I change what needs changing and what or who can help me with this task?' Note the answers for your client. Make sure the client comes back to the centre and stays there for a while, internalizing the experience that the wheel keeps moving, but we can come back to the centre, being and staying calm in it.

Now, depending on the answers received by the client, you can evaluate the outcomes of this process and work towards the necessary change.

Touching on deeper life questions: the dream

An interesting journey around the wheel is to touch on more existential questions. The following is a simple exercise, which works well when it is set up in the right way. I would only advise you to attempt it if your client is ready and if you can spend time setting up a wheel in a ceremonial way, call in spirit and lead the client into an altered state before instructing her to turn in each direction, asking the specific questions:

South: Who am I?

North: What is my true work?

West: What is my source of power? Where do I come from? How do I manifest?

East: What is my direction? Where am I going? For what service has spirit given birth to me?

Ask the client to get images as well as words, hunches and feelings in relation to the question. The overall picture will emerge.

CASE EXAMPLE: LETTING THE PICTURE EMERGE

A group participant, a mother with two young children, received the following answers to the questions:

SOUTH
She saw herself with her two children. They played happily, whilst she was watching, feeling tired and 'empty'.

- I am a mother.
- I am a woman.
- I am a confused person.
- I am a person who has much, but is searching for something.
- I am not stimulated enough.

NORTH
She saw herself dancing together with a group of women and children.

- I am a dancer of life.
- My work is to dance and teach people how to dance.
- I am a whirling dancer.
- My work is to help people to dance themselves alive.

WEST
The image was the phoenix, which she associated with:

- I am a spark.
- I rise from the ashes of fire.
- My power source is fire, movement, passion.

EAST
My direction is Joy.

- I am to spread joy by being more 'in joy'.
- I experience great joy when I dance.
- I experience joy when I hold my children.
- Joy is my teacher.

This simple journey around the wheel confirmed for Kathryn what she had already contemplated, namely to offer after-nursery dancing classes for three and four-year-olds. She had trained as a dancer before becoming a full-time mother, but couldn't envisage, for several reasons, returning to the highly competitive world of professional dancing. She opened the after-nursery dance club two months later together with a friend at her local nursery.

Connecting and balancing the 'inner beings'

One of the basic ways we can use the wheel concentrates on the union of the male and the female and the adult and the child within us. We all suffer, to a lesser or greater extent, from the so-called four 'shamanic shields of balance', the West/East and the North/South, being anything but in balance. Whilst western therapeutic practices are well equipped to work with the North/South axis of the wheel, the inner child and the inner adult, it rarely addresses the East/West axis, which represents, when we use the concept of shields, the inner opposite gender spirit child in the East and the inner opposite gender adult in the West. We achieve inner balance if we integrate all four.

To understand this concept and to work with it is beneficial for every client, but it is especially important for clients who struggle within their relationships. We, in this world and in this age, are completely brainwashed into seeking everything we feel is missing outside ourselves because we are, in aboriginal terms, all 'broken half people'. Nowhere does this become more apparent than in our search for the 'perfect partner'. Many of us have had the thought that we are in a relationship with the wrong person, or that we are married to the 'wrong person', and especially that our lives would be perfect if we could find our soul mate. In searching for this perfect person we go through relationship break-ups and marital divorces, produce immense heartache, leave children behind and start again and again or, alternatively, we stay within a relationship that keeps us dissatisfied, blaming the other person for everything that seems missing.

In shamanic views this kind of thinking doesn't touch the core issues, as wholeness can only be achieved by integrating aspects of ourselves, not by 'having the perfect relationship'. In accordance with the Medicine Wheel we have four cardinal inner shields in the directions of East, West, North and South. The North and South shields, which lie along the visible reality axis, are our current gender adult and child. The East and West shields, which are located on the spiritual axis, are the residence of our opposite gender child and adult. The centre point of the two axes, where they meet, holds the key to wholeness. To create wholeness, the East/West axis shields need to be explored, included, brought to life and connected to the North/South axis shields.

> The East shield is the inner spirit child of the opposite gender.
>
> The South shield is the child. It is normally of the same sex as the person.
>
> The West shield is the inner spirit adult of the opposite gender.
>
> The North shield is the adult of the same gender as the person.

The East and West, the spirit shields, teach the North and South shields to 'dance'. The West inner opposite sex adult is the archetypal opposite sex lover with all the qualities of the perfect mate. She or he will court the North, adding the spiritual dimension, the dimension of the intuitive mind. The East child of the opposite gender is the archetypal spirit child, the spirited, adventurous, enthusiastic playmate to the South that teaches the wounded South how to get back into the spirit-magical, the child-magical, and helps it to heal the past (Magdalena 2011a).

> By accessing, identifying, and giving 'life' to the wisdom of all of the internal shields, we become whole, balanced, integrated and functional beings. Universal truths are

gifted us as we consummate this inner marriage. It is said in shamanic terms that when North dances with West and South with East, wellness prevails. (Magdalena 2011b, p.1)

I like to journey for each of these inner parts and then use a ceremony around the wheel to integrate them with each other. These journeys can be done with the same intent, adjusted to the direction. In the West, for instance, we state the following intent: 'I am journeying to meet my inner spirit adult in the West.' Once the client has journeyed in all four directions, found an image for each and explored the figures, we can begin to work with them. The West adult needs to meet the North adult. Quite often, without saying anything beforehand to the client, this will happen of its own accord. They will often dance together. The South child needs to meet the East child. They need to play together. This, too, will also often happen spontaneously.

You can also use the wheel for more integration. Instruct the client to sit in the centre and imagine that each of the inner figures floats out of their direction into the centre and into the client's body. Another way to work with them is to craft something that represents all four aspects. You can also use a visualization with the client imagining that the opposite directions, South and East and West and North, work together or do something together, have a dialogue or just have fun together. You can treat them generally as you would treat ego-states. The West and East figures can also be used in future sessions to give advice, complementing the North and the South. But even if you do not carry out much work with those energies after the initial exploration, it is beneficial for every client to make contact with those energies, have images that represent them and get to know them.

THERAPEUTIC WORK WITH EIGHT DIRECTIONS

Working with eight directions is a bit more complex, but I want to give one example of how we can use the wheel to explore and change particular, rather debilitating behaviours. As already stated, once you have used the wheel a few times, it becomes easy to formulate questions in each direction that will serve the issue at hand.

Here I am using an example of a client who self-sabotaged in a rather indirect form. She found all kinds of rational arguments to 'give up' or concluded that the world around her seemed to work against whatever she tried to achieve.

When you work with eight directions it becomes even more vital that you write down whatever the client receives in every direction and that you remind them briefly what the directions stand for as well as the questions that might be asked. Encourage the client to 'listen' for answers in every direction with all senses, to see the image, to sense what is there, to hear words and get ideas and to pay attention to their feelings. Give it time and encourage your client 'to let things show themselves and come to mind'. Sometimes nothing comes to mind in one direction, or there are contradicting ideas and images. There is no right or wrong. This is an exploration and the overall picture will emerge.

CASE EXAMPLE: SELF-SABOTAGING BEHAVIOUR AND 'GIVING UP'

SOUTH: What did I learn about myself when I was a child? What have I been told about myself? What are the stories I keep telling myself when I 'give up' or when the world doesn't support me?

SOUTHWEST: How does 'giving up' influence my dream?

WEST: Which part that I don't like showing to anybody helps me to 'give up'? What stops me taking responsibility?

NORTHWEST: What are the rules and laws I follow when I begin to stop doing what I really want to do?

NORTH: What are my thoughts when I 'give up'? What do I believe to be true?

NORTHEAST: How do I use my energy? What do I do when I 'give up'?

EAST: How do my creative power and my spirit look and feel shortly before I stop?

SOUTHEAST: What is my self-image, my self-concept? How do I see myself?

Circling round

Now, go into the second round, without stopping and discussing the first exploration, staying in the Southeast and then moving on:

> SOUTHEAST: How would my self-concept feel, look and sound if I had achieved what I set out to achieve?
>
> SOUTH: What would I believe about myself?
>
> SOUTHWEST: How would my dream have changed?
>
> WEST: Which aspect of myself would I not need to hide? How would it feel to have taken responsibility?
>
> NORTHWEST: Which rule or law would I have had in place?
>
> NORTH: How would I think? What belief would be there to support me?
>
> NORTHEAST: How would I design and use my energy?
>
> EAST: How would I stay 'in spirit'? What would be different in the East?

Once we have obtained all the answers we can take the next step. Now we can begin to work with each direction if we choose to do that, or use the diagonals. We can create affirmations for each direction, find out what we need to let go or implement, we can dance the positive outcomes, we can embody the positives, we can create goals and design steps to achieve them, we can create ceremonies or use whatever we use within our therapeutic practice to achieve goals.

WHAT WE ARE WORKING TOWARDS

Generally, when working with the Medicine Wheel, it is beneficial to keep the overall aims, which relate to the different directions, in mind:

> *South:* We choose to reclaim our authentic self. We are born with trust, innocence, openness and willingness to learn, with the ability to try things, to experience, to be playful. We are born with a range of feeling states, which we want to reclaim without being at their mercy. We open up to life and love and stop avoiding because we fear pain.

Southwest: We set out to define our own dream. What we want life to be, what has meaning to us, what makes sense to us. And we begin to work, focused and consistently, setting achievable goals.

West: We take responsibility and begin to actualize our dreams. We take concrete, creative action moving our dream from the imagination into the grounded place of earth. We also take responsibility for our bodies. We introspect when needed instead of avoiding. The West is the body of the mother and the child is healing by passing through the body of the 'mother'.

Northwest: We begin to implement 'sacred laws', rather than seeing the laws of society and other people's wishes and needs as our guidelines. We look at the rules and laws and ask ourselves: do they serve me, my higher goals, my higher self and with that also 'all my relations', or do they hinder me?

North: We question our beliefs and ways of thinking, seeking to touch our innate sense of knowing more often, flow easier and become aware of coincidences and 'nudges from spirit', and try to be open to knowledge that comes our way. The North is the father and the child can heal through passing 'through the father'.

Northeast: We choose from a place of balance and harmony. We design our energy to act and create, instead of react and follow. We develop focus and co-operation and remember our dream in the Southwest.

East: We open our imagination to unlimited possibilities. We enter the 'realm of the magician'. We engage in spiritual practice, follow our bliss, ask for and receive spiritual vision and create lives that contribute purposefully and meaningfully to our own growth and the growth and balance of all humanity.

Southeast: We are grateful to the ones that came before us, we seek to develop a self-concept that affirms ourselves as worthy, loveable and unique co-creators of the human race, a role that is life affirming and joyful.

Centre: We will find that our whole self becomes more balanced, that the conflicts lessen, that we live increasingly from our spiritual (higher) self and walk a path that has heart. We find stillness in the centre, developing a deep knowing that whilst the wheel is turning we have a still centre that is eternal.

Notes

1 See also Chapter 6. The wheel can be utilized in many ways. The following can only be a brief introduction. I have already mentioned several books in Chapter 6. If you want to learn more about the Medicine Wheel and its applications in therapeutic practice please consult my website for forthcoming training courses for therapists on the subject.

2 In some cultures the totem animal of the West is the bear. The bear hibernates; she goes into the cave to give birth. The 'dream lodge' is also situated in the West. We retreat to 'dream', to be with spirit, away from the world so that we can bring forth our lives.

16 TRAVELLING HOME

Reconnecting with Nature

Nature is one of the best healing and teaching environments that still exists. It is available to all of us and free of charge. Our increasing disconnection from it creates many of the ills of our times, and research tells us that, if we can reconnect with it on a deeper level, it contributes vitally to the development of the positive facets of our psyche.

The most insightful teachings we receive from indigenous spiritual teachers are informed by their intimate knowledge of nature and their intense connection to it. Even if they dwell in villages surrounded by natural habitat, shamanic practitioners will spend time in nature, away from where they live, whenever they feel the need. They travel into nature to be alone, to heal, to revitalize and re-energize their powers, to reconnect with their initiation commitments, to converse with natural spirit allies and helpers, to be inspired and to generally fill themselves with the connection to 'All there is', with the sacred, so that they can come back to the job with more strength, power and balance.

Of course we cannot pretend that we can turn back the clock. Our densely populated world with its sprawling cities is a far cry from the wild and few of us have the privilege to live in natural environments whilst also earning a living. Nevertheless, if we want to balance and develop, or even survive as a species, it is essential that we change our relationship with nature, reconnect with it and redefine our place within it. We are now dissociated from nature to an extent that is, in my opinion, extremely harmful to our psyche and to our individual and collective development. Bill Plotkin, an eco-psychologist who has worked with people in wild nature for over 20 years, observes that 'healthy human development requires a constant balancing of the influences and demands of both nature and culture... By suppressing the nature dimension of human development...industrial growth society engenders an immature citizenry unable to imagine a life beyond consumerism and soul-suppressing jobs' (Plotkin 2008, p.6).

It is not easy to transfer the nature teachings, tools and techniques used by shamanic practitioners into a consulting room. However, it is vital that professionals understand how our separation from nature has greatly contributed to the disenchantment of our psyche, how profoundly the natural environment can nurture and balance us emotionally and mentally, give our bodies pleasure and enchant our souls, and that they encourage clients to reconnect with it. I will therefore briefly describe some research that supports these claims and incorporate some ideas about how to encourage clients to reconnect with nature.

People who are still embedded in – or in some form connected to – their indigenous traditions will experience being in a natural environment as being close to creation, the creator and the divine. Miriam Rose Ungunmerr-Baumann, an Aboriginal teacher and artist from Daly River, who received an honorary doctorate for her work, expresses this beautifully when she writes about the quality of being silent in nature:

> In our language this quality is called dadirri. It is inner, deep listening and quiet, still awareness. Dadirri recognizes the deep spring that is inside us. We call on it and it calls to us... When I experience dadirri, I am made whole again. I can sit on the riverbank or walk through the trees; even if someone close to me has passed away, I can find my peace in this silent awareness. My people today recognize and experience in this quietness the great Life-Giving spirit, the Father of us all. It is easy for me to experience God's presence. When I am out hunting, when I am in the bush, among the trees, on a hill or by a billabong; these are the times when I can simply be in God's presence. My people have been so aware of Nature. It is natural that we will feel close to the Creator. (Ungunmerr-Baumann 2007, p.1)

The reverence of indigenous people for the earth, the mother of all beings, is remarkable and can be observed in their daily lives. It is, in their belief system, the healthy connection to Mother Earth that keeps us alive, safe, healthy, strong and focused. For me, this is one of the contrasts with orthodox religious teachings, especially those with a focus on an afterlife somewhere 'out there'. They seem to have little understanding that 'God' can be directly experienced through 'his/her' creation. The Mamas, the shamanic teachers and custodians of Kogi cosmology, from northern Colombia, the only known indigenous tribe/people who have survived the Spanish conquest and have managed to keep themselves apart and preserve their own culture completely up to today, have been leaving their mountain repeatedly lately to warn about the catastrophic effects the destruction of the earth will have for mankind. The Kogi know that it is the earth that teaches us right from wrong, but that we have long stopped listening. Their teachings and their powers are profound; their insights and their knowledge about creation and its 'unseen' forces as well as their sustainable, spiritual ways of life are inspirational.[1]

Others, who are to a certain extent not connected to contemporary society, such as the Yachak shamanic family I learned from, still keep a strong connection to 'Pachamama', to Mother Earth, which influences their way of life profoundly and beautifully. They live at the foothills of three powerful volcanoes in Ecuador. The three mountains that surround them are directly connected to their work. The male mountain, Imbabura, who stands in the East, symbolizes the masculine. He is the leader and protector; he gives strength and power. The female mountain, Huarmeraso, the woman of snow, symbolizes the feminine. She stands in the West, opposite Imbabura, connected to him by marriage. She is the giver of birth, of the nurturing, the soft, intuitive and creative. Mojanda, a mountain range that borders the Valley of Dawn, represents the balance between the masculine and the feminine, the old and the young. In a sense, it represents the family: the father, mother, grandparents, male and female children.

All three mountains have to be climbed, explored and honoured often. Pilgrimages are made to them for Vision Quests and to collect sacred water and the plants and stones that are used during healing ceremonies. The mountains are known intimately and honoured regularly by the shamans as well as their families. Food for the spirits of the mountains is left, smoke is blown, and ceremonial work is done when climbing the mountains. The Yachaks use seven earth elements in their work: earth, fire, water, air, rocks, plants and birds, which represent all animal life on earth. All of these are represented with objects and plants from those mountains on the altar in their healing room. The spirit of each mountain is called in and asked for help before a healing ceremony is attempted. Their fire ceremonies in the village also honour the three mountains: three fires are lit, one for each. As the mountains are volcanoes, fire is the strongest element the Tamayos work with and fire, which is blown all over the body to cleanse the body, soul and spirit of the person, is part of their traditional healing ceremony. Don Esteban Tamayo is head of the family and keeper of the family's traditions. These have lasted over many generations and he is passing them on to his two sons, who work with him. Don Esteban had his most profound visions on one of those mountains. Outside their working hours the Yachaks I met still treat everything they resource from nature with respect, as they know that life itself and their abilities are directly bestowed on them by the natural forces that surround them.

I see three reasons for encouraging clients to 'get out and involve themselves in the natural environment'.

1. We need to regain some balance. We are immersed in artificial environments during most of our waking hours. We work in buildings, look at screens, are surrounded by artificial lights and have to cope with constant noises and sounds. We are overloaded with information and bombarded by images via the internet, emails, texts, phone apps, TVs, I-players and game stations – to name just a few. Whilst all of these might stimulate, indeed over-stimulate, certain parts of our brains, our bodies and senses are under-stimulated.

2. Maybe more importantly, the barriers we have erected between the natural world and ourselves keep us disconnected from the longings of our souls to be known by us. Ventures into the wild can help reveal the inner: that which is beyond what we access in daily life. Nature, if we sharpen our awareness, reflects back our most intense fears and also our highest joys. Being in wild nature reinstates a sense of the power, beauty and awesomeness of basic life forces, and a relationship that we cannot nurture within urban settings. It calms the mind, opens the senses and nourishes us on deep levels. I couldn't define it better than Allen Holmquist, who writes: 'Because being with nature inherently leads to connection with the deepest parts of our being where self knowledge, inner balance, and inherent healing abilities already exist, we become naturally more peaceful, wise, and healthy in our professional lives' (Holmquist 2007, p.344). In fact, I would postulate that wilderness resonates on the level of soul. Our soul is, after all, our inner wilderness, that intra-psychic land, of which most of us only experience glimpses until we have the courage to attempt the hero's journey.[2]

3. It is essential for our very survival that we begin to re-experience that we are part of the natural world and understand and respect her laws. Every breath we take, everything we eat, every drop of water we drink comes from nature. For the shaman, the quality of our relationship with nature reflects our consciousness, and our consciousness can be enhanced through striving for a loving and honouring relationship with nature, as we are made of the same elements as everything else and, most importantly, we depend on nature much more than she depends on us. The idea that we 'need to save the planet' might tell us more about our self-centredness than about the planet. It is, in my opinion, not the planet we need to save, but ourselves as a species. The earth will survive and heal. It has time to do that. We as a species might not.

Of course we know this instinctively, but we don't act upon it often enough. It is interesting that no client of mine ever visualized a busy shopping street or his workplace or his local pub or a club as a place of power or a place of sanctuary. In fact I would say that the vast majority of clients of all age groups visualize a place in nature when asked to find their special place, normally one containing the elements of water, earth, air and fire, in the form of the sun. Parks, a therapist and healer from the Association for the Advancement of Psychosynthesis, reflects that an astonishing quantity of nature symbolism in the form of animals, plants and minerals occur in healing and self-realization experiences. 'Perhaps Nature Herself is the universal healer. This of course has been an axiomatic truth of Shamanism for thousands of years' (Parks 1999, p.40).

RESEARCH INTO THE PSYCHO-SPIRITUAL BENEFITS OF BEING IN NATURE

But not only do we know instinctively that we are depriving our bodies and our psyche and fostering a disconnection that could be fatal to our survival, research into the benefits of nature also shows us increasingly that the more we deprive our children of it, the more we influence their development in ways that are neither beneficial for them individually, nor for society as a whole.

I listened recently to a programme on Radio 4 that discussed the fact that most young people between the ages of 14 and 24 do not find it 'cool' to be environmentally aware and are not willing to give up any of the comforts and entertainment that can be provided by electricity. The discussion centred on the question: why do the majority of young people not get involved in environmental issues and why has all the environmental education and raising of awareness not worked for the majority of the young generation? I found it astonishing that nobody seemed to recognize the level of disconnection we have reached within our society and that theoretical education lacks a vital ingredient, namely being properly connected via experience.

Connection to something cannot start with being asked to 'care for it'. It has to start with being given time and opportunity to be in a space, to use it and to have fun. A Natural England report from 2010, for example, reports on the benefits of wild nature on children's and teenagers' emotional well-being and mental health, stressing that being in nature as a child promotes emotional stability in young adulthood. It also identifies emotional, educational and social benefits: the learning of social skills; promotion of language; development and socialization; improved self-esteem and ability for goal setting; enhancement of self-control; enhancement of self-efficacy; encouragement of responsibility; development of flexibility and adaptability to changing surroundings; development of ecological consciousness. It states that 'a growing body of recent literature suggests that childhood experiences of nature play a crucial role in an individual's sense of connectedness with nature in later life' (Natural England 2010).

Those benefits don't only apply to children and teenagers during formative years. A recent project, conducted by Peggy Bartlett, Professor of Anthropology at Emory University, shows that reconnecting with nature can have astonishingly wide-reaching effects on adults also. The project, which was designed for the academic faculty, explored the idea of 're-enchantment' through spending time in nature. Interestingly, it was based on the hypothesis that the valuing of reason and logic over emotion and intuition has led to an overvaluing of the objective study of nature phenomena compared with the enhanced understanding that comes from subjective, direct experience. This dominance, according to Dr Bartlett, reveals a disenchantment within us and within our world that is based on a long-term cultural suppression of our collective relationship with nature, which has removed from our lives the real connection with authentic divinity. But not only have we lost this connection with authentic divinity, we have in the process become increasingly separate from valuing our own connection with nature and even our own nature and, as Dr Bartlett rightly concludes, we cannot urge each other to care about the environment unless we have a sense of our primal at-one-ment with the created world (Bartlett 2008, pp. 1077–1098).

The project consisted of occasional two-day gatherings of around 90 faculty members in nature and ongoing lunchtime walks across wilder areas of the campus. The reflections reported by the participants show that 'experiencing nature' is transformative on more levels than we would expect:

Sensory expansion: Participants reported experiencing connection with the sensual, alive, wide-awake world of nature, including their own bodies, accompanied by joy. Some felt a deeper connection to moral goodness as well as to the awareness that goodness and beauty are intrinsic values that exist within us.

Being lost in wonder and awe: Participants reported a sense of being outside themselves, of being 'caught up or lost in wonder'. Many experienced a profound 'sense of the mysterious' in which everything around them, including their relationships, was more intensely felt and more richly lived.

Feeling peace, serenity and restoration: Some reported that their time spent in nature had led to feeling more serene, more at peace, with an increased sense that all of their faculties had been restored.

Increasing attachment to life and identification with living systems: An enhanced sense of belonging to a larger system of living beings created a shift in identity as participants developed a sense of being part of the web of life.

Connection to childhood experiences: Participants displayed enhanced memories of childhood experiences; many recalled positive and important experiences in nature from a formative phase and felt delight in making these reconnections.

Reconnection to religious, moral or ethical commitments: The experiences in nature connected many directly with moral precepts for living, personal commitments or ethical guidelines.

Deepened sense of care: For many, it created a breakthrough in their sense of empathy that was transferred to a deeply felt ethic of care for, and action on behalf of, all living things.

Dr Bartlett draws many conclusions from those results, including a fostering of imagination, playfulness and creativity, which extend beyond the boundaries of this book. Nervertheless, the results above speak for themselves, and we have to ask ourselves why we do not put more effort into reconnecting with nature regularly and recommend 'being in nature' within psychological/therapeutic treatments.

HELPING CLIENTS TO RECONNECT WITH NATURE

Contemporary shamanically orientated practitioners will work in nature with a range of means and tools. The most profound, transformational experiences can be had during Vision Quests, especially when experienced facilitators conduct them in a wild environment. Vision Quests, which I will come back to later, lead us into the wilderness, on our own, for days and nights. The sweat lodge ceremony is also conducted in and connected to nature and so are most Medicine Wheel ceremonies. Solstice, sun dance and medicine plant ceremonies, and many other ceremonies and rituals, are performed outside. Nature awareness walks, meditation exercises, the burial of the warrior and training for seeing and connecting with the essences/spirits of plants, rocks and trees are all part of the 'shamanic nature repertoire'. In fact, the entire middle world, the world around us, is where the shaman communicates with the essence aspects of nature. As all things are seen as having a spiritual essence, we therefore have the ability to connect with all of nature, communicate with it and learn from it.

Education

As I have already said, it is not possible to transfer such ways of working in and with nature into a consulting room, but we might want to try with the means we have at our disposal. I believe that we are asked at this critical point in our collective development to encourage clients to reconnect with nature, and with that also with their own deeper selves, by developing a conscious awareness of the many benefits of such connections. It is in a way appalling that we, as a society, still have a tendency to belittle people who try to be more in tune with the natural world, calling them, for instance, 'tree-huggers' or 'eco-freaks'. So, even if we cannot transfer nature exercises easily into our therapeutic practice, we can educate clients by making them aware of the benefits I have listed. We can encourage outdoor activities and outdoor sports, rather than suggesting exercising in the gym, where most of us put on our headphones and either watch TV or listen to music to overcome the sterile boredom of the treadmill or the rowing machine. Another way is to encourage clients to replace the 'city-break' with a 'nature-break' or to engage in one of the many nature activities on offer, such as participating in wilderness camps, nature foraging courses or nature survival courses, or learning how to cultivate vegetable gardens and so forth. I personally would also encourage certain clients, especially those who struggle to find their path in life, to consider a Vision Quest, provided the facilitator is experienced, trained and provides integration afterwards.

Being seen by nature

A powerful, quick way of reconnecting with nature, in my experience, is to instruct clients to be seen by nature. We have a tendency to 'look at', forgetting that we are also 'being looked at'. You can give this exercise as homework, or, if your practice is set in an adequate environment, you can do this exercise at the end of a session. I have used it with individual clients many times, normally at the end of the session, especially when the session was emotionally demanding or distressing, usually allocating 10 to 15 minutes for it.

I ask the client to take a note pad outside, spend a few minutes breathing deeply, with their eyes closed, and then imagine that they are seen by Mother Nature, and that Mother Nature is looking at them, as one of her cherished children, with love. I ask the client to trust their inner clock, open their eyes again when they feel the urge to do so, and write down what they experienced, what thoughts came into their minds and how they felt. What clients experience seems always to be beautiful and feels loving and nurturing. Although it might bring up some tears, these are mainly tears of gratitude or of feeling blessed. Again, it changes the perspective and establishes connection with the natural world and with something bigger. If this exercise works for a specific client, ask them to repeat it twice a week. With time, the connection deepens and the positive loving regard of nature will work its magic.

Nature walks with a twist

Most therapists will recommend exercise. Exercise is good for the depressed client, for the anxious individual, for the grieving client, for the person with low self-esteem, for the stressed-out high-achiever and for the overweight. Whenever we recommend physical exercise, we can ask clients to take walks between sessions. A nice way to turn a walk into something more than physical exercise is to use it to sharpen awareness for – and connection with – nature.

Awareness walks

Ask your client to do two 20-minute walks between sessions, either in a park, if you work in an urban area, or along a river or somewhere else in nature. Turn these into awareness walks. Ask the client to listen intently for five minutes, noting all the sounds; then for five minutes to experience/feel the sensations produced by air, wind, warmth, coolness, rain, sun; then for five minutes to notice the trees and plants and all the wildlife the client can spot; and finally, for the last few minutes, to feel his feet firmly on the ground with every step he takes, sensing his connection to the earth. He should then, silently or aloud, bless the trees, the wildlife, the air, the sun and the earth and give thanks for being able to enjoy the natural world. Ask your client to take a few minutes afterwards, when back home or at the end of the walk, to contemplate and write down whatever comes to his mind about the walk. You can use this in the next session.

CASE EXAMPLE: ALAN'S AWARENESS WALK

Alan, a client of mine, went dutifully on the walk and went through a range of feelings. He was quite captivated during the 'listening' phase as he heard subtle sounds to which he had never paid attention before. He then got bored during the 'feeling phase' and felt astonishment when he realized how many different species of trees, plants and wildlife he could identify during the 'spotting phase'. He was surprised at how solid his feet felt on the ground, something to which he had never paid attention. He then 'felt silly' during the 'blessing phase', but was moved and close to tears during the 'thanking phase'. I picked up on the 'feeling bored and silly' and we explored this for a while under the aspect of manliness. I also wondered aloud why he would feel silly during the blessing phase, which turned into an exploration of 'Who am I to have a right to bless anything?' It was when I quietly stated that he had as much right as anybody else to bless the trees that he began to cry and some deep childhood hurts began to emerge.

Let 'something find you' walks

Another way of doing an awareness walk is to instruct your client to walk silently, being aware of his feet firmly on the ground whilst taking deep breaths, relaxing on the exhale by making it consciously a bit longer. After a few minutes of relaxing, the client is asked to state, aloud or silently, but for a few times, an intent along the lines of 'I am practising awareness and I ask for whatever wants to find me, to find me.' After stating this a few times, the client practises silent listening whilst walking, similar to the 'Aboriginal dadirri' described above. Something will find her and, most of the time, what finds the client is wonderfully surprising.

CASE EXAMPLE: LETTING SOMETHING FIND YOU 1

One of my clients was found by her voice. It was a deeply moving experience for her. She walked along as instructed and suddenly found that she had the urge to sing. She was walking along a river and began to hum. Later, when she told me about it, she was absolutely sure that she didn't remember starting to put words to the hum. The songs just seemed to come out of her. She extended the walk and sung the way she had never sung before. Even when she passed the odd person, she just sung more quietly, never interrupting her song. Is it surprising that we had talked in the previous session about her 'finding her own voice' in connection to meetings at work, where she usually stayed silent? She found her voice in a way neither of us had expected, but she found it nevertheless.

CASE EXAMPLE: LETTING SOMETHING FIND YOU 2

Another of my clients was found by her 'wild childhood'. She walked along, not believing for a moment that something would find her, and suddenly remembered quite vividly a day of her childhood when she was cycling in the woods with friends. She remembered the excitement, the feeling of freedom and, most importantly, her courage. When she returned to the next session, she had written it all down, the memory as well as the tears she shed when remembering. We used this as a basis to explore the subject of 'lost courage' as well as 'freedom to be herself'.

There are many ways to create 'awareness walks'. You can adjust the concept to your client's personality and to the condition you are treating. It is important, though, that awareness and focus is directed onto nature, not the client's inner state. The focus on nature will create a resonating inner state, which, if that's what you want, can then be therapeutically explored and worked with.

DAILY NATURE EXERCISES AT HOME
Meditations

Clients who meditate, practise yoga or tai-chi or are engaged in any other regular spiritual practice should be encouraged to add the quality of nature to their activities whenever this is possible. Engaging in mindfulness meditation practices near a stream, river, rock or under a tree can add a wider dimension, with astonishing results.

Brief ceremonies

Another way in which we can bring the healing and connecting qualities of nature into the therapeutic process is through designing brief ceremonies that clients can perform daily in their back yard, on the balcony or in the garden. The first step is to create an altar representing the elements. I discuss this with clients – not everybody, but the ones that are open to such suggestions – during the session. I talk to them about taking a walk somewhere to find four pieces that represent air, fire, water and earth for them and suggest that they then create a small space somewhere in the open and arrange the pieces, either in a way that just feels right or in the four directions of the wheel. I also ask them to find a centre piece that represents that 'which always is and will always be'. A daily small blessing of the elements or a brief meditation or a few minutes of calm thankfulness is then recommended. Give suggestions, but in the end leave it up to the client's imagination.

Greeting the directions

An enchanting way in which we can work outside involves the directions of the wheel. Every shamanically orientated facilitator, every indigenous shaman, will, in one form or another, honour the directions, calling them in before they work, asking them for blessings and so on. It seems that the directions resonate with us, once we begin to work with them. The easiest way to begin is to greet them in the morning. One can simply stand outside, close one's eyes and turn into each direction – the South, North, East, West – and then to the sky and the earth, expressing a greeting. For example, turn East and greet the sun; turn South and greet the plants and the water; turn West and greet the earth; turn North and greet the air; and then look up and greet all there is above and look down and greet all there is below.

One can go further and ask each direction for a piece of advice for the day, or give thanks if it's evening. Over time we feel that we begin to connect with our daily environment differently. We begin to experience it in a more natural and spatially wider sense, feeling more embedded in it.

Honouring the spirit of a place

All teachers I have met, before they begin to work in a place, will honour its spirit. The spirit of a place can be felt and we may call it by many different names, although we don't usually call it 'spirit of a place'. We walk into a place and it feels right, or warm, or cold, or kind of messy, or calming or exciting. The spirit of a place consists of many layers and ingredients: the people who have lived there, the ancestors who dwelled there, the plants, trees, rocks and the water that might be part of it, and the animals which roam around it. The way to honour the spirit of a place is, again, to quiet the mind, close the eyes and ask to connect to it. Once the client feels something like a connection, they thank the spirit of the place or, if they feel inclined to go a step further, an offering can be made with the words: 'I offer this to the spirit of the place with love and thanks.'

There are many more ways to get to know the natural world and connect with her via simple exercises during walks such as exploring the mysteries of the seasons, learning to read terrains, getting to know different plants and herbs, finding answers to questions and so on. A nice, informative book that suggests and describes many of those and more is Ted Andrews' book *Nature-Speak: Signs, Omens and Messages in Nature* (2004). I want to end this chapter with a quote from this book:

> All signs and messages in Nature work to accomplish 1 of 3 things: First to stir a sense of wonder about the world around us, Second to help us solve and handle problems and issues in our life and Third to awaken and quicken us to new potentials and creativity. (Andrews 2004, p.38)

Notes

1   There is a beautiful, albeit long, clip about the Kogi and their message to us on YouTube. It is well worth spending the time watching. See Cultural Anthropology, Ecology – The Kogi; 'The elder brothers' warning': http://video.google.co.uk/videoplay?docid=-521537373096312859#.

2   A wonderful book on the subject has been written by Dr Bill Plotkin: *Nature and the Human Soul: Cultivating Wholeness and Community in a Fragmented World* (2008).

17 | THE CYCLE OF LIFE
When the Body Dies and the Soul Leaves

I was unsure whether to include a chapter about death within this book because I assumed that many readers would find death an uncomfortable topic. Nevertheless, I decided to stay true to the subject of this book. One cannot talk about spirituality, and especially not about shamanism, without addressing the question of death as, far from shying away from death, the shaman faces it, embraces it, and learns from it. In fact, within every spiritual system, questions about death are being raised because, without paying attention to death, and trying to understand what happens when the body dies, we cannot understand life. Both together create the whole, the whole of what we, in a spiritual sense, perceive as being life.[1]

I do not pretend to have definite answers to questions that have been addressed by great minds, by saints, mystics and sages, by religious scholars and by scientists. Nevertheless, I will address aspects of the subject, contrasting the difference between our way of dealing with death and the spiritual/shamanic way, and convey some techniques and tools, which are based on shamanic teachings, and on my own experiences and experiences I have had with clients and students. I will not attempt to adjust the tools and techniques I describe to fit a therapeutic setting, but I hope that you still find this chapter worth reading and can utilize parts within your work.

One of our greatest sorrows and greatest opportunities lies in the fact that we know with absolute certainty that the body we inhabit will one day cease to exist. Unfortunately, it is this single absolute certainty in our lives that we try to remove as far as possible from our conscious awareness. It seems to me that the further we separate ourselves from the rest of creation, the more science demystifies our existence and the more we subscribe to an individualized egocentric materialistic world-view, the more we fear death, pushing it out of awareness. It follows that, as with every fear that we do not face, we feed it unconsciously and we might even project it onto others. I personally believe that death has become one of our shadow subjects in the Jungian sense, with all the negative consequences that this entails, so it is now vital that we reintegrate it into our psyche and consciousness.

I am not disputing that fear of dying has its rightful place. It is, after all, the power of our survival instinct that has helped to ensure that we are still on this planet. The problem lies in our increasing need to pretend that we will live forever, that we can stay eternally young, that our body/mind can be permanently sustained. Today, especially in prosperous, medically advanced societies, we try to prolong youth and life with means that border on the inhumane. Whilst millions of people all over the world live on scraps of food and die of malnutrition and preventable diseases, we spend valuable resources on prolonging 'youth'. Even worse, when we get old and fall seriously ill, we are being artificially kept alive with medication, hooked to machines and fed through tubes. With all the beneficial advancements of medicine, we are in danger of making a travesty out of death.

THE GIFTS WE RECEIVE WHEN FACING DEATH

Refusing to acknowledge that the body/mind in its manifested form has a limited time on this planet, we throw away a most precious gift, namely the focus on things that really matter and the peace that can come with the acceptance of the cycles of all physical life. Whilst we cannot change the fact that this body will die, the confrontation with our own mortality is the best perspective changer that exists. Many minor, unnecessary and unimportant thoughts, feelings and behaviours that deplete us energetically become meaningless if we can only unequivocally acknowledge that the body we inhabit right now will cease to exist one day and accept the naturalness of it. Not only would we live in a more focused way, we would give ourselves the gift of dying in a more dignified and healed way.

Death is not only the best perspective changer, it is also the great equalizer. To know that all living beings are equal in death helps us to understand that all life is precious. I had an experience when I was quite young that had a lasting effect on me. I walked with my family through a market in Lisbon. We stopped at a stall that sold rabbits. The stall owner slaughtered them after the customer had chosen the rabbit she wanted. The rabbits were cramped together in narrow cages, still alive – barely. It was when looking at one of the rabbits that I had a moment of insight that stayed with me. Suddenly and without thinking about it, I realized that the rabbit was afraid and we were equal in one point: we both would die and we both wanted to live. I was only about 14 years of age and had had, up to then, no experience of death. I wish I could say that this experience changed my life, and that it taught me what is important and what is meaningless clutter. It didn't. I guess I was too young. Nevertheless I have ever since rejected the human notion that we are superior to the rest of creation and have believed, from an energetic point of view, that if we take a life prematurely we harm ourselves in the process.

In this context, it might be appropriate to tell you about an interesting chat I had with a Buddhist monk in Sri Lanka. I met him whilst working there for a few weeks after the 2004 tsunami. Somehow the question 'Does Buddhism allow the killing and eating of animals when people are hungry?' entered the discussion. Having been a vegetarian for most of my adult life, I had to think about it and decided that the answer must be 'Yes', as being hungry seemed to justify the killing of an animal. The monk looked at me kindly, as those people do, and I felt the need to rationalize my opinion along the lines of 'Well, animals kill when they need food; it's really the killing of animals by humans for other reasons than hunger that is not right.' The monk smiled and said to me: 'The difference between you and an animal is that you are a thinking human being. You have choices. If there are still animals on this earth you can find and kill when you are hungry, then there will be plant food for you to find and eat. Killing is always bad for your Karma, no matter what the reason.' This hit me hard because I realized how much I, vegetarian by choice, conscious being by my own definition, still thought in terms of humans being superior.

That death is the great equalizer is a learning that has never left me. Later, in my early twenties, especially when I visited the House of the Dying in Calcutta, I observed that to suffer some fear when faced with the death of the body is also a universal experience and that a 'good and dignified death' is important. Only much later did I ask myself whether the fear of death is truly universal or whether it can be overcome by facing it and accepting death as a part of life. There is a saying that we can avoid reality, but that we cannot avoid the consequences of reality. When it comes to dying, we have chosen to avoid reality, and the consequences can be seen daily in the way we live our lives. 'You are unlikely to uncover and embody your soul if you are living as if your ego and body are immortal,' writes Bill Plotkin (2008, p.281), stating the obvious fact that is so very difficult for humans to accept. Facing our own mortality is not easy, but it is most rewarding, as it brings to the fore what really matters to us.

We can, of course, when we contemplate our own death, immediately use avoidance strategies again. We can flee into religions that promise us an afterlife, into the belief that we live many lives or into the idea that we are the 'chosen few'. Indeed, from an energetic/spiritual point of view, it is highly likely that our consciousness will carry on being, long after our physical body has ceased to exist. It is the facing of the ending of this life that is important because, from a spiritual point of view, it matters how we live it. When we don't avoid the issue, when we consciously confront ourselves with it in a way that doesn't deny our fears, but looks at them, holding them in the light of conscious awareness, when we begin to accept reality, life becomes more intense, enriched. We begin to learn what is important and what is not. We become more compassionate with ourselves and others, listen more to our soul's small voice, follow more our hearts' desires, are less concerned with other people's judgements, fear failure less, become less attached to the fleeting pleasures of this physical life and more inclined to yearn for deeper and higher states of consciousness. Choices that we make in the context of our own mortality will be based on what has meaning and value for us, helping us to become more authentic and develop towards expressing our highest potential.

WORKING WITH DEATH IN A SHAMANICALLY ORIENTATED SETTING

In shamanic work, facing physical death is essential. This is, needless to say, easier, or may be only possible, when it is embedded within the walking of a spiritual path that leads us, over time and with practice, into a world of soul, energy and connection, where the manifested world becomes just one of the perceived worlds. In traditional cultures, facing death was, and still is, one of the most important rites that an initiate goes through, sometimes repeatedly, on his or her way to becoming a shaman, as described in Chapter 3. All spiritual teachers are well aware of death, utilizing this for the expansion of consciousness, spiritual connection and development and using death as their advisor. In fact, most traditional shamans, having been through near-death initiations, would state that they are 'already dead' and therefore don't fear death. Thanks to their experiences, they know that they are not just the person that lives in their body and mind, but something that is way beyond and is eternal. In such traditions, death is not dying in the sense we define it, but just another form of reality. In simplified terms, seeing the world energetically, the spirit essence, the light soul, leaves the body at the time of death. It is still alive, just in another dimension. Death is therefore a transition stage between lives.

In shamanism, facing our own death, or going through it in the form of death and rebirth experiences, as described in Chapter 3, has three vital purposes. First, death becomes a teacher: the teacher of death and of life, giving life within this context intensity, choice and direction, which includes living in a way that ensures 'dying a good death'.[2] Second, when we face death, or even go through it, our world-view changes from a material one to an energy-connected one. Third, the shaman goes through death and rebirth experiences to overcome his/her survival instinct. With this mastered, he can access the spirit worlds generally and also learn about the spirit world of the dead, which is a vital ingredient of his work as a psychopomp.

There are different ways of working with death in contemporary shamanism[3] and, as I am not suggesting that you apply these directly in psychotherapeutic or counselling sessions, I will not describe them in depth, but simply for the purpose of raising awareness about the issue and to give you information that you might choose to utilize in your own way.

The burial of the warrior

One of the more profound ways to face 'death' in contemporary shamanism is the 'burial of the warrior'. I participated in one of these rituals. It was led by Victor Sanchez, a shamanic practitioner of the Toltec tradition in North Mexico, which he has written extensively about (e.g. Sanchez 1996). The burial of the warrior is a long ritual, taking five days, including a period of preparation before the burial and some integration afterwards. The main focus is the burial. The apprentice digs his/her own grave and will spend the night in the grave, covered by earth, with only a small hole, the size of a tennis ball, to ensure a sufficient oxygen supply. The preparation period leads into an altered state; strong spirit helper connections are established; and as many fears as possible are addressed and confronted beforehand. The burial is not only about facing death. It is also about confronting fears and overcoming them and about our closeness to the earth. In modern times, especially when participants are non-indigenous, the ritual is done in a group, which is held quite safely, with the facilitator/shaman and helpers holding vigil around the fire whilst drumming through the night. One is also asked to take a torch into the grave, with instructions only to use it when unavoidable. Still, it is not for the faint hearted and certainly brings up many fear issues we usually avoid.

Contemporary initiation rituals

Contemporary shamanism also uses initiation rites to face death and the fear of dying. The Gabonese ritual I described in Chapter 5 is an example. An initiation ritual I participated in was held in Ecuador.[4] The initiation took place in a sulphur cave and the build-up to it was, for me, more nerve-racking than the actual experience, as it included more than one reminder that I could literally die in that cave. Overcoming fears and the instinct to survive was, as far as I can judge, the major aim and I personally found that I have become increasingly fearless over time, more focused and certainly more courageous when it comes to speaking my mind, but also when it comes to holding fearlessly a therapeutic space where people can tap into whatever they need.

Journeys to explore death

Less frightening confrontations with death within contemporary shamanic practices are journeys; either dismemberment journeys or journeys forward in time to your own death, or journeys with the intent of finding out about death. These are done in the journey format, as outlined previously, with spirit helpers being available and the spirit leaving the body, looking down at the body. This dissociated state guarantees that the physical and emotional reactions, in the form of physical pain or fears and anxieties, are kept to a minimum. So the intent to formulate for the journey would be something along the following lines: 'I am going to journey to observe my own death. I will be in spirit form and have my guides and power animals with me.' From then onwards, the journey will unfold. A good learning when you journey in this way is the fact that the moment your spirit leaves the body death loses its sting and is experienced as something quite natural. Roger Woolger (2004), a teacher and friend who recently left this world, used similar approaches in his Past Life Regression workshops, suggesting that the spirit moves first into 'Bardo', the space in between life and death, to finish unfinished business, before departing completely.

Another beautiful and beneficial way to journey is with the quest to be shown the realm: the cosmology of where we go when we die. This journey is accompanied by spirit guides and helpers, which usually show up spontaneously, and often we will also find that the person who journeys meets loved ones who are already in the spirit world. This reflects what seems to happen in reality. Shortly before they die, many people report feeling or even seeing a loved one around who is already in spirit form. My own experience confirms this. My father saw his own mother, whilst my mother spoke to my father, with such conviction and such warmth, three days before dying in my presence, that I had no doubt that she saw him, felt him and was helped by him.

Visualization exercises

Death can also be envisaged via visualization exercises. These are more gentle ways of getting people to begin to confront the fact that they will die and to focus their attention onto the life they really want to create. The Hoffman Process, which I participated in a while ago, includes a good exercise with regards to your own death. It focuses on the people who will be at your funeral. I have found this a good way to begin to approach death, if I do with clients at all. It can be done as a visualization or, as practised in the Hoffman Process, outside, lying on the floor within a marked space. You do some breathing to centre yourself and then imagine the people who will attend your funeral. You imagine that you are already in spirit form, looking down at your own funeral, listening to what they say about you. In a structured way, you can listen first to the negatives, and then to the positives. You instruct yourself that you will let this happen as honestly as you possibly can, without judging. It is essential to have people present in your imagination whose opinions are important – your partner, your children, your friends, your parents and whoever else's opinion matters. Already the imagining of 'meaningful people' shows us something about what is important and what is not. More important than showing what people we care about see in us, positively and negatively, it also shows us where we might want to change, where we behave carelessly and that we are loved.

Dancing your last dance

Another way to work with death and dying is to 'dance our last dance'. This can be done in different ways. We can journey to our power place with the intent to find out about our death. And then we dance it there. Or we can 'dance our last journey', which is a wonderful way to work with our own death. The journey, the dance, will have to last for as long as it takes, with the music being powerful, yet supporting us gently in our quest to dance our last dance. Along the way we might encounter anxieties, sadness, the people we love and memories of good times and not so good times. Usually our guides and power animals are with us and, sooner or later, significant people who have already left this body, such as parents, will show up. Much healing can be done within this dance and much love is always present. All of it we express in our 'last dance' until we are peaceful, ready to let go. Then we dance the spirit leaving our body, which is always a very joyful experience.

Does this sound morbid to you? Let me assure you, it is not. All work with death is done in a 'held' way, including preparation and the creation of a beneficial energy field around people. This kind of work deals with a reality for which most of us in our society are completely unprepared. It gives us some control, it heals wounds and, who knows, it could help us to have some control over the way we die as we can influence the way we envisage it, the way we think about it and the way we want our death to occur. When I was confronted with the possibility of my own death a few years ago due to a life-threatening illness, I felt astonishingly calm, which is not to be confused with the calmness of being in dissociated shock and certainly not with a wish to die. I do love life and I feel that I still have much living to do. Nevertheless, as unsettling as this experience was on one level, it also produced a calm space within me from where I could have yet another look at what needed to change in my life: at what is important to me, which areas I still want to improve, which I want to let go, and if there is anything new I would still like to bring into my life.

WORKING AS A PSYCHOPOMP AND ADDRESSING GRIEF

This brings me to the last point I want to explain: for indigenous shamans, as well as some contemporary practitioners, death is also an important subject because part of their job is to act as a 'psychopomp', with responsibility to guide the dying and the dead. To do this job, the traditional shaman has to be familiar with the spirit world of the dead and needs to visit it frequently. 'The ability of shamans to work as a psychopomp is unique because they have faced the fears of their own death in shamanic initiations and have found their way back to the land of the living. The pathways of death in the spirit world are familiar' (Pratt 2007, p.138). By ritualizing the transition period inherent in the dying process, the shaman helps to make it a time of growth and healing for the dying person and then helps the spirit to leave the earthly realms, travelling into non-ordinary reality, first into Bardo, the realm in-between, and then onwards, completing the passage safely. It is this ritualization of the transition period of death that we have lost. The 'last rites' and the burial rituals of contemporary Christianity are but a shadow of what can be done to turn the time before, during and after death into a healing experience.

Although I have no calling to work as a psychopomp, or even with people who are terminally ill, I have supervised hypnotherapists who have worked in palliative care and have repeatedly found that the ones who have a spiritual connection not only lasted longer within such an environment, but were much less negatively affected by it and could react more calmly and with more substance to the dying patients, as well as to their relatives, than practitioners whose belief system was of this material earth. When we are confronted with crisis, death and/or grief, our own spirituality can put us into the 'right frame of mind' and provide us with the 'right' words.

Connected with the transition of the soul is the grief of the people left behind, which I will only touch briefly upon. All living creatures grieve: animals grieve and humans grieve. It is a natural reaction to loss, to the loss of a person who was close and to the loss of an energy field that leaves literally a 'hole'. Grief can be substantial; it is necessary and its expression needs to be allowed in whatever ways the grieving person wants to express it. It takes time, holding, compassion and sharing to grieve properly without harming ourselves in the long run by suppressing it. Grief is often mixed with emotions such as detachment, when still in shock, guilt, anger and a feeling of powerlessness. We hope that over time the grieving person feels less sadness, can begin to think about other people and things again, that acceptance of the loss grows and that it leads to learning and development as the person moves on in life. What we are missing in societies such as ours are extended rituals to help us with this process, especially when the loss is dramatic and traumatic. More spiritually orientated societies, which take the caring for the soul of the deceased and the caring for the living left behind more to heart, provide such rituals. The Oglala Sioux of North America, for instance, had a tradition that is described in *The Sacred Pipe: Black Elk's Account of the Seven Rites of the Oglala Sioux* (Black Elk and Brown 1989). When a loved one died, a medicine bundle was created that included something from the deceased person. The soul of the person was invited to reside in the bundle and the grieving person would care ritually for the bundle for one year, feeding it, giving it love, sleeping with it, dreaming with it. After a year, at the anniversary of the death, the bundle would ritualistically be opened, the soul would be released and the grieving would cease.

CASE EXAMPLE: A MOTHER'S GRIEF

Whilst writing this I was reminded of a client. I didn't take her on readily; in fact, she should not have been my client at all, as she certainly needed somebody more experienced in bereavement counselling. I saw Louise as an 'emergency client' for a session to cover for her bereavement counsellor, who was on holiday. The bereavement counsellor had arranged cover, but unfortunately the professional who should have covered had developed a bad cold and was unable to see Louise. The professional phoned and asked if I would see Louise, as she felt that Louise, who had been suicidal, needed the session to support her until her counsellor returned from her holiday.

I saw her the same evening. She was the 42-year-old mother of two boys whose infant daughter of seven months had died five months earlier after an attack of meningitis. Louise had broken down with grief, hardly sleeping or eating and unable to look after her other children, while her husband and her sister had taken over running the family. She would spend long periods of time staring into space, or crying, unable to get up. Louise had had ongoing bereavement counselling and was prescribed anti-depressants. It would be too complex to list all that Louise was going through, but all of us who have children, or those of you who know about bereavement, will be able to imagine. The pain of losing a child was compounded by feelings of guilt ('I should have spotted this earlier') and shame ('I should look after my children and get over this, but I can't') and by tension within the marriage, as her husband, who kept the family going, was unable to support her emotionally. She furthermore felt that everybody, except her counsellor, expected her by now to 'get better and get on with life'.

All I could do was to offer an open heart and my time, hoping that this would enable her to 'hang on in there' until her regular counsellor was available again. At one point, after speaking, crying or just staring at the floor, she looked at me, with overwhelming sadness in her eyes, saying, 'This can't ever make sense to me. I loved her so much. She was the little girl I always wanted. I just want to bring it all to an end. Do you understand that?'

'I am not sure,' I said, 'I have never lost a child, but listening to you I imagine that this is hurting on such a deep level that it is not possible for others to really fully comprehend what you are going through. But I am doing my best because I do know about the pain that is of the heart and soul and how it feels to hurt in such a profound way, on a soul level, that everything else fades into insignificance, that one questions the very point of one's existence.' Louise said nothing. Then she looked at me and said, 'This is it. It is as if the part of me that wants to go on living just left. And I am angry with myself because I have two other children. They are alive. But they don't matter to me at all any longer. All that matters is that I lost something that was so precious that was so much a part of me... I am so afraid. I cannot get Gemma out of my mind. There isn't a moment when I don't think of her or picture her or feel her.'

What do you say to that? That you understand? That this is normal? That it will take time? That she can use different techniques? I was sure that her counsellor had worked with her along similar lines and more. I have a tendency to tell a story when I know that everything I could say would sound like a platitude, or when I want to sow a seed but don't want to work with something directly, which I didn't want in Louise's case.

So I told her a true story, saying something along these lines: I worked for a while in Sri Lanka, after the tsunami. And although I never lost a child, I met people who had lost a child. One of the men I met in the camp where I worked had lost his wife and two of his children in the tsunami. And you know what really touched me very deeply? It was the way Buddhists deal with the loss of a loved one. Buddhists believe in death and rebirth. So they believe that after death the soul departs from the body to come back at one point into physical life.

But let me come back to the man who had lost so much. He was devastated. Sri Lankans don't show emotions easily, but he, when he wasn't sitting there just motionless, would be seen running through the camp, shouting, crying, swearing. He was very angry and very sad and very lost, just as everybody else would be in such a situation. Everybody, the monks and the people in the camp, would sit with him, offer him tea, or just walk around with him without saying anything. We, the people from the non-governmental organization (NGO), imitated them, and nobody tried to do more than 'just be there'. Every day, or so it seemed to me, monks would perform one ritual or another for the children and the wife and then, on the seventh day, a traditional alms-giving was offered to the monks to transfer even more merit onto the departed. After the alms-giving, a meal was shared. Food was first given to the monks and then to the extended family and then to everybody else who was there. People talked and prayed and chanted. This is repeated after three months, on the day of the death, and again after a year, which then marks the end of the mourning period. The man invited us all, many from the camp and all the NGO workers, to the rituals. I was extremely touched by that. I somehow could see that the knowledge that the souls of his loved ones were cared for, that merits were bestowed on them and especially that they were set free in the right way, helped him to accept it and to go on living. Of course he was still grieving badly, but he also had the assurance that the souls of his loved ones had been set free in the right way and that everything had been done for them. You know, I wish Christian rites would be more like that.

We sat quite still for a while, I praying silently that I had spoken the 'right words' in the 'right way'.

'I was a kind of spiritual person – not in the sense that I believe in God – but I did meditate on and off,' Louise offered after a while. I said, 'I guess that's difficult to do right now – or?' Louise replied, 'Yes.'

I offered Louise another session in two days, which she accepted. When I saw her again she said, 'I was thinking about the story of the guy in the camp. Do you think it would be a nice idea to do a ritual to set Gemma's soul free? I haven't set her free. I can't set her free. But I could make a start by doing something.'

In a way, this was exactly what I had hoped would happen, that the story would have an effect, but on the other hand, it was exactly what I didn't want, as I knew the ritual would stir up strong emotions. Nevertheless, I had started, so I couldn't backtrack. 'I think we could do this together, next week, with your counsellor. We could do it here, in the garden. We can make it very beautiful. You could, if you wanted, bring your husband or your sister, or both,' I suggested.

And that's what we did. Louise brought her sister along. It was beautiful, very beautiful, and very touching for all of us. We slipped into a different role. We became four women facilitating a ritual for a girl child who had been precious and who needed to rest in peace. Louise spoke the words. We had flowers galore. We build a little altar. We sung and I drummed the 'spirit home'.

Louise's marriage didn't survive, but she did. She now lives with her two boys in a small town near by. I didn't see her for a while after the ritual. Her counsellor resumed the sessions for several more months. Shortly before the anniversary of her daughter's death, Louise contacted me asking if I would be willing to help her with another ritual. Her counsellor and her sister wanted me to be there as well. After seeking reassurance from her counsellor, I agreed. We did this and, although there was still grief, Louise had also included her boys in the prayers she had written and celebrated their lives, which was a sign for me that all was as well as could be under the circumstances.

Notes

1   In shamanism, we also pay attention to 'coincidences' and 'hunches', so it is significant to me that I finish this chapter, after a week of sadness, on the day one of my teachers and friends, Roger Woolger, left his body, peacefully and much healed, according to his children, who were with him.

2   I have described this in Chapter 12.

3   One of the ways is through hallucinogenic plants, which can lead to profound 'out of body experiences' and visions of death and dying, which are illegal in most of the western world but are used in South America and some of the Asian countries. I am not describing these within the context of this book. Heaven and Charing wrote an interesting book on the topic, *Plant Spirit Shamanism* (2006).

4   Eve Bruce, a plastic surgeon from the USA, includes in her book *Shaman, M.D.* (2002) her experiences with the same shamans in more detail.

PART IV

Back to the 'Bigger Picture'

The purpose of our lives is to give birth to the best which is within us.

Marianne Williamson (1992)

18 | ABOUT INDIVIDUAL AND COLLECTIVE PURPOSE IN TODAY'S WORLD

In the introduction I stated that if we want to move forward we need to work towards a change in paradigm from the material and self-centred to the energetical and interconnected and from the ego to the soul, integrating the psycho-spiritual aspect of humans in a grounded (nature-orientated) form within all areas of life. When making a case for the inclusion of the spiritual in psychology, in Chapter 1, I quoted Andrew Powell, the psychiatrist leading the Royal College of Psychiatrists' spiritual interest group, who remarked: 'Where else should that fundamental loss of meaning and purpose in life go except to the psychiatrist's consulting room when, for many people, the established faiths seem to be so divorced from the realities of daily life?' (Powell 2001a, p.2). I would like to widen this question by asking: 'Where indeed should that fundamental loss of meaning and purpose go if the field of psychology, counselling and therapy doesn't work towards integrating the spiritual aspect as an essential facet of human life? Can we really help our clients with questions of meaning and purpose by staying within the narrow field of the body/mind?'

From a shamanic/spiritual point of view, purpose and meaning cannot be defined if we stay solely on the level of the material world and on the level of the body and mind within this reality. Only if we dare to widen and change our perception, through spiritual practices and altered state experiences, will we know that consciousness is not local, that the brain and the body are only our current vessels and that the underlying reality consists of an energetic web, a symphony of interconnected frequencies. Once we arrive at an energetic world-view, we can begin to address the question of meaning and purpose. From this view of the world, it is in the first place this web, this 'dance of energy', from which we arise, which we are part of, which we influence via the way we live our lives and to which we return when we leave the physical body.[1] From a spiritual/shamanic point of view we do not arrive here as an empty vessel. We are a spirit (consciousness) in a body, and spirit wants to express itself through us to the highest form possible. This 'field of possibilities' is already within the field of our soul, but we have to give birth to it in this world.

Within this energetic reality we are co-creators, and it is my understanding from the teachings I have received and the experiences I have had that our purpose is twofold: first, to develop individually to our highest possible level and, second, to contribute positively to the world, because it is in this material world that we have the exciting and painful experience of being a spirit in a body and where spirit expresses itself through us in manifested form. Both our own development and our contributions are intertwined. The traditional shaman in a small, indigenous community is a prime example. His or her development and explorations of 'the whole' are not for him or herself, but rather, by the very definition of his role, in the first place for the service of that community, where his or her main job is to achieve connection, balance and harmony between the physical and the metaphysical.

TOWARDS A PURPOSEFUL, INDIVIDUAL LIFE: SHAMANIC TOOLS

Before I come back to our collective purpose and the role of psychology, therapy and counselling within it, I want to give you some ideas about how shamanism specifically, and spirituality generally, supports individuals to lead a more purposeful life. For each of us individually, as I have shown, shamanism provides much that can help us on our path towards an integrative development, and within the wide field of shamanism there is more on offer, which couldn't be included within the framework of this book.

Shamanism also provides teachings, techniques, ceremonies and exercises to 'stalk' and bring forth our individual purpose. I am using the word 'stalk' here deliberately, as for many people their individual contributing purpose isn't obvious, but needs to be 'stalked'.

Before I describe some of those means and tools, I would like to talk a bit about the expression 'soul's purpose', which has led many people to search endlessly for 'that one big task'. What's more, given the nature of our society, seekers usually think it has to be something they do professionally, almost as if they are looking for their soul's purpose in the hope of finding a 'job title'. I have encountered clients, friends and acquaintances who have been searching for a long time, only to give up at some point when they think that they are now too old. Unfortunately, they are right and wrong simultaneously. There is no contentment without feeling useful, without purpose. In that sense, the search is justified. Nevertheless there is no 'job title', as vessels for purposeful actions will show up as we unfold.

When we address this issue from a shamanic point of view, we need to shift our thinking from matter to energy. Our soul's purpose, seen energetically, is already there, within us. It has to do, as Marianne Williamson (1992) so rightly observes, with giving birth to the best we can be. With this 'unfolding of our becoming', with each of us striving to express 'spirit to the highest possible form', we contribute positively to the energetic field of the whole, and the more we step out of narrow confinements, the more we will unfold. What, precisely, we do is the vehicle for our purpose, not the purpose itself. What gives us individual purpose will show itself when we integrate the facets of ourselves and when we begin to live in more soul-centred, authentic ways.

Nevertheless, there are specific tools we can utilize when we search for our specific purpose and I will describe a few of these first, before I convey some ideas about living a soul-centred life, which will help us to 'unfold' and lead, in my experience automatically, to living a life that makes sense and has purpose.[2]

Vision Quests

An important tool is the Vision Quest. Traditional Vision Quest ceremonies last a few days, or even longer. These are spent alone in the wilderness, without food and water, deeply entranced in prayer, observation and openness to spirit. Quests can confront us with our own mortality and can be intended to gain insights into life, into our personal visions and tasks from now on. Contemporary quests are usually shorter, done in groups and one is advised to take water and torches. However long the quest, its objective, besides questing for 'vision', is to go inwards to observe and explore what we experience, and to sharpen our awareness and connection to the natural world in its manifested and essence form. It is astonishing how strongly the inner and the outer connect for us when we quest over a longer period of time.

Vision Quests certainly confront us with our fears. In that sense alone, Vision Quests contribute to our 'unfolding'. Christ was on a 'Vision Quest' when he spent 40 days and nights in the desert. He came up against Satan – the inner and the outer – and had to overcome his fears, his loneliness, his demons and his survival instinct to be all he could be.

Vision Quests, no matter whether challenging or not, do not necessarily lead to a 'vision about one's purpose' for everybody, but they contribute. In the world of shamanism, Vision Quests are a part of the ongoing spiritual life and are attempted either regularly or when necessary. Some people come away from quests with great insights right from the start; some will receive a clear message or even have a great vision and will walk a different path afterwards, one with more purpose.

Journeys

Besides the purpose of 'development to the highest possible level', there are streams in shamanic thought that teach that we arrive on this earth with a specific purpose (which, of course, is not in contradiction to developing to our highest level possible) and that we therefore come into this life with an individual birth vision. This is based on the idea that we live many lives, that we are here to learn certain lessons and that our birth vision for every life gives us the opportunity to learn the lessons we are meant to learn. If we subscribe to this view, we need to acknowledge that the circumstances we are born into are just right. Not necessarily pleasant or good, but right for the lessons we have to learn. So we need to look at 'the negatives', the things that repeat themselves and the shortcomings of our upbringing, the 'addictions' we have developed, the shadow sides we don't want to acknowledge, and more. Armed with those insights, we can begin to formulate 'purpose' and then look for the vehicle that allows us to contribute to society within our purpose. A good example is people who have overcome addictions and who later begin to work in such fields, having found their purposeful way to contribute positively, whilst still healing and developing themselves.

Besides examining such issues, we can journey with the intent to be shown our 'birth vision'. We can also journey to our 'origins' and will get a good idea about what we came to this earth to accomplish and heal. I have described such journeys in Chapter 10. Journeying to the upper world to receive advice from guides with regards to the issue of purpose also often brings results. In fact, if we formulate different intents, such as 'What would fulfil me?' or 'What is my task in life?', we can use the shamanic journey extensively with the quest to find information about our individual purpose.

Medicine Wheel

The Medicine Wheel can be used to explore — and later create — 'the dream' by helping clients to ask the appropriate questions in each direction and letting the picture emerge, as I have described in Chapter 15. An easy and accessible way to let the picture emerge is also to address deeply the following questions:

South: What did I love doing as a child?

North: What are my values? What do I value?

East: What nourishes my soul/spirit? What can I be inspired about?

West: What does the world need from me? What is my unique gift to the world?

Such questions, asked within the 'right meditative, altered state set-up, with spirit present', will provide us with valuable insights.

LIVING SOUL-CENTRED AND CONTRIBUTING

In my experience, most people will find their unique way of leading a purposeful life when they begin to lead a more soul-centred life, becoming increasingly authentic as this soul-centred life unfolds. The more we become involved in spiritual practice and discover our own truth, the more we receive ideas, hunches and insights and, more often than not, the opportunities are presented to us. We suddenly find ourselves involved in something that 'feels just right' and then we develop it from there. I have observed this more often than not with group participants and clients. The question then changes from 'what' to 'are we aware enough and courageous enough' to take the offer, or are we still waiting for the 'job title'. Purpose is not, as certain religious teachings would have us believe, about being charitable; it is about our own psycho-spiritual development first and it is, second and parallel to this, about contributing to the wider field in a beneficial way.[3] If we take the concept of energy seriously, we already contribute more positively when we begin to live a soul-orientated, instead of a materially orientated, life. Both our development and our contributions will over time become one, but, according to all spiritual traditions, one has to start with oneself first.

> *Spiritual practice:* Including spiritual practice in our lives is vital. An essential step is to make catering for our souls a priority, putting our spiritual practice first, rather than habitually getting busy with small things. The systems in our societies have diverted us into a focus on consuming materialism and one-sided development. The will to step away from this and begin to focus on humanness, on the soul, on the spiritual,

is a major step to discovering that we are connected to the consciousness of the wider field and that this field nourishes us. It doesn't matter which spiritual practice, as long as we incorporate it into our daily lives. Spiritual practice can, and will, change over time. What's essential is that we tune into 'the field' daily, be in it and let it be in us. We can meditate, pray, chant, journey, practise yoga, commune with nature, create a ceremony, bless, give thanks – or all of those, or some of those, or more. We can do this by ourselves or with other people. Most people who walk a spiritual path will do both. With spiritual practice, we develop ourselves, widen our world-view and, energetically speaking, contribute to the change of the energy field and the dream, which manifests as our concrete individual and collective reality.

Being inspired: A purposeful life cannot be found, expressed and sustained without being able to feel inspired (in-spirit) and passionate. For some people, therefore, another important step is to cultivate passion, not in the head but as a physical flow of energy. We must cultivate this to be able to feel enthusiastic, inspired and joyful. You could write a list about the things you are passionate about, that which really gets your juices flowing. What makes you want to jump up and do it? If one can't find anything, it might be advisable to look back. We all had the ability to be inspired when we were children, and what inspired us when we were children can be brought back to the fore. Whatever it was, it is advisable to do it again (or something of the same quality) to rekindle passion. In shamanic terms, one must cultivate passion, otherwise one gets lost again and again. The shaman is after all a 'master of ecstasy'. Whatever inspires us will connect with a deep truth inside us.

Truth: Practising to find, be, speak and live one's truth as much as possible is another contributing practice. This takes courage and discernment. That which resonates as 'truth' within us is part of our purpose. Truth resonates in the heart. It 'feels right'. Truth is about being authentic, about having the courage to be oneself. The courage to say 'no' to things that 'don't feel right' is a step in the right direction. The courage to attempt to do things and to be in the world in a way that 'feels right' is another. To be honest, even if it's uncomfortable, and to stand up for our own truths, to step beyond the boundaries of rules that restrict us in our own truth, is a practice that will bring us closer to our own self-expression, which in turn is part of our purpose.

Following the heart and taking responsibility: Truth lies in the heart. To practise making decisions that are based on what the heart says leads us deeper into authenticity. What we feel with the heart is ours; what we have to talk ourselves into, or out of, is not. It also makes it so much easier to take responsibility for our choices when we follow our hearts. We might make mistakes in the sense that we find out later on that the decision wasn't right for us after all, but if we follow our heads or succumb to pressure from outside ourselves, we are always in danger of transferring the responsibility and the blame for our choices onto others. To take responsibility is a vital teaching in shamanism, based on the understanding that we have the right to – and responsibility for – our own personal and spiritual development: that we will not be delivered into salvation by an outside force.

Openness and trust: To be 'open' is a practice that will open the field of possibilities that is already within the soul. Openness to whatever life throws at you, openness to criticism as well as praise and openness to receive, to give and to learn. Practising trust means that we take risks, that we practise trusting life, that we know we can learn from whatever hurt or pain gets thrown at us and that we develop strength from it. When we were children, life was an adventure – why not remember this more often?

Gratitude: We have lost gratitude as a society, the habit of being grateful for what we have, for our children's health, for the roof over our head and the opportunities we are offered, and thankful that we do not starve. Instead of expressing gratitude, we tend to moan and find fault. Opening our hearts and expressing gratitude as a daily exercise shifts our focus and creates a positive energy field, produces generally a more positive way of thinking, all of which in turn help us to blossom.

Being involved: This practice is about doing something with others, contributing to a whole. It can be a circle of friends, a project, a community. When we develop to a certain extent, when we integrate our different facets and lead a spiritual life, we will automatically contribute. It will come naturally to us, as I have described in Chapter 1. We can practise by getting more involved.

Ask and you will be given: Practise asking for what you want and need. Journeying, meditating or praying, sending our questions, needs, wants and visions out into the field, can bring miraculous results. I do not subscribe to the idea that we manifest easily (if this were the case, anybody who followed the laws of attraction would by now be rich, famous and 'content'). In my experience, there are many forces out there and especially within us that can work against our manifesting; nevertheless, I know that we do have the ability to manifest and we are asked to practise it.

Reconnect with nature: Shamanism sees reconnecting with nature as a 'spiritual practice'. I have outlined the reasons in Chapter 16. Reconnecting will help us to unfold 'our wild soul', integrating us with – and bringing to the fore – facets that are innately natural, humane, courageous and sacred.

Practising love: And now to love. There are as many definitions of love as there are people. Practising 'love' in the spiritual sense in which I am using it here is about cultivating and practising to see 'the spirit, the Buddha nature' at the core of everything. We will develop kindness, tenderness and compassion in the process for all living beings, without condoning the dark and without becoming passive. In fact, it is only from this place that we can contribute effectively. For me, Nelson Mandela is a good example and so is Aung San Suu Kyi. They are political figures, and fighters for humanity, but the place they come from is their heart.

Much will happen when we begin to lead a soul-centred life. Most importantly we will experience a sense of wonder, a sense of connection, a sense of openness and flowing that seems to produce 'miracles' in our lives. Things happen to us and purpose and meaning unfold as we unfold.

THE INTERCONNECTION OF INDIVIDUAL AND COLLECTIVE PURPOSE

To understand purpose in a shamanic sense, we also need to put ourselves into the perspective of our time. Collectively, we are at a different point of our development, compared to, for instance, small indigenous communities or to the times when our now institutionalized, monotheistic religions were founded. Our world is large and heavily populated. It is diverse in its belief systems, ranging from the secular to the fundamental, yet it is increasingly connected and interdependent via a global economy and a global information system. And, most importantly, our economic, monetary and social systems have reached their limits. Our materially orientated leaders cannot provide us with answers, and certainly don't show the will and courage to implement adequate solutions, and our monotheistic religions waver between turning more fundamentalist and not having any answers to our pressing issues. Our world is in crisis. The global economic, ecological and social crisis we face is completely of our own making, based on our individual and collective state of mind. Underneath the manifestations there is a crisis of the collective soul.

I personally think that if we wait for the 'one (or few) big visionary' to lead us through the current crisis in which our old, inadequate social and economic structures are breaking down, we will wait forever. The same applies, in my opinion, to the spiritual. There will be no saviour who will miraculously appear to bring our religions together, or create a new spiritual system, and lead us to paradise.

The answers to our challenges can only be found in growing movements that consist of transformational communities with humanity, equality and spirituality at their centre. In the long run, assuming we can move forward before we destroy too much, we will rely on those worldwide communities that try to explore the wider realms of consciousness, moving away from the material to the humanitarian/spiritual. We will slowly work towards a shift in paradigm, which will be, as far as I can see, supported by the development and discoveries of science. As with every shift, we will, at the same time, see a fundamentalist countermovement that wants to turn the clock back and force us back into systems that are materially orientated, divisive, controlling and hierarchically structured, working to keep us in line through instilling fear. On an energetic level, we could see this as a battle between 'dark' and 'light' forces.

Collectively, according to contemporary shamanism, our purpose at this moment in time is to contribute to the new emerging paradigm that sees the world and all life within it as an interconnected web, energetic in essence, with consciousness/spirit as the driving force. Only a new paradigm can bring the fundamental changes of thinking, being and behaving that we need if we are to treat the planet we inhabit, the people we share it with and, indeed, ourselves in a way that will honour the 'spirit' at the essence of everything and help us to lead more soul-centred lives. How we achieve this, and how, concretely, we do that, is up to us, individually and in groups. 'We may as well consume, pollute and war our way into social collapse or even species oblivion. Alternatively we may find our way through our current global crisis via a forced collective maturation. To achieve this however will require development of our inner world as much as our outer one' (Walsh 2010, p.270). It will take a substantial number of people and many groups, on different levels of society, all working towards this inner maturity, rejecting the current world-views and trying, with their means and in their own ways, to change their ways of seeing, being and acting in this world. The vessels for concrete purposeful action will (and already do) show up as they are created and perceived whilst we walk a path that leads us towards a more soul-centred, care-taking and humane way of being.

Individually, if we want to 'live wisely, love wholeheartedly, mature fully and contribute effectively' (Walsh 2010, p.28), we had better begin to understand that we are spiritual beings in essence and to cater for our souls, rather than just our minds and bodies, developing into humans that deserve the attribute humane. The same applies collectively. Whatever we attempt, our concepts and social structures need to incorporate the humanistic/spiritual. If we wait for the one integral theory to emerge, and the scientific proof to underpin this one integral theory completely, we might find that we are running out of time.

One of those groups is the growing psycho-spiritual movement in all its diversity, which includes certain strands of psychology, therapy and psychiatry. I wrote this book in the hope that the fields of psychology, therapy and psychiatry will continue to widen their definition of what constitutes a human, rather than staying on the narrow scope of body/mind, so that we can cater more for the souls of our clients and integrate the knowledge of the psychological with the age-old wisdom of the spiritual.

Notes

1   It is our thought processes, our feelings, our intents and our actions that create collectively the reality we are in. This collectively created reality will also influence our individual reality. How much individual power we have, and to which level the energy fields around us determine our reality, is the subject of another book and also currently the subject of debate. For certain, if we do not want to 'go under', in fact drown within those influences and just drift along, being at the mercy of what is happening to us, we need to consciously and seriously get and stay in touch with the deeper and higher levels of ourselves, the wider field and contribute to it consciously, first by working towards integrating all the facets of ourselves and second by consciously co-creating from there.

2   In traditional indigenous cultures of South America as well as Asia, mind-altering herbs are used as well to quest for vision. Seekers will travel to such places to work with plant medicines, but they are not part of this book because they are classified as illegal substances and are not available in Europe and America.

3   If we look at people who have had a profoundly positive influence, we realize that they all spent time – some not necessarily voluntarily – on their spiritual development before their greatest and wisest actions took place, e.g. Nelson Mandela, the Dalai Lama, Mother Teresa, Buddha, Jesus, Aung San Suu Kyi, Mahatma Gandhi, Black Elk. I personally believe, as Aung San Suu Kyi (2011) so wisely remarked in her Reith lecture, that political, charitable and generally 'contributing' action has to come from an inner place of peace and freedom, rather than from a place of 'needing to do good', which can be tainted with all kinds of needs, such as self-gratification, power and control.

References

Achterberg, J. (1985) *Imagery and Healing: Shamanism and Modern Medicine.* Boston: New Science Library.

Alper, K.R. (2001) Ibogaine: A Review. *Alkaloids, 56,* 1–37.

Alper, K.R., Lotsof, H.S. and Kaplan, C.D. (2008) The Ibogaine Medical Subculture. *Journal of Ethnopharmacology 115,* 1, 9–24. Accessed 19/1/2012 at www.ibogaine.desk.nl/subculture.html.

American Psychiatric Association (2000) *DSM-IV-TR – Diagnostic and Statistical Manual of Mental Disorders. Fourth Edition. Text Revision.* Washington, DC: American Psychiatric Association.

American Psychological Association (2011) Topics. Accessed 10/6/2011 at www.apa.org/topics/index.aspx.

Andrews, T. (2004) *Nature-Speak: Signs, Omens and Messages in Nature.* Jackson, TN: Dragonhawk Publishing.

Assagioli, R. (1965) *Psychosynthesis: A Collection of Basic Writings.* New York: Viking.

Association for Humanistic Psychology (2011) Humanistic Psychology Overview. Accessed 10/8/2011 at www.ahpweb.org/aboutahp/whatis.html.

Bartlett, P. (2008) Reason and Re-enchantment in Cultural Change: Sustainability in Higher Education. *Current Anthropology, 49,* 1077–1098.

Bastien, J.W. (1992) *Drum and Stethoscope: Integrating Ethnomedicine and Biomedicine in Bolivia.* Utah: University of Utah Press.

Beauregard, M. and O'Leary, D. (2007) *The Spiritual Brain.* New York: HarperOne.

Beck, A.T., Rush, A.J., Shaw, B.F. and Emery, G. (1979) *Cognitive Therapy and Depression.* New York: Guilford Press.

Black Elk, N. and Brown, E.J. (eds) (1989) *The Sacred Pipe: Black Elk's Account of the Seven Rites of the Oglala Sioux.* Norman: University of Oklahoma Press (first published 1953).

Blacker, C. (1975) Two Kinds of Japanese Shamans: The Medium and the Ascetic. Republished in J. Narby and F. Huxley (eds) (2001) *Shamans through Time: 500 Years on the Path of Knowledge.* London: Thames & Hudson.

Bohm, D. (1983) *Wholeness and the Implicate Order.* London: Arch Paperbacks.

Bonenfant, R. (2006) A Comparative Study of Near-Death Experience and Non-Near-Death Experience Outcomes in 56 Survivors of Clinical Death. *Journal of Near-Death Studies, 22,* 3, 155–178.

Bourguignon, E. (1973) *Religion, Altered States of Consciousness and Social Change.* Columbus: Ohio State University Press.

British Psychological Society (2011a) Introduction to Psychology. Accessed 10/8/2011 at www.bps.org.uk/psychology-public/introduction-psychology/introduction-psychology.

British Psychological Society (2011b) Transpersonal Psychology Section. Accessed 10/8/2011 at http://transpersonalpsychology.org.uk.

Bruce, E. (2002) *Shaman, M.D.: A Plastic Surgeon's Remarkable Journey into the World of Shapeshifting.* Rochester, VE: Destiny Books.

Campbell, J. (1968) *The Hero with a Thousand Faces.* New York: World (first published 1949).

Campbell, J. (2002) *The Inner Reaches of Outer Space.* Novato, CA: New World Library (first published 1986).

Caplan, M. (2009) *Eyes Wide Open: Cultivating Discernment on the Spiritual Path.* Boulder, CO: Sounds True.

Castaneda, C. (1969) *The Teachings of Don Juan: A YaQui Way of Knowledge.* New York: Ballantine.

Chopra, D., Ford, D. and Williamson, M. (2010) *The Shadow Effect: Illuminating the Hidden Power of Your True Self.* New York: HarperCollins.

Cowan, T. (1993) *Fire in the Head: Shamanism and the Celtic Spirit.* San Francisco: HarperSanFrancisco.

Crowley, N. (2005) *Holothropic Breathwork: Healing through a Non-ordinary State of Consciousness.* London: Royal College of Psychiatrists.

Culliford, L. (2011) *The Psychology of Spirituality: An Introduction.* London: Jessica Kingsley Publishers.

Devereux, G. (1956) The Shaman is Mentally Deranged. Republished in J. Narby and F. Huxley (eds) (2001) *Shamans through Time: 500 Years on the Path of Knowledge.* London: Thames & Hudson.

Eliade, M. (1964) *Shamanism: Archaic Techniques of Ecstasy.* Princeton, NJ: Princeton University Press (first published 1951).

Elkin, A.P. (1945) Aboriginal Doctors Are Outstanding People. Republished in J. Narby and F. Huxley (eds) (2001) *Shamans through Time: 500 Years on the Path of Knowledge.* London: Thames & Hudson.

Ellis, A. and Dryden, W. (2007) *The Practice of Rational Emotive Behavior Therapy.* New York: Springer (first published 1997).

Elvin, V. (1955) The Shaman Performs a Public Service with Grace and Energy. Republished in J. Narby and F. Huxley (eds) (2001) *Shamans through Time: 500 Years on the Path of Knowledge.* London: Thames & Hudson.

Ereditato, A. (2011) On 'Unexpected Results' at CERN. BBC Science 23.9.2011. Accessed 1/10/2011 at www.bbc.co.uk/news/science-environment-15034426.

Estes, C.P. (1992) *Women Who Run with the Wolves: Contacting the Power of the Wild Woman.* London: Random House.

Fenwick, P. (2011) The Neuroscience of Spirituality. London: Royal College of Psychiatrists. Accessed 5/7/11 at www.rcpsych.ac.uk/members/specialinterest groups/spirituality/publicationsarchive.aspx.

Frankl, V. (1973) *The Doctor and the Soul: From Psychotherapy to Logotherapy.* New York: Pelican Books.

Gagan, J.M. (1998) *Journeying: Where Shamanism and Psychology Meet.* Santa Fe, NM: Rio Chama Publications.

Gilma, H. (ed.) (2011) *Selected Writings of Ralph Waldo Emerson.* New York: Signet Classics (first published 1965).

Goodman, F. (1988) *Ecstasy, Ritual and Alternate Reality: Religion in a Pluralistic World.* Bloomington: Indiana University Press.

Grigori, J.W. (2002) Nature of the Soul. Accessed 24/8/2011 at www.shamanic.net/index.php/articles/25-article-nature-of-the-soul.

Grigori, J.W. (2010) Winter Solstice: A Time of the Shaman's Gift Bringing. Accessed 24/8/2011 at www.shamanic.net/index.php/articles/82-article-winter-solstice-a-time-of-the-shamans-gift-bringing.

Grof, S. (1985) *Beyond the Brain.* Albany, NY: SUNY Press.

Grof, S. (1993) *Holotropic Mind: The Three Levels of Human Consciousness and How They Shape Our Lives.* San Francisco: HarperSanFrancisco.

Grof, S. (1995) Frontiers of the Mind. Interview with Daniel Redwood. Accessed 9/7/2011 at www.healthy.net/scr/interview.aspx?Id=200.

Grof, S. (2006) *When the Impossible Happens: Adventures in Non-Ordinary Realities.* Boulder, CO: Sounds True.

Grof, S. and Grof, C. (2010) *Holotropic Breathwork: A New Approach to Self-Exploration and Therapy.* Albany, NY: SUNY Press.

Halifax, J. (1979) *Shamanic Voices: A Survey of Visionary Narratives.* New York: Viking.

Halifax, J. (1982) *Shaman: The Wounded Healer.* London: Thames & Hudson.

Harner, M. (1982) *The Way of the Shaman: A Guide to Power and Healing.* New York: Bantam.

Heaven, R. and Charing, G.H. (2006) *Plant Spirit Shamanism: Traditional Techniques for Healing the Soul.* Rochester, VE: Destiny Books.

Hellinger, B. (2003) *Farewell: Family Constellations with Descendants of Victims and Perpetrators.* Heidelberg: Carl-Aver-Systeme-Verlag und Verlangsbuchhandlung GmbH.

Hillman, J. and Ventura, M. (1992) *We Have Had a Hundred Years of Psychotherapy – And the World's Getting Worse.* New York: HarperSanFrancisco.

Hoelzel, B.K., Ott, U., Gard, T., Hempel, H., Weygandt, M., Morgen, K. and Vaitl, D. (2008) Investigation of Mindfulness Meditation Practitioners with Voxel-based Morphometry. *Social Cognitive and Affective Neuroscience, 3,* 1, 55–61.

Holmquist, A. (2007) *Alternative States of Consciousness in Shamanism, Imaginal Psychotherapies, Hypnotherapy and Meditation.* Boca Raton, FL: Dissertation.com.

Hultkrantz, A. (1973) A Definition of Shamanism. *Temenos, 9,* 25–37.

Ingerman, S. (1990) *Soul Retrieval: Mending the Fragmented Self.* San Francisco: HarperCollins.

Ingerman, S. (2004) *Shamanic Journeying: A Beginner's Guide.* Boulder, CO: Sounds True.

Ingerman, S. and Wesselman, H. (2010) *Awakening to the Spirit World: The Shamanic Path of Direct Revelation.* Boulder, CO: Sounds True.

International Indigenous Leadership Gathering (2011) Third Annual International Indigenous Leadership Gathering: Protecting the Sacred. Fountain, British Columbia, Canada. Accessed 30/8/2011 at www.iilg.ca/the-gathering.

James, O. (2010) *Britain on the Couch: How Keeping up with the Joneses has Depressed Us Since 1950.* Reading: Vermillon (first published 1998).

James, W. (1958) *The Varieties of Religious Experience.* New York: New American Library.

Joralemon, D. and Sharon, D. (1993) *Sorcery and Shamanism: Curanderos and Clients in Northern Peru.* Utah: University of Utah Press.

Jung, C.G. (1959) Archetypes and the Collective Unconscious. In H. Read, M. Fordham and G. Adler (eds) *The Collected Works of C.G. Jung* (trans. R.F.C. Hull), Vol.9, Pt 1. London: Routledge and Kegan Paul.

Jung, C.G. (1961) *Memories, Dreams, Reflections.* New York: Vintage.

Jung, C.G. (1967) Symbols of Transformation. In *The Collected Works 5,* Bollinger Series XX, 2nd edn. Princeton, NJ: Princeton University Press.

Jung, C.G. (1977) *Symbols of Transformation.* Princeton, NJ: University Press.

Kalweit, H. (1988) *Dreamtime and Inner Space: The World of the Shaman.* New York: Shambhala.

Kim, S., Reed, P., Hayward, P.D., Kang, Y. and Koenig, G. (2011) Spirituality and Psychological Well-being: Testing a Theory of Family Interdependence among Family Caregivers and Their Elders. *Research in Nursing & Health, 34,* 2, 103–115.

Kleinman, A. and Sung, L. (1979) Why Do Indigenous Practitioners Successfully Heal? *Social Science and Medicine, 13B,* 7–26.

Koenig, H.K., McCullough, M.E. and Larson, D.B. (eds) (2001) *Handbook of Religion and Health.* Oxford: Oxford University Press.

Krippner, S. (2002) Conflicting Perspectives on Shamans and Shamanism: Points and Counterpoints. *American Psychologist, 57*, 11, 962–977.

Kübler-Ross, E. (1997) *On Death and Dying*. New York: Scribner Classics.

Kyi, A.S.S. (2011) Liberty. BBC: Reith Lectures 2011. Accessed 15/7/2011 at www.bbc.co.uk/programmes/b0126d29.

Laszlo, E. (2004) *Science and the Akashic Field: An Integrative Theory of Everything*. Rochester, VE: Inner Traditions.

Levi-Strauss, C. (1949) Shamans as Psychoanalysts. Republished in J. Narby and F. Huxley (eds) (2001) *Shamans through Time: 500 Years on the Path of Knowledge*. London: Thames & Hudson.

Lyons, O. (1980) An Iroquois Perspective. In C. Vecsey and R.W. Venables (eds) *American Indian Environments: Ecological Issues in Native American History*. New York: Syracuse University Press.

Magdalena, A. (2011a) *Beyond the Four Agreements: Mastering the Inner Shields of Transformation*. Bloomington, MN: Author House.

Magdalena, A. (2011b) Shamanic Shields: Creating Peace in Your Inner World. Institute for Shamanic Synthesis. Accessed 17/10/2011 at www.instituteforshamanicsynthesis.com/blog.htm.

Mash, D.C., Kovera, C.A. and Pablo, J. (2000) Ibogaine: Complex Pharmacokinetics, Concerns for Safety and Preliminary Efficacy Measures. *Annals of the New York Academy of Sciences, 914*, 394–401.

Maslow, A.H. (1968) *Towards a Psychology of Being*, 2nd edn. Princetown: Van Nostrand.

May, R. (1969) *Love and Will*. New York: W.W. Norton.

McClain, C.S., Rosenfeld, B. and Breitbart, W. (2003) Effect of Spiritual Well-being on End-of-life Despair in Terminally-ill Cancer Patients. *The Lancet, 361*, 9369, 1603–1607.

McTaggart, L. (2001) *The Field*. San Francisco: HarperCollins.

Mental Health Foundation (2011) Mental Health Statistics. Accessed 10/8/2011 at www.mentalhealth.org.uk/help-information/mental-health-statistics.

Metzner, R. (1998) *The Unfolding Self: Varieties of Transformative Experience* (rev. edn of *Opening to Inner Light*). Novato, CA: Origin Press.

Mindell, A. (1993) *The Shaman's Body: A New Shamanism for Transforming Health, Relationships and Community*. New York: HarperSanFrancisco.

Mindell, A. (2000) *Quantum Mind: The Edge Between Physics and Psychology*. Portland, OR: LaoTse Press.

Mindell, A. (2004) *Quantum Mind and Healing: How to Listen and Respond to Your Body's Symptoms*. Charlottesville, VA: Hampton Roads Publishing.

Mitchell, E. (2011) Consciousness, Quantum Physics, the Zero Point Fields and the Quantum Holographic Model. Accessed 10/6/2011 at www.quantrek.org/Dyadic_model_and_QH/Dyadic_model_and_QH.htm.

Moody, R. (2001) *Life after Life*. San Francisco: HarperCollins.

Murphy, M. and Ballou, R. (eds) (1960) *William James on Psychological Research*. New York: Viking.

Myerhoff, B. (1974) I Found Myself Impaled on the Axis Mundi. Republished in J. Narby and F. Huxley (eds) (2001) *Shamans through Time: 500 Years on the Path of Knowledge*. London: Thames & Hudson.

Narby, J. and Huxley, F. (eds) (2001) *Shamans through Time: 500 Years on the Path of Knowledge*. London: Thames & Hudson.

National Institute for Clinical Excellence (2008) Summary of Cognitive Behavioural Therapy Interventions Recommended by NICE. Accessed 28/9/2011 at www.nice.org.uk

Natural England (2010) Commissioned Report-NECR025: *Wild Adventure Space: Its Role in Teenagers' Lives.* Accessed 12/8/2011 at http://naturalengland.etraderstores. com/NaturalEnglandShop/NECR025.

Neidhardt, J. (1988) *Black Elk Speaks: Being the Life Story of a Holy Man of the Oglala Sioux.* Lincoln: University of Nebraska Press (first published 1932).

Noll, R. (1987) Shamans, 'Spirits' and Mental Imagery. Republished in J. Narby and F. Huxley (eds) (2001) *Shamans through Time: 500 Years on the Path of Knowledge.* London: Thames & Hudson.

Parks, J. (1999) *To Be a Body or Not to Be a Body: Reflections on Psychosynthesis.* Amherst, MA: Association for the Advancement of Psychosynthesis Monograph.

Perkins, J. (1990) *Psychonavigation: Techniques for Travel beyond Time.* Rochester, VE: Destiny Books.

Perkins, J. (1994) *The World Is as You Dream It: Shamanic Teachings from the Amazon and Andes.* Rochester, VE: Destiny Books.

Perkins, J. (1997) *Shapeshifting: Techniques for Global and Personal Transformation.* Rochester, VE: Destiny Books.

Perkins, J. (2006) *Confessions of an Economic Hit Man: The Shocking Story of How America Really Took Over the World.* London: Ebury Press (first published 2004).

Perkins, J. (2009) *Hoodwinked: An Economic Hit Man Reveals Why the World Financial Markets Imploded and What We Need to Do to Remake Them.* New York: Broadway Books.

Perls, F. (1969) *Gestalt Therapy Verbatim.* Lafayette, CA: Real People Press.

Perry, J. (1986) Spiritual Emergence and Renewal. *ReVision, 8,* 2, 33–40.

Peters, L. (1989) Shamanism: Phenomenology of a Spiritual Discipline. *Journal of Transpersonal Psychology, 21,* 115–137.

Peters, L.G. and Price-Williams, D. (1980) Towards an Experiential Analysis of Shamanism. *American Ethnologist, 7,* 405–406.

Plotkin, B. (2008) *Nature and the Human Soul: Cultivating Wholeness and Community in a Fragmented World.* Novato, CA: New World Library.

Powell, A. (2001a) Mental Health and Spirituality. London: Royal College of Psychiatrists. Accessed 5/7/2011 at www.rcpsych.ac.uk/members/specialinterestgroups/ spirituality/publicationsarchive.aspx.

Powell, A. (2001b) Beyond Space and Time – The Unbounded Psyche. In D. Lorimer (ed.) *Thinking Beyond the Brain: A Wider Science of Consiousness.* Edinburgh: Floris Books.

Powell, A. and MacKenna, C. (2009) Spirituality and Psychotherapy. London: Royal College of Psychiatrists. Accessed 5/7/2011 at www.rcpsych.ac.uk/members/ specialinterestgroups/spirituality/publicationsarchive.aspx.

Pratt, C. (2007a) *An Encyclopedia of Shamanism: Volume 1.* New York: Rosen Publishing.

Pratt, C. (2007b) *An Encyclopedia of Shamanism: Volume 2.* New York: Rosen Publishing.

Rankin, L. (2011) The Difference between Sick, Well and Whole. *Psychology Today.* Accessed 1/11/2011 at www.psychologytoday.com/blog/owning-pink/201110/ the-difference-between-sick-well-whole.

Read, T. (2006) Non-ordinary States of Consciousness and the Transpersonal Journey. London: Royal College of Psychiatrists. Accessed 5/8/2011 at www.rcpsych. ac.uk/members/specialinterestgroups/spirituality/publicationsarchive.aspx.

Reichel-Dolmatoff, G. (1975) Shamans Are Intellectuals, Translators, and Shrewd Dealers. Republished in J. Narby and F. Huxley (eds) (2001) *Shamans through Time: 500 Years on the Path of Knowledge.* London: Thames & Hudson.

Rogers, C.R. (2003) *Client-centered Therapy: Its Current Practice, Implications and Theory.* London: Constable & Robinson (first published 1951).

Rogers, S. (1982) *The Shaman.* Springfield, IL: C.C. Thomas.

Rosenblum, B. and Kuttner, F. (2006) *Quantum Enigma*. New York: Oxford University Press.

Rossi, E.L. (2004) *A Discourse with Our Genes – The Psychosocial and Cultural Genomics of Therapeutic Hypnosis and Psychotherapy*. Genoa: Editris S.A.S.

Royal College of Psychiatrists (2010) Spirituality and Mental Health. Accessed 16/7/2011 at www.rcpsych.ac.uk/mentalhealthinfo/treatments/spirituality.aspx.

Rutherford, L. (1997) *Principles of Shamanism*. London: Thorsons.

Rutherford, L. (2008) *The View through the Medicine Wheel: Shamanic Maps of How the Universe Works*. Rapley, Hants: O Books.

Sams, J. and Carsons, D. (1988) *Medicine Cards*. New York: St Martin's Press.

Sanchez, V. (1996) *Toltecs of the New Millennium*. Vermont: Bear & Company.

Schermer, V. (2003) *Spirit and Psyche: A New Paradigm for Psychology, Psychoanalysis and Psychotherapy*. London and New York: Jessica Kingsley Publishers.

Secunda, B. (2011) Dance of the Deer Foundation. Accessed 6/7/2011 at www.danceofthedeer.com/brant-secunda/huichol-shaman-healer.

Siegel, R.K. (1989) *Intoxification: Life in Pursuit of Artificial Paradise*. New York: Dutton.

Somé, M.P. (1994) *Of Water and the Spirit: Ritual, Magic and Initiation in the Life of an African Shaman*. New York: Penguin.

Somé, M.P. (1998) *The Healing Wisdom of Africa: Finding Life Purpose through Nature, Ritual and Community*. Los Angeles: Jeremy P. Tarcher.

Somé, S. (1999) *The Spirit of Intimacy: Ancient Teachings in the Ways of Relationships*. New York: William Morrow.

SPSIG (2011) The Spirituality and Psychiatry Special Interest Group. Royal College of Psychiatrists. Accessed 17/5/2011 at www.rcpsych.ac.uk/members/specialinterestgroups/spirituality.aspx.

Storm, H. (1997) *Lightningbolt*. New York: Thorsons (first published 1994).

Strubelt, S. and Maas, U. (2008) The Near-Death Experience: A Cerebellar Method to Protect Body and Soul. Lessons from the Iboga Healing-Ceremony in Gabon. *Alternative Therapies, 14*, 1, 30–34. Accessed 5/6/2011 at www.ebando.org/en/docs/strubelt.doc.

Swindon, J. (2001) *Spirituality and Mental Health Cure: Rediscovering a Forgotten Dimension*. London: Jessica Kingsley Publishers.

Tart, C. (ed.) (1992) *Transpersonal Psychologies*, 3rd edn. New York: HarperCollins.

Teish, L. (1991) *Jambalaya: The Natural Woman's Book of Personal Charms and Practical Rituals*. New York: HarperSanFrancisco (first published 1985).

Teish, L. (1994) *Carnival of the Spirit: Seasonal Celebrations and Rites of Passage*. Sydney: HarperCollins Australia.

Townsley, G. (1993) Twisted Language: A Technique for Knowing. Republished in J. Narby and F. Huxley (eds) (2001) *Shamans through Time: 500 Years on the Path to Knowledge*. London: Thames & Hudson.

Turner, S. (2005) *A Hard Day's Write: The Stories behind Every Beatles Song*, 3rd edn. New York: Harper Paperbacks.

Ungunmerr-Baumann, M.R. (2007) Dadirri Inner Deep Listening and Quiet Still Awareness. Accessed 12/8/2011 at www.liturgyplanning.com.au/documents.

Van Lommel, P. (2004) About the Continuity of Our Consciousness. Paper presented to the Royal College of Psychiatrists, London. accessed 4/8/2011 at www.rcpsych.ac.uk/members/specialinterestgroups/spirituality/publicationsarchive.aspx.

Van Lommel, P. (2010) *Consciousness beyond Life: The Science of the Near-death Experience*. New York: HarperOne.

Vaughan, F. (2000) *The Inward Arc: Healing in Psychotherapy and Spirituality*, 2nd edn. Lincoln, NC: Blackinprint.com.

Vivoldo, A. (2010) in S. Ingerman and H. Wesselman (eds) *Awakening to the Spirit World: The Shamanic Path of Direct Revelation*. Boulder, CO: Sounds True, 90–91.

Walsh, R. (1990) *The Spirit of Shamanism*. Los Angeles: Jeremy P. Tarcher.

Walsh, R. (2010) *The World of Shamanism: New Views of an Ancient Tradition*. Woodbury, MN: Llewellyn Worldwide.

Wasson, R.G. (2011) Seeking the Magic Mushroom. Accessed 20/5/2011 at www. imaginaria.org/wasson/life.htm (original article in *Life Magazine*, 10 June, 1957).

Weil, A. (1972) *The Natural Mind: A New Way of Looking at Drugs and the Higher Consciousness*. Boston: Houghton Mifflin.

Wilber, K. (2000) *Integral Psychology*. Boston: Shambhala.

Wilber, K. (2006) *Integral Spirituality*. Boston: Shambhala.

Williamson, M. (1992) *A Return to Love: Reflections on the Principles of a Course in Miracles*. New York: HarperCollins.

Winkelman, M. (1989) A Cross-cultural Study of Shamanistic Healers. *Journal of Psychoactive Drugs, 21*, 17–24.

Woolger, R.J. (2004) *Healing Your Past Lives: Exploring the Many Lives of the Soul*. Boulder, CO: Sounds True.

Yanez, B., Edmondson, D., Stanton, A.L., Park, C.L., Ganz, P.A. and Blank, T.O. (2009) Facets of Spirituality as Predictors of Adjustment to Cancer: Relative Contributions of Having Faith and Finding Meaning. *Journal of Consulting and Clinical Psychology, 77*, 4, 730–741.

Subject Index

Author Index

Printed in Great Britain
by Amazon

75871063R00183